WONDERLANDS

Also by Charles Baxter

WONDERLANDS

Essays on the Life of Literature

Charles Baxter

Graywolf Press

Eight lines from the poem "Two Poems about President Harding" from *Collected Poems* © 1971 by James Wright. Published by Wesleyan University Press. Used by permission.

Clothes on Hooks, Home Place, 1947; photograph by Wright Morris. Collection Center for Creative Photography. Copyright © Estate of Wright Morris. Courtesy of the Center for Creative Photography.

Excerpt from "The Teeth Mother Naked at Last" copyright © 1973 by Robert Bly. Copyright renewed 2001 by Robert Bly, from *Collected Poems* by Robert Bly. Used by permission of W. W. Norton & Company, Inc.

This publication is made possible, in part, by the voters of Minnesota through a Minnesota State Arts Board Operating Support grant, thanks to a legislative appropriation from the arts and cultural heritage fund. Significant support has also been provided by the McKnight Foundation, the Lannan Foundation, the Amazon Literary Partnership, and other generous contributions from foundations, corporations, and individuals. To these organizations and individuals we offer our heartfelt thanks.

MINNESOTA
STATE ARTS BOARD

CLEAN
WATER
LAND &
LEGACY
AMENDMENT

Published by Graywolf Press
212 Third Avenue North, Suite 485
Minneapolis, Minnesota 55401

This is a work of nonfiction. It is also a work of memory and craft. On occasion, names, places, and events have been altered in the interest of personal privacy and artistic intent.

www.graywolfpress.org

Published in the United States of America

ISBN 978-1-64445-091-8 (paperback)
ISBN 978-1-64445-179-3 (ebook)

2 4 6 8 9 7 5 3 1
First Graywolf Printing, 2022

Library of Congress Control Number: 2021945925

Cover design: Adam Bohannon

Cover art: Rob Evans, *Marietta Train*, oil on panel, 1993

In Memory

Lewis Daniel Baxter

Contents

Preface

What I offer in this book is a set of essays about features in narratives that have had an obsessive grip on me: requests and lists; and hauntings; toxic subject matter and Hell; dreams and urgent narratives; and images. These topics do not yield up a set of suggestions and pieces of practical advice, although now and then, as in the "Captain Happen" essay, the writing may stray into that territory. I apologize for any inconsistencies, of which there are several in these pages. The essays are often subjective and autobiographical. My parents (especially my mother), my siblings, my friends and loved ones are here, and sometimes they speak up.

Years ago, when I was in graduate school, one of my teachers was asked what he wanted in the final term paper he had assigned. "Try to be interesting," he said to us with a smile. In that spirit, I have done my best in these essays to be interesting and to be as courageous as I could be in uniting the personal and impersonal, the subjective and the objective.

As I write, we have recently passed through a presidential election. The candidate who lost, Donald Trump, claimed that he did not lose, that he could not have lost. Such a thought was impermissible: it did not square with his view of himself, and as a fact, and a thought, it had to be rejected and exiled to that place—a kind of psychic sub-basement where unthinkable thoughts reside. Donald Trump does not write stories, poems, or novels. But his refusal to concede the presidential election derives from a narrative that was toxic to him—namely, that he had lost and was a loser. In this book you will find an essay on toxic narratives. That essay does not exactly explain Donald Trump's behavior and it does not exactly explain how to write a toxic narrative. But it does its best to give an account of what an unthinkable thought is, and what its contradictory elements may contain, and why unthinkable thoughts often produce stories.

All the stories we tell each other are hybridized: parts of them come from the "real world" (scare quotes attached) and parts of them come from somewhere else, a place I have called "Wonderland," very close to the land of possibility and the land of dreams. In front of every story and novel and poem, there is a WELCOME mat. You step on the mat as you enter. Once you're in, you're somewhere else.

Welcome.

WONDERLANDS

The Request Moment,
or "There's Something I Want You to Do"

My uncle, a combat veteran of World War II, once told me that when he was a little boy, he had been bossed around by his older sister. Every day from morning until night, she would say to him, "There's something I want you to do." He would scurry through the house doing the various chores she had requested. When he asked her *why* he should follow her orders, she replied, "If you do what I ask, I won't get mad at you. *That's* your reward."

Sometimes family members act as if they were gods. They can enforce their own laws. If you don't do what they ask, you get punished. The hierarchy of enforcement in both families and society at large runs from the modest suggestion to the more urgent request, to the military order, and at last to the Supreme Authority's decree. The level of enforcement is in proportion to the intensity of the demand and the power available to the authority for a punishment if the demand isn't followed. If you don't follow a *suggestion*, you don't get punished (it's only a suggestion, after all). If you ignore or disobey a *command*, hell may await you.

Suppose that when you were a pre-teen, or a teenager, one of your friends dared you to do something. *Let's get drunk and steal your dad's car! I dare you.* Someone daring someone else is a classic and solid

basis of many stories, mostly because the dare may involve a dangerous or criminal action, and partly because the objects of the dare are
having their courage tested. More than that, they are having their
character challenged and defined.

When I first started writing short stories, I would show them to a
friend of mine whom I will call Duffy. Away from books, he was fun
to be around, but confronted with the printed word, he lapsed into
brutality. He had a mean streak. He also fancied himself a writer, as
I did. We thought we had to toughen each other up in preparation for
what the world would do to us, so we pronounced the harshest judg-
ments on our stories that we could think up. Brutal criticism can be
helpful if you can stand to listen to it and not become depressed or
enraged. Duffy looked like a hippie, smoked a lot of weed, and had
hair down to his shoulders, but as a critic he enjoyed being abusive.
Literature had seduced and betrayed him. For him, literature was the
scene of an ongoing crime that had been perpetrated in silence and
secrecy against him.

One time in a greasy spoon he returned one of my stories to me.
The pages had been marked up and bloodied with red ink, and there
were some very creepy-looking stains on them. I asked Duffy what
he thought of my story. "Well," he said, "the *sentences* are okay; I
guess. But the story just sort of sits there." Whaddya mean? I asked.
I thought my story was pretty good and that Duffy was lost in a
stoner haze. "Just what I said," he told me. "Your story just sits there.
Nothing happens." He gave me a probing look. His eyes were blood-
shot, with capillaries like tiny trails to his brain. "You know, Baxter,"
he said, "nobody in your stories ever takes action against bad guys,
and nobody ever asks anybody for anything. Why's that? You scared
of something? What kind of a world do you live in? Do people just
give you stuff?" He gave me a smug, drug-infused smile. "Me, I live
in the grip of necessity."

Necessity was a word that Marxists liked to deploy in those days. But Duffy had his nerve, using that word on me. No, people did not just give me stuff, but I felt like murdering him for not liking my fiction. *That* felt like a necessity. In hindsight, I recognize that he was doing me a favor by talking about necessity, the force that leans on characters to do what they do.

The years pass; the calendar pages fall from the wall. The scene changes, and I'm sitting in the audience at the Guthrie Theater in Minneapolis watching a production of Shakespeare's *Macbeth*. One of the first features I notice about the play this time is that almost as soon as Macbeth is reunited with Lady Macbeth in act one, she begins issuing requests, or orders, to him in the imperative mode: "To beguile the time," she says, "Look like the time; bear welcome in your eye, / Your hand, your tongue: look like the innocent flower, / But be the serpent under 't." This is neither advice nor a suggestion. She's telling her husband what he should do: commit a murder. For the sake of his own ambitions, he must murder Duncan, but first he must act hospitable when Duncan arrives as a houseguest. When Macbeth quails at the prospect of murdering Duncan, Lady Macbeth informs him that if he were a real man, he'd do it. The act constitutes the proof of manhood. "But screw your courage to the sticking-place, / And we'll not fail," she instructs him, noting, by using "we," that they're in this together. At this point in the play, Macbeth's worries about being judged a weakling by his wife are worse than his worries about being a murderer.

I dare you.

Macbeth begins with prophecy by the weird sisters and a request moment from Lady Macbeth, and both drive the play forward. A month or so later, by coincidence, I happened to be watching another Shakespeare production, this time of *Hamlet*, when in the first act something clicked and I sat up. When the ghost of Hamlet's father appears in act one, scene five, he has three requests that he passes on to his son: (1) *avenge my death by killing Claudius*, (2) *honor your mother*, and (3) *remember me*. Without the request moment that's set into motion by the ghost, there's no dramatic tension and no play. That request is the play's dramatic core, and, for Hamlet, the central problem. Here are the ghost's words:

> If thou has nature in thee, bear it not;
> Let not the royal bed of Denmark be
> A couch for luxury and damned incest.
> But, howsoever thou pursuest this act,
> Taint not thy mind, nor let thy soul contrive
> Against thy mother aught: leave her to heaven
> And to those thorns that in her bosom lodge,
> To prick and sting her. Fare thee well at once!
> The glow-worm shows the matin to be near,
> And 'gins to pale his uneffectual fire:
> Adieu, adieu! Hamlet, remember me.

This request puts Hamlet into a corner: the request is a huge one involving murder—and regicide—but Hamlet can't decide whether he's obliged to fulfill it and strong enough in will to honor it. Some of us may not be capable of murder even for a good cause. What starts out the play also ends it: with his dying breath, Hamlet gasps out a last request to Horatio: "If thou didst ever hold me in thy heart, / Absent thee from felicity awhile, / And in this harsh world draw thy breath in pain, / To tell my story." It's as if requests animate the play from start to finish and therefore have a second and third life: the first one sets others into motion, like a repetition compulsion of four words: *Do what I ask*. In the world of the play, one request engenders another, and another.

Once you notice request moments as sparkplugs to Shakespearean drama, they seem to crop up everywhere. In *King Lear*, act one, scene one, Lear makes the preposterous request to his daughters that they should, or must, tell him how much they love him. This request frames the condition—of parceling out his kingdom to them. As he says, "Tell me, my daughters,— / Since now we will divest us both of rule, / Interest of territory, cares of state,— / Which of you shall we say doth love us most? / . . . Goneril, / Our eldest-born, speak first." Cordelia, of course, regards her father's request as ridiculous, and she refuses to follow his instructions. And, as a consequence, we have the drama of a refusal that sets all the dramatic machinery into motion.

Measure for Measure begins with a request, from the Duke to Angelo. Sophocles' *Oedipus the King* begins with an urgent plea from the citizens of Thebes to Oedipus: please lift the plague that's destroying the city. There are many, many other request moments in Shakespeare and in dramatic literature generally, too many to count. What is it about these requests that set stories with a particular urgency into motion?

Many of our models for writing and for thinking about plot and plot construction go back to common questions: What does this character want? Or: What is this character afraid of? According to the conventional wisdom, if we know what the protagonist desires or fears, we know what's at stake in the story—that is, the goal, what stands to be gained or lost: status, a love object, riches, a particular identity, whatever it may be. Those desires and fears provide us with the emotional logic of the story. This is standard fiction workshop orthodoxy.

Partial truths can quickly turn into rule-of-thumb conventions and then into clichés. Literature doesn't always work through simple desires and fears because real life doesn't always work that way. Social life often requires a disguise. Much of the time in our lives, we aren't doing what *we* want to do; we're performing actions that other people want us to do. We're acting on the basis of a transferred desire, a desire that has been unhoused from its owner and sutured onto us. In this way, we lose ownership over our behavior. Beyond that, we lose control of our lives by trying to fulfill all the requests that others have placed on us. Your spouse or partner wants you to do something small or large; your children want you to do whatever they can think up; your boss has various demands or requests; and God has several commands, and if his commands are sometimes hard to live up to, well, that's life. The Bible is an inventory of humanity's failures to do what God has asked. The story of Adam's fall is the story of how Adam and Eve fail at the first command that God makes of them. And that's the *ur*-story, the original story at the beginning of time, that moment, and its subsequent punishment.

If you divide imperatives into three general categories—suggestions, requests, and commands—you're forced to consider the size and scope of rewards and punishments. Advice or suggestions often function as dramatic preludes, but they typically feel light and inconsequential. *The Great Gatsby* opens with a remembered piece of advice from Nick Carraway's father, and this easygoing and almost weightless suggestion starts off the novel: "Whenever you feel like criticizing any one . . . just remember that all the people in this world haven't had the advantages that you've had." Okay, fine. Advice can usually be ignored because it involves no obligation on our part to follow it. By its very nature, it's unenforceable. We may take someone's advice or not, and no one will pay much attention to what we do one way or the other. In *Hamlet*, the character of Polonius is famously long-winded and dull. In act one, scene three, he dishes out tiresome advice to his son, Laertes. "Neither a borrower nor a lender be," he says, and so on and so on.

At the other end of the spectrum are the orders and commands that presuppose no real choice on our part unless we choose to disobey or violate them at our peril (torture, prison, the firing squad, one of the circles of Hell). Those with great power have the means to enforce what they ask for. But if the enforcer's power is not absolute, the person who is the object of the request may still have a choice. Suppose in the midst of a pandemic you are asked to wear a mask. This request will not be enforced everywhere. The conditional proof it implies is as follows: *Wearing a mask will help to contain the disease and protect you from infection. If you care about other people, you'll wear it.* However, most of the time, you are not commanded to wear a mask, there is no penalty for not wearing one, and the request is not a mere piece of advice. You have some freedom to choose. Your choice, furthermore, may be a reflection on your character, and it may have consequences in the real world. People who don't like to take orders will claim that their liberty is at stake. (We are not at liberty, however, to drive while drunk or to commit murder. There are limits to what we are free to do when our actions cause harm to others, which complicates the problem of masks.)

Dramatic interest and dramatic structure usually involve a character's *decision* to go in one particular direction. That's a crucial difference: requests contain a certain obligation but also imply a choice on your part, whereas commands assume that you have no choice but to obey. The Ten Commandments are not requests; they're orders. They're not the Ten Suggestions. God has issued the order, and you follow it, or else. You're not supposed to have a better idea about how to behave.

Somewhere between advice and commandment, we find the requests that produce dramatic tension. Typically, they have three components: (1) the request itself, (2) what the enactment of the request will establish or prove, and (3) the time frame.

For example: (1) Please get that dog down the street to stop barking. It's driving me crazy. (2) If you're smart, you'll figure out a way to do it. (3) Please do it now; I'm going nuts.

Another example: (1) Kill King Duncan and fulfill your dream and mine. (2) If you're a real man and want to enact your ambitions, you'll do it. (3) It must be done tonight.

A final example: (1) Save the city of Thebes from this terrible plague. (2) We are dying, and you're the king. Prove your kingship. (3) Do it now.

Because request moments happen in a social world between two or more characters, they often reveal the particular society or subculture in which the characters are living, the nature of obligations in that world, and thus the social contract. In this way, a request may reveal the norms by which people live.

The movie of *The Godfather* begins with an Italian American undertaker, Bonasera, making a request of Don Vito Corleone. Some men have assaulted Bonasera's daughter, and the undertaker wants Don Vito to kill these men in retribution. The request illuminates the web of social obligations that the two men and their families inhabit, and Don Vito refuses the request as out of proportion and unjust. The request has to be scaled down, or the Godfather won't give the order. Also, because Don Vito has been offended by Bonasera's behavior, there's a condition: Bonasera must agree to be Don Vito Corleone's friend. Don Vito tells the undertaker that he himself may have a request someday—that is, as I've noted, requests are by nature often reciprocal by giving birth to other requests. (He does in fact have such a request, eventually: Bonasera must make the body of Don Vito's older son presentable in his casket, after the son has been shot up on the causeway.) The Godfather finally agrees to the scaled-down request. He says magnanimously to Bonasera, "Accept this justice as a gift on my daughter's wedding day." For the reader or viewer of *The Godfather*, the request shows us the inner workings, the dynamics, of this complex social structure, the family and its related criminal organization.

What if someone with power over you asks you to perform an unethical action? That's part of Hamlet's problem, and Macbeth's, but also Don Vito Corleone's: they've all been asked to perform violent acts that may be unjust. What if you say, "If you love me, you'll do what I ask"? This statement is a turning point in Raymond Carver's story "Cathedral." The narrator's wife has befriended a blind man who's coming to the house tonight for dinner. The narrator's wife asks her husband to be hospitable to the blind man, with this condition: "'If you love me,' she said, 'you can do this for me. If you don't love me, okay. But if you had a friend, any friend, and the friend came to visit, I'd make him feel comfortable.'"

Request moments function so well in stories because they may reveal power relationships in a social matrix: they show us who's got the power, and who has little or none, and what people do, or *think* they can do, when in the grip of such power. Can a particular person resist power? Can Hamlet resist the request that his late father, now a ghost, makes of him? Power sometimes moves in unexpected directions. One is not always the master, and the other is not always the servant.

Until you're a parent, for example, you may not realize how much power infants actually have, or how much power our children may have over us as they grow up. We always assume that power goes in the other direction, from parents to children, but it's not always so. Romantic relationships involve a constant shifting of power between one person and another—the power of sex, of attraction, of money, of charm, of love. The stories of request moments reveal the bizarre manner in which power can sometimes displace our best intentions and make us into people we didn't think we were. But the point is that the revelations don't arrive on the scene until after the request has been made. First the request, then the revelation.

By exposing the ethical obligations that we feel we owe to others, request moments reveal what other people want from us and what their claim on us may be. Requests often force a choice that reveals our inner self, and they create narrative momentum by forcing a character to decide to do something when that person would rather not make any decisions at all. We often forget about urgency and momentum in workshops because we know that the supervisor and the workshop group have to finish the story. But in the real world, no one has to finish any literary work—not the poem, or the story, or the novel. Decisions, especially bad decisions, are the lifeblood of narrative.

One of the most common statements you hear in writing workshops is that this or that character is "passive." The passive protagonist is regularly thought to be dull and uninteresting. But Hamlet, the prince of Denmark, is *the* passive protagonist of Western drama, and he is absolutely compelling. People have talked about him for a few centuries now, including, very recently, Simon Critchley in his book *Stay, Illusion!* (2013). Critchley's study is about the persistence of Hamlet in our consciousness. Why this nagging interest in Hamlet? One reason, one among many, is that if there has been a request moment in a story or a play, as there is in *Hamlet*, the situation may remain dramatically charged whether the recipient of the request does anything or not. Suddenly, inaction becomes significant. It stands in the shadow of the request, and it tells you about the norms of the society in which the protagonist happens to live. And inaction can create suspense. Do the dead have any real power over us? Is Hamlet obligated to do what his ghost father asks? What about Laertes and his (murdered) father? Do the dead tell the truth? How would we know? What is the nature of their hold over us? The dead have many good reasons to lie about everything. Hamlet says he's uncertain. Hamlet may be mad. He temporizes. If he follows the request, he may be only a "rogue [or] peasant slave." But as long as he does nothing, the request hangs in suspension; the obligation remains open.

To return to my friend Duffy's talk about necessity: Hamlet is not just doing little or nothing: he feels the *necessity* to do little or nothing because lives are at stake: his father's, his own, and that of King Claudius. The consequence of his father's request, like that of Lady Macbeth, would be murder.

Not all stories need request moments. But sometimes stories and plays and poems stall out because the request hasn't been clarified. There may be a request in the air, or an obligation, but the obligation hasn't been articulated properly. We don't quite know what the request is. To quote Duffy again, the story just sits there. But once a request is uttered, the story may be saved, its power relationships revealed. Its narrative flow acquires momentum as the character moves—tragically or not—in the direction of the request's fulfillment.

Maybe we are asking two questions about such stories: Not only *Who wants what favor?* But also *Who wants what, and from whom?*

I can imagine the poets saying, "What does this have to do with us?" The history of lyric and dramatic poetry, however, is partially the history of requests and how they're planted like little time bombs inside poems. Any request demonstrates that the poem is populated by more than one person.

In the spectrum of poetry, Shakespeare's sonnets often constitute pieces of advice to the young man. At the other end of the spectrum are commands, or orders. William Butler Yeats' last poem, "Under Ben Bulben," a poem of the public-address system, consists of requests ("Irish poets, learn your trade") that sound like commandments, though they are unenforceable. Shelley's "Ozymandias" contains an empty command at its center. A poem may also be made up of directives, as witness Robert Frost's "Directive," a sly and somewhat enigmatic guide to conduct. More often the poetic request is a kind of invitation, as in Auden's "Lay your sleeping head, my love, / Human on my faithless arm." Such requests are not coercive: their power is neither absolute nor negligible because they involve a choice.

Here, as another instance, is poem thirty-two from A. E. Housman's *A Shropshire Lad*:

> From far, from eve and morning
> And yon twelve-winded sky,
> The stuff of life to knit me
> Blew hither: here am I.
>
> Now—for a breath I tarry
> Nor yet disperse apart—
> Take my hand quick and tell me,
> What have you in your heart.
>
> Speak now, and I will answer;
> How shall I help you, say;
> Ere to the wind's twelve quarters
> I take my endless way.

This little poem from 1896 has occupied considerable mental space among twentieth-century novelists: E. M. Forster quotes from this poem in *A Room with a View*, and Ursula Le Guin titled one of her novels *The Wind's Twelve Quarters*.

What does this melancholy poem ask for? Its meaning is relatively straightforward. In stanza one, the poet says that fate and time and the universe have knit him together into his human form. For a brief period, he exists. He is suspended here in time. But note that the clock is ticking and there is a sense of urgency—from "the stuff of life" he will turn to dust soon. In the third line of the second stanza, he now turns to address you, or another. The situation has taken a leap; it has grown anxious and tense—and therefore dramatic. Take my hand *quick* (because time is short), he asks, and tell me what's in your heart. For God's sake, he implies, don't remain silent. Tell me what you feel right now and tell me how I can help you. Do it quickly, do it now, because we come from cosmic dust, and we're going to go back to that dust soon enough. Speak up. Save yourself, and save me. Something is unspoken and must be articulated. How can I help you? Say.

The point is, a request alone may not energize the story or poem. The request must have some urgency of time and the condition behind it. The speaker is not asking his listener to do a load of laundry or to take out the garbage; he's asking the listener to say what is in his heart before time runs out. This is the landscape of emotional necessity.

Notice that the poet doesn't ask or demand that his listener *love* him, as is the case in so many Elizabethan and Romantic lyrics. A request for love is slightly ridiculous because love can't truly be requested. This speaker does not make that mistake. Instead he asks, "How shall I help you, say." The "help" *may* be love, or sex, or something else, such as comfort. The entire poem pivots on that next word, *say*, and in present narrative time, it stays suspended there. Note the absence of the question mark. *Say* is the word that will give life, and the response to it will also give life. On either side of that word *say* yawns an eternal silence. Silence is the abyss, the cosmic dark reach of empty space. So *say something.*

Somewhere behind this poem is its antagonist, the deadly stultifying silence of the English stiff upper lip, which resists expressions of feeling, and also behind it lies the repressive silence of polite society.

Compare A. E. Housman's reticence to a more overt but rhetorically similar request at the conclusion of Danez Smith's poem "bare" from *Don't Call Us Dead* (2017):

if love is a hole wide enough
to be God's mouth, let me plunge

into that holy dark & forget
the color of light. love, stay

in me until our bodies forget
what divides us, until your hands

are my hands & your blood
is my blood & your name

is my name & his & his

This statement has a timeless, classic root. Sometimes it seems as if half the love poems ever written have sought a way to re-frame and to re-state the soul and body's request: *love, stay*. Don't leave me alone here. Don't abandon me. Don't let this feeling we share slip away. Don't take your body away from mine. Let the two of us be one being, forever. Those requests may be directed toward the speaker's lover, or they may be directed toward the feeling of love, the experience of it—love itself. Love, don't go away. Let me feel this particular emotion, yours, from now on.

A request moment could also be a prohibition. Here is the opening of the Blue Ridge folk song "Silver Dagger":

Don't sing love songs, you'll wake my mother
She's sleeping here right by my side
And in her right hand a silver dagger,
She says that I can't be your bride.

All men are false, says my mother,
They'll tell you wicked, lovin' lies.
The very next evening, they'll court another,
Leave you alone to pine and sigh.

My daddy is a handsome devil
He's got a chain five miles long,
And on every link a heart does dangle
Of another maid he's loved and wronged.

Go court another tender maiden,
And hope that she will be your wife,
For I've been warned, and I've decided
To sleep alone all of my life.

This story has a classic form: it begins with an unstable triangle, of mother, daughter, and would-be lover. The prohibition comes from the daughter and is spoken to her suitor, who is probably standing outside a window, but that prohibition sits on top of another rather dire prohibition from the seduced and abandoned mother. The power, the condition, is punishment by murder: the mother's gleaming silver dagger is patiently waiting to be used. Terrible violence is threatened. We are not so far from the plot of Alfred Hitchcock's film *Psycho*. The third stanza constitutes the explanatory flashback: the mother once loved a faithless man. The song ends with another request: go away, court someone else, leave me alone, or else.

I have two more brief examples in mind: one from Alice Munro, one from Shirley Jackson. For Shakespeare, the request moment is often the starting point of a play. For *these* writers, the request moment often serves as the turning point, the Aristotelian reversal. The request changes the situation and sends the story into its last act.

Shirley Jackson's "The Lottery" (1948) is one of those classic stories that many Americans were once required to read in high school, as if it were a secret parable about the behavior of adult groups or mobs—something that you just had to learn about the behavior of our fellow citizens. The story concerns a small American town where a ritual stoning of one of the town's residents occurs once a year, in springtime. The person who is stoned to death is the winner or more exactly the loser of the town's annual lottery. The story is written so that the reader gradually figures all this out (through a trick of point of view, no character's thoughts are ever paraphrased). No one in the town seems to know how the ritual got started, or what it's good for, but it goes on year after year nevertheless. The story begins with David Lynch–like small-town sunshine, "the fresh warmth of a full-summer day," and ends with a David Lynch–like collective murder of that year's lottery loser, Tessie Hutchinson. Even the little children help to kill her.

The near invisibility of the request reflects the story's brilliant strangeness. There isn't a request moment, you could claim, unless you count Old Man Warner's "Come on, come on, everyone" at the story's end. That is, there's no explicit request. Who wants this murderous collective action performed? Who asked the town to do it? Who set it into motion? We don't know and are never told. The story is about an obligation being paid off for a reason that no one seems to remember, the very definition of the unsourced request.

And that may be the point. Sometimes a story benefits by having the request clarified, but Shirley Jackson's fiction thrived—in both her stories and her novels—on desires over which no one has staked a claim, desires that no one really wants to have anymore, in answer to dead obligations. We might call these *orphaned* or *zombie desires* that have turned into empty traditions, and they're visible whenever individuals or groups are in the grip of a compulsion or a habit. With zombie desires, you need to perform some action but can't remember why you're doing it. Orphaned desires are hauntings and are the first cousins to addictions. Under these conditions, people say, the devil made me do it. Okay, I (sort of) did it, but the action I performed was not something I would ever do. I can't exactly own up to it.

In Shirley Jackson's fiction, people have a tendency to act as if they're under a spell. Some authority may once have asked this town to perform a springtime sacrifice, but that person has been long forgotten, and the reason for the request has been lost. The action goes on being performed anyway, automatically, mindlessly. You wash your car on Saturday. Why? *Because you always wash your car on Saturday.* You go around performing habitual actions because you're supposed to do them, but you can't remember why you're supposed to do them, or what the obligation was and who set it into motion. One good premise for a story is the enactment of a dead tradition that no one believes in. No one in Shirley Jackson's town remembers why everybody's supposed to stone a fellow citizen; all that they remember is that they *have to do it*. The *why* has been lost; the *what* remains. The reason this works dramatically in "The Lottery" is that the result is terrible violence. Poor Tessie Hutchinson. Her last words are, "It isn't fair, it isn't right."

We all have behaviors over which we disclaim ownership. Under a compulsion, we do what we don't want to do, and we perform these actions only because we're supposed to do them, or we do them because we've fallen into the habit of doing them. The rationale for the action has disappeared, shrouded by time's passing. Shirley Jackson's *The Haunting of Hill House* (1959) has a character named Eleanor whose life was formed by her caretaking of her mother. This caretaking hollowed her out, and now she scarcely has any free will at all. It is as if she has always answered the request claims of others and has no idea anymore what she actually wants for herself. The haunted house—haunted by her unlived life—therefore begins to speak to her once she's inside it. Her bloated and fugitive subjectivity, having no other place to go, moves into the landscape and into the walls. The house even writes letters to her. The letters, written in blood on the wall at night, say, COME HOME ELEANOR. This invitation comes directly from the land of the dead.

You may feel dead inside if you have spent your life doing the bidding of others. This is the zombie feeling of the perpetually oppressed, the deadness of the butler as dramatized in Kazuo Ishiguro's *The Remains of the Day* (1989).

The art of writing horror fiction usually depends on an evil person or entity making a request or a demand on an innocent who cannot resist. Given their particular nonstandard appetites, vampires always have an agenda. Victorians by temperament, they may at first ask politely for favors by seducing the victim, but sometimes their patience runs out. This is not true of zombies. Zombies are past all that because they're dead and are entirely unconscious but are still crazed consumers, heading for the mall.

Speaking of Gothic fiction, Alice Munro has a wonderful and very disturbing story in her collection entitled *Too Much Happiness* (2009) that turns on a request moment. The story is "Child's Play," and it concerns two girls, Marlene and Charlene. Marlene is the narrator, Charlene is her friend, and the story is Marlene's account of her childhood in proximity to a special-needs, cognitively challenged girl named Verna. At summer camp, when they are ten years old, Marlene and Charlene do something terrible to Verna, an action that, under most circumstances, would be the climax of the story. Together, they hold her under the water at a lake during the swimming hour, drowning her.

But "Child's Play" has a second, and even a third act, and the story is not really about the terrible thing that the two girls do to Verna, or Verna's death. What the story tracks is how different the two girls are from each other, and how they differ when they're adults, and whether they feel the need to be forgiven. Marlene notes that the terrible thing they have done to Verna occurred "as if we were doing just what was—amazingly—demanded of us." But the action (as in "The Lottery," a collaborative murder) results in two forms of response.

Marlene, the narrator, does not believe that she can ever be forgiven. What she has done to Verna is unforgivable, and she will not confess the murder to anybody—partly out of shame, and partly because she believes no perpetrator is ever really released and restored after such an action. Some actions may be unforgivable—you can't undo them. Accordingly, the story picks up at the moment when Marlene and Charlene are in late middle age, and Charlene is dying of cancer. Charlene sends Marlene a note: "I am writing this in case I get too far gone to speak. Please do what I ask you. Please go to Guelph and go to the cathedral and ask for Father Hofstrader. . . . He will know what to do. This I cannot ask C. [Charlene's husband] and do not want him ever to know. Father H. knows and I have asked him and he says it is possible to help me."

Marlene does, more or less, what Charlene has asked her to do. And the reader wonders, Doesn't the narrator want forgiveness for herself? The request has created a contrast, which is crucial to the story. Most people, after all, want to be released from the burden of their past guilt and obligations. But Marlene does not:

Was I not tempted, during all this palaver? Not once? You'd think that I might break open, be wise to break open, glimpsing that vast though tricky forgiveness. But no. It's not for me. What's done is done. Flocks of angels, tears of blood, notwithstanding.

For Marlene, Catholicism is no help, and confessing is useless (though the story itself becomes a form of confession), and forgiveness is the stuff of dream worlds that only children believe in. Marlene apparently believes that the wish to be forgiven is essentially sentimental. The phrase that Marlene uses, "what's done is done," is the language of the unforgiven and the unredeemed. The story achieves a kind of moral clarity because Marlene's behavior contrasts with that of Charlene, who cannot die peacefully with the burden of her childhood actions weighing on her. Marlene doesn't buy in to any form of institutional confession and forgiveness. "What's done is done," Marlene writes. This may remind some readers of the words of Lady Macbeth. "What's done," Lady Macbeth says, "cannot be undone." She's gone through a one-way gate.

Having done an errand of mercy for her dying friend, Marlene cannot manage a similar act of mercy for herself.

Request moments charge things up and change the situation. I began with a frame story about my mother, and I want to end with another one. My mother passed away in 1978, may she rest in peace. Several years after that, I was having coffee with a college friend, a woman who had been the coeditor with me of the literary magazine at Macalester College in the 1960s. We have coffee now and then, and we talk about old times. There was a pause in the conversation, and she said, "I have to tell you something."

I asked what.

"I've had two dreams about your mother," she said. My friend has always been a bit psychic, so I was not entirely surprised.

"You did? But you never met my mother. What happened?" I asked.

"Well, the first time, she told me that she wanted me to tell you something." At this point, my friend told me what my mother had said in the dream. My friend was supposed to pass on a request to me of what my mother wanted me to do, and to keep my mother's privacy in the hereafter I won't repeat what my mother's request was, but it was reasonable, and since then, I have tried to do it. This is my own small-scale and personal version of Hamlet being visited by his father's ghost. "Anyway," my friend continued, "after she came to me in the dream the first time with that request, I thought the whole thing was so completely weird that I didn't tell you about it the last time you and I had coffee together."

"Oh," I said. "Okay."

"So anyway," my friend said, "when I didn't pass on your mother's request to you right away, I had a second dream in which your mother reappeared. Your mother was very upset with me that second time, and she said, 'I'm very disappointed in you. You didn't do what I asked you to do. You didn't tell Charlie what I asked. So I have to ask you again now.'"

At this point I got the shivers, because that business about being disappointed in someone really sounded like my mother, as did the double undying request carrying the unmistakable maternal note, in an ordinary and apparently immortal haunting over a cup of coffee on a bright, sunny day.

Inventories and Undoings

To start with, imagine the most basic act of reading. We open the book, we read the first few sentences, and there in front of us is a person who somehow has to come alive on the page. As writers ourselves and as readers, let's suppose for the sake of argument that this character happens to be someone we have never heard of, someone we must become acquainted with as soon as we start to read the story. Perhaps this person has a name strange to us, uncommon in some way, like Job or Desdemona or Ahab or Genji or Flem Snopes or Bathsheba Everdene, or Milkman Dead, the sort of name you might never expect to hear or see outside of the story in which the person resides. They *are* their story; they exist almost entirely as creatures of literature, and their claim to their identity is so great that no one else may ever be called that name again—after being used, the name has been retired. There have been no prominent Ahabs in literature following the ship's captain found in *Moby-Dick*, and there probably won't be.

And Job? Whoever he is, he exists entirely in his book as a character with whom we're familiar because of what happened to him and not because of his accomplishments or what he made of himself. He exists as a figure in the Bible and in the history of literature because of his suffering, his *undoing*.

The anonymous author of the Book of Job does not begin with an action in order to establish his central figure on the page. He does not start with what creative-writing textbooks advise: a small dramatic attention-getting device that leads inexorably toward a possible goal and the central conflict and the dramatic development that follow, although these elements are certainly visible in the story and contribute to it. No: the author of the Book of Job begins with a statement of a human being who existed somewhere, followed by another statement about this man, in the form of an inventory. In the New Revised Standard Version: "There was once a man in the land of Uz whose name was Job. That man was blameless and upright, one who feared God and turned away from evil. There were born to him seven sons and three daughters. He had seven thousand sheep, three thousand camels, five hundred yoke of oxen, five hundred donkeys, and very many servants; so that this man was the greatest of all the people of the east."

The story continues with an account of Job's sons, of their feast days and of how they invited their sisters to these feasts; it tells us of how Job blessed his children, and made offerings to God, and asked forgiveness for any sins those children might have committed. In effect, the first scene ends here. With great majesty, narrative dignity, and beauty, we have been given all the earthly background we need concerning this person.

But stories begin when things start to go wrong. Stories begin when trouble is visited upon the characters. They cannot be tested otherwise. As a friend of mine once said in answer to a question about how he writes his stories, "I think of characters whom I love, and then I visit trouble upon them." And so, in the Book of Job, the scene shifts to God and to a debate he has with an entity called Satan. This debate, one of the most gravely important ones in Western thought, is about Job's faith and whether this faith means anything at all if it is subjected to intolerable pressures. God believes that Job's faith is infinite, and he therefore allows Satan to undo Job's successful life, which Satan is happy to manage, touching everything belonging to Job and even Job himself. The story, then, becomes one concerned with the meaning of suffering, and of how, given a belief in God, we might think about our own suffering and how we will act when we are in its grip.

But it is not Job's undoing that I want to discuss here, or the significance of the enormous weight of human sorrow and suffering narrated to us in this book. I want to draw our attention to something smaller and seemingly insignificant, the little inventory at the start of the story—those seven thousand sheep, the three thousand camels, the five hundred yoke of oxen, the five hundred donkeys, and the servants. And what I want to say about this inventory seems to me both obvious and, just possibly, difficult and mysterious.

A literary inventory, as opposed to any sort of list, is an accounting, a reckoning of possessions. And it seems to be in the nature of inventories to suggest not only what's been gained, but more properly what's about to be lost and what the prospects for further loss might be. Inventories are at the center of many characterizations, and every inventory implies a plot involving loss, leading to an odd reversal implicit in most inventories: by adding up what seems to be an account of fullness, they seem to create exactly the opposite effect, which is that of an emptying out. In such cases, the shadow is more visible than the body that casts it. Inventories give us an addition, but metaphorically and narratively they imply removal, de-acquisition, and nothingness—the subtraction effect of narrative undoing, which will imply the undoing of the character. You start with the accumulation, but you end up with an erasure. You begin with the person in possession of ten million dollars and then wait for the money to be stripped away; that's the logic of storytelling. B. Traven's *The Treasure of the Sierra Madre* (1935) is not really about finding the gold but about how the characters go about losing it and then losing themselves. Most stories about gold are about losing the gold.

In what is obvious about these inventories, we are invited to witness an Aristotelian reversal. In Aristotle's thinking about tragedy, a great man is brought low through the forces of circumstance in tandem with flaws in his own character. To tell a story about a great person, we may need an inventory of the possessions: in contemporary terms, the Porsches and the swimming pools, the Armani suits and Manolo Blahnik shoes, and the square footage of the houses in the Hamptons and Pacific Palisades. We may also need a statement or an illustration of this person's great human qualities—that he is blameless and upright, a God-fearing person, who turned away from evil.

These inventories stay with us as cultural markers and in recent years have intensified. During a gilded age, people pay constant attention to everyone else's inventory. You're measured by what you own. In Ayad Akhtar's *Homeland Elegies* (2020), the narrator's acquaintance reports on the riches owned by a man of consequence, Riaz Rind, a Pakistani American who has been very successful as an investor. To measure his success, his importance as a character, we are given an inventory of his possessions. In its shine of admiration and awe, this inventory constitutes a very American moment, as if the possessor of these precious objects has been touched somehow by a God who dispenses both good and bad luck. A friend reports back to the narrator about Riaz Rind's riches this way:

> "East End Avenue. He's got the top four floors. You take an elevator to the first floor, and then he's got his own elevator for the floors inside the apartment. There's an indoor pool. And I don't mean a Jacuzzi. A pool. It's not small. Moroccan tile, foil arches. He took us into this room he's got full of Sufi manuscripts. Another room, just for bourbon, bigger than my living room. The walls on

two sides are covered, floor to ceiling, with bottles—a butcher-
block bar in the middle. I saw the Van Winkle [a rare bourbon]
on the shelf and flipped out. I mean, I just wanted to hold it, but
he brings it down and breaks the seal, then pours me a snifter. I
almost fainted. He watched me drink it. I must have looked like
I was having an orgasm."

In the modern age, when the possessions proliferate, a sexual fire—
an increase of the sensual temperature—is lit and begins to burn.

Now, over two thousand years after the writing of the Book of
Job, we have probably come to another stage as writers in this age of
commodities. The possessions I have just listed do not, in fact, play
the same positive role that the possessions did in the Book of Job. In
the Book of Job, possessions are an indication of stature and quality
of character. In our time, the possessions themselves, the very nature
of the possessions, have turned into features of character but not necessarily of stature. The brand name is attached to the product and to
the person who owns it. It's not just an Armani suit; the person who
wears it is an Armani-suit sort of guy. In this way, certain features of
setting subliminally turn into features of characterization.

Setting and characterization are not so separate as they might appear. A person with houses in the Hamptons and Pacific Palisades,
who wears haute couture and drives a Porsche and owns a bottle
of Van Winkle bourbon, might be a powerful human being, but the
other feature of Job's character—his goodness—is conspicuously absent from the inventory of objects I have named. It's not only absent,
it's slightly contradictory to it. If you said that the man who wears the
Armani suit was blameless before God, you would be under clouds of
narrative suspicion. The indoor swimming pool and the Van Winkle
bourbon and the town house in New York City make the "blameless and upright" harder to put over as features of our modern Job's

character, simply because of what we know about what it may take to acquire those objects in a society like ours, and because God and Satan are not quarreling in the background anymore. That quarrel is over.

You can say something about a person by listing the surrounding objects, and how that person looks. I'm not arguing that this is a complete mode of characterization, only that it is a start.

No modern writer would shift the scene from Job to a discussion between God and Satan. We are not permitted, or we do not usually permit ourselves, such a change in scene or context. But with the loss of this sort of faith goes a loss of context and proportion, so that if we want to write about a person's undoing, any person's suffering, we're stuck with that person, and the place, and the time, and the culture. Satan is no longer available to use as an ethical marker. (Wallace Stevens notes Satan's absence in his poem "Esthétique du Mal": "The death of Satan was a tragedy / For the imagination.") We can begin with the inventory, we can pile up the lists, in showing a character's downfall or undoing. What we don't always think about, but what the Old Testament narrator could summon easily, is the ethical importance of this undoing and the resulting suffering and what that suffering may mean and whether it means anything at all. Sometimes we think the fact of suffering is enough, that any suffering is sufficient for a story. But does such suffering really have *any* meaning? After all, at times we want to see the affluent punished, just because they're luckier, or smarter, or richer, than we are. But what if the affluent are generous, and kind, and magnanimous? Poor people who suffer: What does that mean, if it means anything? How do we think about the good person's suffering, their undoing? We enter the realm of Dostoevsky's *The Idiot* with such a question. Here is a puzzling and mind-bending statement that I first heard from the critic Lionel Abel in 1971: "Prince Myshkin [the protagonist of *The Idiot*] is good without anybody thinking that he is."

Does this statement make any sense, philosophically or otherwise? How is it even possible?

Putting an inventory together is not so difficult until you realize that not everything can go into the list of possessions, and you, the writer, must decide which objects may carry personal meanings and which ones do not, and what slant, what angle of approach, you may need.

In the days when I was teaching introductory creative writing classes, I used to assign exercises of characterization in which the students had to put together "ten things I know about them." One of these ten things had to be a secret. And I also used to advise everybody to think about particularized details that would give the reader an insight into character. For example, you can say, "She likes chocolate," but almost everybody likes chocolate. It's better to say, "The only chocolate she will eat is imported from Mozambique." That immediately gives you a little sense of her character—not much, but it's a start.

Almost invariably I got interesting responses from the students after they had completed this exercise. At first they grumbled about it, but then they discovered that they were happening upon facts concerning these imaginary characters that they didn't know they knew. Simply by inventing imaginary facts, by forcing themselves to invent them, they made them true. When you invent a fact in a story, it becomes imaginatively true, as long as it doesn't contradict the logic of the story. This is one of the great mysteries and secret delights of writing fiction. As Nathanael West wrote, "Possibilities became probabilities and wound up as inevitabilities."

When you start to make such lists, you discover a principle of inner consistency. If the list gets long enough, the inventory first of possessions, then of personal appearance, including beauty or handsomeness, and finally of personal qualities, you begin to realize that some items belong on the list, and some items don't belong there, and you take out the ones that are wildly inconsistent with the rest of the list. If you make a list about an imaginary character named Harold, you will discover, eventually, that some of your facts don't belong on your list: if Harold belongs to an Alaskan hunters association and drives a Hummer, he probably doesn't spend the rest of his time playing the viola, working for Earth First!, and translating the poems of Jorge Luis Borges. He might, but you'd have some explaining to do.

You begin to discover something else when you start to make lists like this. You discover that you can say "She is brave" as an important statement that feels unsubstantiated, thin, and unsound until some proof is offered. "She is brave" is a claim about an inner quality, as is "He is timid." You can make a lot of claims like this, but sooner or later you have to establish their validity, unless you happen to believe what Lionel Abel said about Prince Myshkin—that some people are intrinsically good or bad without anyone thinking that they are. But how, on what grounds, would you believe such a thing? Claims about character are like promissory notes or claims in court, and they require actions or evidence to back them up. You can say, "Over this dresser, there on the wall of his bedroom at home, this teenager has a poster of the band Grätüitöüs Ümläüt." Or: "This young adult male has a tattoo of a roaring lion on his right calf." These assertions are not claims; they're statements, markers, about possessions, and therefore are parts of inventories. When you start to write fiction, you can help yourself out by noticing the difference between making a claim about a character (that is, what a character is), and making an inventory (that is, what a character has). Every claim sooner or later may have to have some proof. But statements, inventories, start to build a world immediately. They *are* the proof. And notice this: you can describe characters in absentia, sometimes, just by describing what they've accumulated in their rooms. Tell me what those particular teenagers have in their rooms, and I will begin to tell you who they are.

Something in the nature of fiction loves inventories and lists. Fiction's subject matter is often related to sheer accumulation. Fiction loves to pile things up, the bricks and the mortar. Writing fiction is about accumulating *stuff*—details about setting, details about clothing and behavior and actions and speech patterns and all the rickrack of objects that we surround ourselves with. If you don't like amassing this bargeload of material, you may not be comfortable with fiction itself, or at least realist fiction, which has a tendency to fill up the page with accretive details. Someone like Tom Wolfe, dressed in his white suit, stood near other writers for years complaining about them and claiming that contemporary writers simply don't collect enough information, enough material evidence, about characters and their possessions in their stories and novels. Wolfe himself became compulsive about this and had a tendency to substitute inventories (the brand names of shoes and suits and hats and cars and furniture and vodkas) for other forms of characterization. He was wrong to be so tiresome about it. But he had a point about material life, and he stuck by it.

I am about the last person on earth to defend Tom Wolfe or his fiction, which I find unreadable, as opposed to his early nonfiction, which I loved. But it strikes me that when we wish to dramatize a character's fall or undoing, our canvas often benefits by being crowded with *stuff*. The more details there are, and the more the front and the back of the story are filled in with material details of this kind, the more we are likely to feel the second context I was referring to in the Book of Job: that is, the moral importance of the experience that we are being shown, the background of the suffering.

An inventory of objects surrounding characters helps to define those characters, and, perhaps, to measure the size of their fall. But the inventory is typically unable to give a sense of the importance or significance of that fall; other means must be found for that. Some materialists are corrupt, but others may be innocent. When their possessions are taken away, we learn which are which. If I take away all of your possessions, what sort of person will you be? It is doubtful that you will be the same person that you are now.

Here, for example, is an eruption of brand names in Toni Morrison's *Song of Solomon* (1977). Hagar has got it into her head that the only way to get Milkman Dead to love her is by her acquisition of clothes and makeup. As she says, "I have to buy some clothes. New clothes. Everything I have is a mess." What follows is a feverish paragraph whose delirium matches Hagar's nearly hopeless wish to gain love from a loveless man by buying cosmetics to make herself pretty:

> The cosmetics department enfolded her in perfume, and she read hungrily the labels and the promise. Myrurgia for primeval woman who creates for him a world of tender privacy where the only occupant is you, mixed with Nina Ricci's L'Air du Temps, Yardley's Flair with Tuvaché's Nectaroma and D'Orsay's Intoxication. Robert Piguet's Fracas, and Calypso and Visa and Bandit. Houbigant's Chantilly. Caron's Fleurs de Rocaille and Bellodgia. Hagar breathed deeply the sweet air that hung over the glass counters. Like a smiling sleepwalker she circled. Round and round the diamond-clear counters covered with bottles, wafer-thin disks, round boxes, tubes, and phials. Lipsticks in soft white hands darted out of their sheaths like the shiny red penises of puppies. Peachy powders and milky lotions were grouped in front of poster after cardboard poster of gorgeous grinning faces. Faces in ecstasy. Faces somber in achieved seduction. Hagar believed she could spend her life there among the cut glass, shimmering in peaches and cream, in satin. In opulence. In luxe. In love.

This paragraph is painful to read for any reader who has com-passion for Hagar, but its technical virtuosity—the lipstick in those telltale "white" hands, the innocent/corrupt "shiny red penises of puppies," and then the conclusive, gaspingly ecstatic "In opulence. In luxe. In love" can only excite writerly admiration. This admi-ration comes at a high cost. Two pages later, Hagar is caught in a thunderstorm, and the downpour drains the makeup from her face and causes her shopping bags to split. By the time she arrives home, she has been deprived of everything she had bought and hoped for (negative inventories often arrive quickly): "the wet ripped hose, the soiled white dress, the sticky, lumpy face powder, the streaked rouge, and the wild wet shoals of hair." Hagar takes to her bed and falls into a feverish delirium. The scene of her dying is one of the most pain-fully beautiful passages in Toni Morrison's fiction, and it suggests that someone who lives by material acquisition risks dying from it as well.

Here, by contrast, is a characteristic paragraph from Thomas Hardy's *The Return of the Native* (1878):

Along the road walked an old man. He was white-headed as a mountain, bowed in the shoulders, and faded in general aspect. He wore a glazed hat, an ancient boat-cloak, and shoes; his brass buttons bearing an anchor upon their face. In his hand was a silver-headed walking-stick, which he used as a veritable third leg, perseveringly dotting the ground with its point at every few inches' interval. One would have said that he had been, in his day, a naval officer of some sort or other.

We tend to avoid inventory descriptions like this in contemporary fiction. We don't believe in the narrative distance required by such a description; we distrust physical descriptions of this sort, includ-ing the hat, the boat-cloak, the brass buttons, and the walking stick; we're much happier with mental states—we side with Virginia Woolf against Arnold Bennett in the quarrel of the inner life against the outer object (you can find this quarrel staged in her essay "Modern Fiction" in *The Common Reader*). But still and all: Hardy has planted an image in our heads, and he is strong where contemporary writers are often weak: that is, you can always see his characters. When Eustacia Vye comes into the story, Hardy spends virtually all of chapter seven describing her by doing a human inventory, starting at her hair and moving downward. Thomas Hardy's novels are often about someone's undoing, and he almost has a blind spot as a writer in piling up of detail. He will confidently stop his novels in order to give the reader a list. There is an insistence in Hardy, as there is in Edith Wharton, Willa Cather, William Faulkner, and Toni Morrison, on both a character and a world, and there is a tendency in all those writers to create those characters and that world by means of detailed inventories.

Here I need to stop and offer a digression, which is the real starting point of this essay.

In 1998, my brother Thomas died. He had been in poor health for a long time, and his heart and kidneys were not in good shape. He lived in Saint Paul, Minnesota, in an apartment located in a building—named the Commodore—whose bar was once frequented by F. Scott Fitzgerald. My brother died of congestive heart failure, and he was living alone when it happened.

My surviving brother and I were ordered by the court to go into his living quarters and to exercise what is called "due diligence" in searching for his will. This we did. But Tom's apartment was like many apartments inhabited by single men; it was not so much a space for living as it was a space for accumulating things, particularly papers. In my brother's apartment I was greeted by official-looking papers piled up everywhere. The apartment smelled of these papers.

But that wasn't all. There were also the rustic-cabin pieces of furniture, the fly rods and shotguns, the yearbooks and diplomas, the collections of kitchen gadgetry (including a meat dehydrator and a Veg-O-Matic), the aftershaves and the colognes, the clothes, the computers, the radios, the police scanners, the audio system, the CDs, and the vinyl LPs.

Part of the experience of losing anyone includes the activity of going through their possessions after a death. In my brother's case, they carried him, or he carried them, and the inventory of these things is finally an inventory not just of possessions but also of being itself, one person's being-on-earth. Every picture tells a story, and every object that we have acquired leads somewhere into our most secret selves.

My brother was not a materialist, but like the rest of us, he lived in the material world, and his objects and their display would have visibly opened a door into his inner life. His possessions did not give off an air of melancholy while he was alive, but once he was gone, they did. At that point, they were his leavings, orphaned, and they were all the material life we had left of him.

The impulse to list the things belonging to someone, starting with appearance and then moving on to possessions, is a traditional starting point in a narrative. That impulse to make lists probably goes back to childhood. It gives us a certain security: "That's mine!" And I think that we tend to put that security-inducing process to work whenever we are traumatized, as Job was, as Hagar was, as anyone is whenever what you have is taken away.

Around the turn of the century, novelists specialized in the patient, lengthy, slow-tempo list. Contemporary writers continue to make lists and to take inventories, but an air of impatience and panic has been introduced to this procedure, as if no one's attention span can sustain it. Perhaps we are now in the age of the panic-stricken list.

William Maxwell managed to be both a regionalist and a cosmopolitan writer, and he inherited and in some sense employed the techniques of both Virginia Woolf and Theodore Dreiser, as odd as that may sound. That is, he was painstaking in the depiction of consciousness, but he also noted, with the care of a jeweler, the material life of his characters.

So Long, See You Tomorrow (1979) is a formally unusual book, in its double narrative track using surrogate narratives and its mixture of the real and the fictional. However, both of the book's narratives are about a death, and both are about being stuck in time, traumatized by events. In both narratives, inventories are absolutely crucial to the development and elaboration of the story. What is unusual about this book is that other people are not minor characters in the pageant of the author's life. The author and narrator is a rather minor character, though his pain is so great that it powers the heart of the book. Clarence Smith and Lloyd Wilson and their wives and children stand at the center of the actual narrative. The novel hands off its narrator's preoccupations to other characters, in a series of surrogate stories.

How does this book go about its business? It first establishes a scene of violence, a gravel pit, where a pistol shot is heard. It then flows out from this specific site and event to Lincoln, Illinois, and to the influenza epidemic of 1918–19, in which the author's mother died. We find out about the author's sorrow as a little boy over his mother's death, and the "commonplace objects" that helped him through it: "an umbrella stand, a glass ashtray backed with brightly colored cigar bands, the fire tongs . . . the two big elm trees that shaded the house from the heat of the sun, and the trumpet vine by the back door, and the white lilac bush by the dining-room window, and the comfortable wicker porch furniture and the porch swing that contributed its *creak . . . creak . . .* to the sounds of the summer night." The narrator says that with the help of these things, he got from one day to the next.

Every time a list like this appears, someone is about to lose something or has already lost it. Lists like this one have an arc, perhaps by their very nature, toward the mournful. They caress details lovingly in compensation for something else somewhere that's gone. In a state of grief, we may do inventories.

So Long, See You Tomorrow signals, about a third of the way through, that it is about to move out of journalistic reporting into imaginative reconstruction. It must do so in order to free itself from a past and in partial restitution for the narrator's slight against a childhood friend. It first sets forth inventories to construct a world, and then dismantles that same world, as violence enters it.

The narrator does his best to imagine his friend's, Cletus Smith's, house. First he imagines a dog. Then he imagines a bicycle (it is painted bright blue) and a horse (it's a workhorse, but it loves the boy) and finally he imagines the kitchen in the boy's house.

For several decades William Maxwell was the fiction editor of the *New Yorker*. We might take that to mean, mistakenly, as it turns out, that he was uninterested as a writer in plain commonplace objects. In fact, he was fixated by them. The minute particulars of his scenes are so loved that he is willing to lay them out before us, as presents. Like a Victorian novelist, he is quite willing to stop time so that we can stare at the objects in front of us.

Here is the paragraph about the kitchen:

Let us consider the kitchen the dog is not allowed into. Steam on the windows. Zinc surfaces that have lost their shine. Wooden surfaces that have been scrubbed to the texture of velvet. The range, with two buckets of water beside it ready to be poured into the reservoir when it is empty. The teakettle. The white enamel coffeepot. The tin matchbox on the wall. The wood-box, the sink, the comb hanging by a string, the roller towel. The kerosene lamp with a white glass shade. The embossed calendar. The kitchen chairs, some with a crack in the seat. The cracked oilcloth on the kitchen table. The smell of Octagon soap. To the indifferent eye it is like every farm kitchen for a hundred miles around, but none of those others would have been waiting in absolute stillness for Cletus to come home from school, or have seemed like all his heart desired when he walks in out of the cold.

Somehow these objects feel like preserves stored in the basement of a house. Maxwell has preserved *these* objects against time so that Cletus Smith could walk into that kitchen and not be as stunned into stillness by wonder, as we are. This inventory seems observed and not merely imagined because of that comb hanging by a string and the wood scrubbed to the texture of velvet. Why is the comb hanging on the string? In the kitchen? Because, my guess is, the kitchen in the summer is a place where the woman of the house works, and she combs her hair back to keep it out of her eyes, and the family is poor and cannot afford to lose a comb.

Let's move now to a much later point in the novel, when a love affair has broken up Cletus' household. How does Maxwell signal that Cletus' mother, Fern, has grown negligent? He doesn't say so, in so many words. He simply says, "All his socks had holes in them. The strawberry bed was loaded with fruit and she didn't bother to pick it. She left the beans on the vines until they were too big to eat." Large inventories, and small ones.

Here is a final inventory, a subtractive listing of what is taken away from Cletus when his parents' marriage begins to dissolve. This listing follows in almost absolute parallel the coming-home scene at the beginning of the novel. Addition in the beginning of the novel is bookended by subtraction near its end. Marriages use addition; divorces specialize in subtraction:

Whether they are part of home or home is part of them is not a question children are prepared to answer. Having taken away the dog, take away the kitchen—the smell of something good in the oven for dinner. Also the smell of washday, of wool drying on the wooden rack. Of ashes. Of soup simmering on the stove. Take away the patient old horse waiting by the pasture fence. Take away the chores that kept him busy from the time he got home from school until they sat down for supper. Take away the early-morning mist, the sound of crows quarreling in the treetops.

His work clothes are still hanging on a nail beside the door of his room, but nobody puts them on or takes them off. Nobody sleeps in his bed. Or reads the broken-backed copy of *Tom Swift and His Flying Machine*. Take that away too, while you are at it.

Take away the pitcher and the bowl, both of them dry and dusty. Take away the cow barn where the cats, sitting all in a row, wait with their mouths wide open for somebody to squirt milk down their throats. Take away the horse barn too—the smell of hay and dust and horse piss and old sweat-stained leather, the rain beating down on the plowed field beyond the open door. Take all this away and what have you done to him? In the face of a deprivation so great, what is the use of asking him to go on being the boy he was. He might as well start life over again as some other boy instead.

This inventory employs virtually all of the senses: smell, with the smell of the soup and of wool drying, of hay and dust and horse piss and old sweat-stained leather; sight, with the sight of the rain beating down on the plowed field, and the cats sitting in a row in the cow barn with their mouths open waiting for the squirts of milk; hearing, with the sound of the crows quarreling in the treetops; and touch, the dry and dusty pitcher and the bowl.

If you are Satan and you want to undo Job, you first take away what is most precious to him. By taking away the objects he loves, you may take away his faith. If you take away his faith, he's no longer the man he was. If you are going to undo Cletus Smith, you take away everything that created his world and therefore made him into the boy he was. The undoing of a character in a story and indeed in life first involves removing from individuals the accessories that made them who they were. But I think it's important to notice how William Maxwell avoids the problem of self-pity and authorial bullying, what I would call the problem of where to put the pathos.

The author does not bother to explain Cletus' own feelings about losing these features of his life. Such a paraphrase is unnecessary. In this sense, the author's negative inventory takes over from his character; the evidence completely overshadows the expository argument. There are no statements such as "Cletus felt terrible. He felt as if the bottom had dropped out of everything. His sadness would not go away." In sentences such as these, the pathos is so clear and obvious that it has no narrative function except to bully the reader into agreeing.

A second notable feature about the passage I have just quoted is the sense of scale. Maxwell makes sure that all the objects and sights and sounds are relatively humble. The immediate effect is one of humanization. Pathos can live in small and apparently trivial objects better than it can in large, grandiose ones. Grandiosity may lead to comedy: "Oh my god, they took away my swimming pool, and now they're taking away my Bechstein piano, and I'm living in a motel." Statements like that constitute one basis of comedy, as in the TV series *Schitt's Creek*. Pathos will not exist comfortably in an inventory of luxuries—it flees from it so quickly that incongruity is the instantaneous result. In fiction, small objects work better than large ones. Large objects have a tendency, like elephants, to become comical.

Every character in So Long, See You Tomorrow is undone by divorce or death, but there is also an effect of great distance that allows these events some air to breathe in, and a counterbalancing sense of friendship and generosity that finally gives the story a saving grace that rescues both the narrator and Cletus. Often writers may undo their characters by means of disease or afflictions, but the touch tends to be so hard and so pressing, and there is so little attention to the world surrounding the characters that an effect of authorial bullying is never far from the reader's consciousness. This is particularly evident whenever the protagonists of a story are explicitly located as victims. After a while it almost doesn't matter to whom these events are happening; the characters are as anonymous as mice. When a protagonist actively participates in his or her own undoing, the story wakes up—such a state of affairs gives the reader more to think about and more to watch for.

Tim O'Brien's "The Things They Carried" (1987) has become a contemporary classic in part by creating a series of inventories. The story makes its narrative way toward the American soldiers in Vietnam by means of lists and inventories that start with objects that the infantry soldiers carry around and end with feelings that they also carry around, that have them in their grip. The story includes one pivotal death and the partial undoing of its protagonist, Lieutenant Jimmy Cross, who stops being the person he was (a sentimentally lovelorn young man) and starts being a dehumanized human being and, therefore, a more effective platoon leader. In this story, a soldier doesn't just carry his gear and his obsessions; he becomes those things.

Jamaica Kincaid's "Girl" (1983) is an instruction manual, a conduct lecture, a code of behavior that begins innocently and then swerves into the mother's judgment against the girl and to a sense of what the girl, the listener, is getting herself into. This brief story combines request moments with inventories, and the effect is overwhelming, as if the person hearing these sentences has no air to breathe except for the air grudgingly donated to her by her mother. The story is in one paragraph. Here's a sample:

> Wash the white clothes on Monday and put them on the stone heap; wash the color clothes on Tuesday and put them on the clothesline to dry; don't walk barehead in the hot sun; cook pumpkin fritters in very hot sweet oil; soak your little clothes right after you take them off; when buying cotton to make yourself a nice blouse, be sure that it doesn't have gum on it, because that way it won't hold up well after a wash; soak salt fish overnight before you cook it; is it true that you sing benna in Sunday school?; always eat your food in such a way that it won't turn someone else's stomach; on Sundays try to walk like a lady and not like the slut you are bent on becoming; [etc.].

All those punishing semicolons! Each semicolon is a little marker of rage, *Don't-interrupt-me-I'm-not-finished* punctuation, informing you that you are not permitted to stop, rest, or breathe. The story won't let you take a break from its one long paragraph, and all those nagging demands pile up in parallel horizontal lines; to use another metaphor, they are like little arrows that the listener (and, finally, the reader) has to dodge. As instructional norms, they're generally given without justification and with the accompanying sense that the listener will fail to follow them. *You do these things because I tell you to do them, and it is not your place to ask why. Besides, you'll never do them right.* These requests and instructions directed at the girl of the title create an entire world from the inventory of what she must do, how she must behave, and instead of getting a sense of an enlarging world, this instruction manual defines the world while diminishing it, as if a girl's growing up was the equivalent of learning *this* particular inventory, the rules for living in a homemade penal colony.

Because I have been arguing that in our times trauma has been associated with lists and inventories, I have also been thinking of collective and social traumas, disasters that our country and culture have faced. In my lifetime, nothing ever felt so traumatic as the war in Vietnam until the COVID-19 coronavirus struck, and it interests me that the form our culture has found for grieving the Vietnam War and its losses was . . . an inventory. The memorial to the dead in Vietnam is not, as has been true in past wars, a heroic image, or, for that matter, much of any image at all. Instead, it is a reflecting black slab in the shape of an inverted V, if you look at it from the front. In this reflecting marble you see your own reflection, and you see, superimposed on your own features, the names of the dead. Nothing is said about them. They are just listed there. No one standing in front of this monument would be able to say whether this list constitutes an addition or a subtraction, but it may be exactly the absence of a context of meaning, apart from your own face, that gives this place and this object such power.

The Vietnam memorial is a text, a kind of story. You can't help but read it like any story, but with this inventory, you don't know where to begin. You get lost in the names of the dead, and finally the names defeat you; you are overwhelmed. No claims are made. The fact of their deaths is sufficient. Those people were here, and then they were taken away. These days, such a list may be all the editorializing we need.

Things About to Disappear:
The Writer as Curator

For Emily Sinclair

1.

A few months ago, I was reading an account of a controversy that had to do with standards and conventions for Muslim women, especially regarding burqas and veils. Midway through the article, I had one of those moments that come more frequently as a person gets older, which is to say that I was transported into the past and my childhood.

The year is 1953, and I am six years old, and my mother is about to go into downtown Minneapolis, and she has dressed up for the occasion, as she always does when she goes into the city. She's wearing a blue skirt and a matching jacket or blazer, I can't remember which, over a white blouse accessorized with a pin. She's wearing white gloves. She's also put on a hat. I remember that hat: its color was a close match for the dress and the jacket, and it was held in place with a hatpin. On her dresser, she had a collection of these hatpins, which were quite sharp and frightening to me. They looked like weapons. The other detail about this hat that I remember was its delicate black veil that dropped down over my mother's face. A veil! I haven't seen a veil of that kind over a woman's face for almost fifty years, although when I went to Google, I found quite a collection of them in websites for antiquarian clothing.

I myself had to be clothed in a white shirt, a tie, and a blue suit—the costume of white middle-class urban propriety in the 1950s.

In all our discussions of time in fiction, the past and the future, we often get stuck talking about the present tense versus the past tense in fictional narratives. These discussions are useful, but they are local, as if we were discussing an entire city by describing a single street corner. There are, however, much larger projects related to time that fiction has always taken on: the first project is that of prophecy of the future, and the second is what I'll call *emotional re-membering* of both the present and the past.

About the prophetic gift, I have little to say, though great fiction, from Jules Verne, and Nathaniel Hawthorne in his short stories, up through H. G. Wells (whose works gave Leo Szilard the idea for the atom bomb), Octavia Butler and Samuel Delany and Ursula Le Guin and Neal Stephenson and Philip K. Dick—these writers have always trafficked in predicting the future, sometimes with great accuracy. But what I'm interested in is something else: the act of noticing and remembering *settings*, and *objects*, and *feelings* before they go away. Both poets and fiction writers may find themselves remembering and preserving what everyone else is discarding, and by doing so, they may keep alive whatever is fading out.

Given the tendency of America to lay waste to its cultural products, this project is essential, as if we were all in emergency vehicles with the sirens on rushing to save the patient, which is our culture. Anarcho-capitalism is very happy if you have no memory of anything except yesterday's TV commercials, and in an age of anarcho-capitalism, one of the most subversive of all activities is to remember how things were, and how they felt, and what people did. Such remembering is not nostalgia. This is what it means to be alive at a particular time with a functioning memory.

At the time of writing this essay, I found myself in an elevator in downtown Minneapolis with approximately six other people. I was the only person on the elevator who was looking at the display indicating which floor we were approaching. Everyone else was gazing downward at their iPhones. Gertrude Stein once said that the only thing that changes from generation to generation is what people are looking at. Every time I see someone tapping away at an iPhone, I think of Gertrude Stein.

2.

Early on in Samuel Beckett's novel *Molloy* (1955), the narrator says, "Let me try and explain. From things about to disappear I turn away in time. To watch them out of sight, no, I can't do it."

Beckett's phrase "things about to disappear" has had an interesting subsequent history. The writer Allen Wier used the phrase as the title of his 1978 collection of stories. But other writers have been struck by the phrase, too. It turns up as the epigraph to Wright Morris' 1968 collection of photographs and text, *God's Country and My People*. Wright Morris' photographs in this book are largely of farms and farm people, all of them weathered and aged, on the cusp, you might say, of disappearance. Both the objects and the people in these photos have the nobility acquired from years of use.

This book of photographs inspired another midwestern writer, William Maxwell, when he was preparing to write his novel *So Long, See You Tomorrow*, published in 1979. Maxwell prepared himself to write that book by looking at Wright Morris' photographs of farms and by reading his accounts of farm life. In a society afflicted with chronic amnesia, looking at photographs may prove to be a source of inspiration, a catalyst, a saving grace.

3.

In the previous essay, I wrote about the inventory method and how William Maxwell employed it in *So Long, See You Tomorrow*. A kitchen is described through a listing of its contents. In Wright Morris' novel *Fire Sermon*, published eight years before *So Long, See You Tomorrow*, there is a similar passage that I need to quote from at some length. It appears in chapter two of the third section of *Fire Sermon* and is filled with left-behind objects:

> This had once been the dining room, and the round oak table is now backed into the corner behind the door. The top of it is littered with pillboxes, medicine bottles (some of them with the skull and crossbones on the label), a lamp with a broken chimney, the wick in an empty bowl, glass salt and pepper shakers, cases for glasses, a cigar box without a lid, full of pins and bone hairpins, a cigar box with the lid made into a pin cushion, stuck full of threaded needles, hatpins, and a lady's cameo. There is a ball of tinfoil, a pocket watch with a chain, a flashlight, a pocket knife with a broken bone handle, two bed casters, a shaving strop, and a shoebox full of black and red checkers.

> —

> Fearing to look behind him, he went forward yelling, "Uncle Floyd! Uncle Floyd!" as he went up the stairs. At the top of the stairs the door ahead of him stood open, jammed with boxes and barrels like an attic. . . . Floyd Warner sat there, or rather he sagged there, his hands hanging limply between his knees, his head tilted as if to catch small sounds from the yard. . . .
> "Uncle Floyd," the boy said, but remained standing in the door. . . . Within [the room], captive, he saw the figure seated on the narrow-backed armless rocker, both the seat and the back

covered with pads made of patchwork quilting. . . . Everything
left over had been put into it, as into this house. The old man
who sat there did not impress the boy as his own great-uncle,
Floyd Warner, but another object preserved from the past. . . .
The boy . . . brought so little to what he saw, he saw what was
there.

When does a mere listing of objects acquire pathos and unexpected grandeur? At the moment when those objects are about to
disappear, when they are about to be gone. There is no good word for
this particular feeling or mode, but it has to do with the beauty of an
obsolete, aged, and weathered thing.

One obvious feature worth noticing about this passage I've just
quoted is that all the objects in it are old. From the hatpins and the
lady's cameo to Uncle Floyd, they're worn out. Sometimes when entering the house of an old person, you feel as if you've been admitted into a museum, one that gives glimpses of a past life, complete
with doilies and antimacassars and odors that no one smells anymore. A particular eerie stillness haunts such places. This passage
has that museum quality, of things lovingly preserved when others
of their kind have become extinct. One additional effect of this passage is that it is anti-narrative: it stops time. Only Kermit, the boy,
is moving here, and even he has been startled into silence and im-
mobility. The busy reader is likely to skim this passage or skip over
it completely. The busy reader wants to get to the murders, the violence, the sex, the drug-taking, the boasting, the atrocities. Who
wants to love something old? Very few of us. It takes a certain act of
curating, a certain gift of focused attention, to admit to the mind's
inner chamber a cigar box with the lid made into a pin cushion. The
reader has to take on an inward quietism simply to read such a passage properly. Things about to disappear do not register when we
are speed-reading; they just disappear faster. Any writer takes a risk

in stopping time to preserve a moment and artifacts from the past, and none of it will work without love. But after all, every novel takes place in the past. When the book is printed, the narrative, whatever it is, is over.

4.

In Don DeLillo's story "Human Moments in World War III," collected in his book *The Angel Esmeralda* (2011), Vollmer, an astronaut in his twenties, gazes down on Earth as he and the narrator collect imagery data on troop deployment. Radio signals from decades earlier somehow infect their transmissions from mission control. "A quality of purest, sweetest sadness issued from remote space." As they work to control the "lethal package" they are dealing with, they look at Earth and fall into reverie: "The cities are in light, the listening millions, fed, met comfortably in drowsy rooms, at war, as the night comes softly down." The story feels like an elegy to the planet and takes its place in the growing literature of pre-apocalyptic writing, intensified in this particular case by the narrator's distance (he's in orbit) and his sense that he and Vollmer are observing a planetary body that is about to disappear altogether with their willing cooperation. The grief over the fate of Earth infuses the story with a tone of immense melancholy, a particular note that has been struck repeatedly in DeLillo's recent work.

5.

A few years ago, I was supervising a graduate student, a wonderfully talented and very smart writer, Emily Sinclair. I learned at least as much from her as she may have learned from me. At one point, we were working on a story of hers called "In the Valley." The situation in the story is that Ed, a middle-aged guy who has been a bit of a philanderer and is now separated from his wife, wants to go to a bar where his friends won't find him. He may pick up a woman at the bar (in fact he does, a young woman named Janie), but Ed stubbornly wears his wedding ring, in spite of his extramarital intentions.

The bar he goes to is called the Parrot. Once there, he thinks of Houston in detail that would do honor to a nineteenth-century realist: "The Bayou, the smell of sea air on some days, the humidity, the raw noises of the streets, the lush foliage, threatening to take over everything manmade." Now, suppose you're going to set the scene in this bar, the Parrot, and you've got your character, Ed. How much detail concerning the bar do you need to put into your story? Are you Balzac, describing the bar in all its wonderful detail as part of the great human comedy, or are you Chekhov, sketching in the background quickly so that you can get efficiently to the dialogue between Ed and the young woman he encounters?

This is not an easy question to answer—of course, it's a judgment call. I personally felt that my student needed to ditch some of the detail concerning the bar so that she could get to the interaction between Ed and Janie. I felt that she needed to be Chekhov here, or, let's say, Eudora Welty; and not Balzac, or, let's say, Edith Wharton. As you can see from the names I've cited, both these traditions are great and honorable ones. And they are not mutually exclusive: Welty sometimes writes social detail as if she were Edith Wharton. *The Optimist's Daughter* is a case in point.

One factor, however, would certainly have decided matters for this writer: if bars like the Parrot are on the verge of disappearing, you would work to get them on the page in all their glorious detail: how they look and sound and smell, the faded cigarette smoke—people don't smoke in bars anymore—and the peanut shells on the floor, the pinball machine in the corner, the tired server with streaked mascara, the lighted rows of liquor bottles, shelf after shelf, rising to the tin stamped ceiling: one lapidary detail after another, a preservation project. You would work hard and diligently to get that noisy and half-elegant, half-sleazy bar right there on the page before it's gone.

The quiet bars of my youth, dark and mournful, whose tables were polished with the tears of the clientele, have given way to noisy sports bars with multiple TV sets, where the patrons shout raucously to each other. It's another, newer way of being lonely.

6.

Henry James, viewing New York City in 1904 and reporting on it in his book *The American Scene*, sees, not a great city, but a principle of colossal destructiveness that feeds upon itself. American culture wastes things and people and places, just out of habit, he notes; if you live long enough, what you saw when you were young will be gone by the time you're old. Waste is the one thing Americans really believe in. Henry James described the result as one that feels like an amputation from a person's own history. The annihilation of everything, he says, reflects a process that *does not even believe in itself.* All it really believes in, he says, is money, and enthusiastic destruction that produces more money.

7.

When I entered Macalester College as a freshman in 1965, the entire freshman class was required to read an etiquette manual called the *MacDo* book, written by Mary Gwen Owen. Among the instructions that I still happen to remember is this particular one: *Always butter your bread one bite at a time.*

Things about to disappear, according to the internet: Paper money. Keys. Corner mailboxes. Your privacy. Landline telephones. "Dear ———" as an opening salutation in a letter. Plows. Fast-food workers. Department stores. Clock radios. Clutch pedals. Family farms. Truck drivers. Effective antibiotics. Saying "you're welcome" (instead of "no problem") after someone says "thank you." And something else about to disappear, according to a former chief executive's campaign spokesperson, Scottie Nell Hughes: facts. Our public life—I am far from being the first person to say this—may in large part have become postfactual.

8.

When my mother took me to the dentist in the 1950s, there was, in the Medical Arts Building in downtown Minneapolis, a waist-high canister next to the elevators, which in those days were operated by elevator operators wearing uniforms and little green caps. In the elevator, the operator sat on a fold-out stool attached to the wall. The canisters just outside the elevators had sand at their top surface. I liked to put my fingers in the sand and would do so until my mother started to yell at me, which she invariably did, telling me not to do that. The sand, she said, was dirty and was there for putting out cigarettes before a person entered the dentist's office, where, next to the dentist's chair, there was a water-swirled spit bowl often streaked with bloody sputum from the previous patient. I haven't seen canisters like that, with sand in them, for at least fifty years. Or spit bowls, either. Or elevator operators.

9.

The great Jewish historian Simon Dubnow was the author of the eight-volume *World History of the Jewish People*. Yiddish was his first language. In school he learned Russian, eventually moving to St. Petersburg, but after the revolution he emigrated to Berlin. After 1940 he moved again to Riga, Latvia, and was condemned to death by the Nazis, but not before he exhorted the Jews of Riga to open their eyes and ears. He urged them to memorize "each detail, each name, every sigh, and the color of clouds, as well as the execution-er's gesture." Dubnow disappeared into the Jewish cemetery of Riga, but his words survive. I first found them in Evan Connell's *Points for a Compass Rose*. Dubnow's instructions are good advice for every writer in any period of historical crisis, to be someone on whom nothing is lost. Saul Bellow said that the best skill for any writer is to be a good noticer. When we write, we are not just writing about indi-viduals, or members of a family, or those whom we love; we are writ-ing about the culture we live in. We can't help but record the zeitgeist of our times, particularly when we are writing about those who are chewed up and consumed by the machinery of the culture and the state apparatus. You never know when the next plague will descend and what's about to be lost.

Each detail, each name, every sigh, and the color of clouds, as well as the executioner's gesture.

10.

So what good are Edith Wharton's novels to us now? One of my for-mer students wrote to me in a moment of despair. Here's one para-graph of her letter:

> *All of a sudden, post-election [of Trump], the problems of rich white people fifty years ago seemed irrelevant. To be Balzac seems inde-fensible, frivolous, a relic of a time when we had the luxury of exam-ining the social order. And I even wonder about Chekhov: what role does quiet and individual despair have in times like these? I recall my sense, during my essay, of Edith Wharton, that she was busily—and conflictedly—serving up and defending New York society at the ad-vent of the first World War, and how backward-looking she seemed to me, how blind to her own conflicts, how studiously irrelevant the condition of one's carriage, parked outside the opera, is at such*

*times. But here we are, still reading her, reading them all, and they
do matter, but I can't quite tell how.*

My provisional answer to this paragraph would be as follows:
Edith Wharton both loved and despised the New York upper-class
society that she depicted, and no one else has been more accurate or
precise about the ways in which a woman like Lily Bart in *The House
of Mirth* (1905) can be chewed up and destroyed by a culture and
society determined to bring her down. There wasn't a single detail
of that society that escaped Edith Wharton's attention. She knew it
the way a watchmaker knows the inside of a watch. And she knew
that its tentacles went everywhere. In *The Age of Innocence*, Newland
Archer says to the woman he loves, Ellen Olenska, "I want somehow to get away with you . . . [somewhere] where we shall be simply
two human beings who love each other; who are the whole of life to
each other, and nothing else on earth will matter." Ellen's answer is
simple and direct: "Oh, my dear—where is that country? Have you
ever been there?"

The Age of Innocence was published in 1920, and the world it presents is New York society of the 1870s—fifty years earlier, a society
that no longer existed. But Edith Wharton remembered all of it, and
how it operated, and she remembered its victims. The way a system
chews up its individuals never quite goes out of style. It is still one of
the great subjects for fiction and poetry.

11.

As if to follow Simon Dubnow's instructions to the Jews of Riga, the
prisoner writes about the prison he is in:

> I couldn't find a way on my own. At that moment I didn't know if
> it was day or night . . . because the toilet drain was rather dark.
> I gathered my strength, guessed the *Kibla*, kneeled, and started

to pray to God. "Please guide me. I know not what to do. I am surrounded by merciless wolves, who fear not thee." When I was praying I burst into tears, though I suppressed my voice lest the guards hear me. You know there are always serious prayers and lazy prayers. My experience has taught me that God always responds to your serious prayers.

But that passage was not written by Simon Dubnow, or one of the Jews of Riga, or Primo Levi. It was written by Mohamedou Ould Slahi, and it is one paragraph from his 378-page book, *Guantánamo Diary* (2015).

12.

In Deborah Eisenberg's "Twilight of the Superheroes" (2006) we are given a story in which the plot is almost nonexistent; it has been subsumed by the situation, which is that of four semi-slackers hanging out in a ritzy Manhattan apartment just before and then just after 9/11. We learn much about these four—Lyle, Madison, Nathaniel, and Amity—and we learn much about their family members, including Nathaniel's parents, and his uncle, Lucien. The four central characters in the story are less interesting as individuals than they are as carriers of particular attitudes: the central feeling is that of not knowing how to say what's happening after the unthinkable has happened. How does one think about the future once the future seems to have been withdrawn? The story is at some pains to be multigenerational: it fits three generations into its limited space, and in several ways it marks the xenophobia of the grandparents as a condition that everyone had thought would disappear but has suddenly and remarkably returned to the stage, stronger than ever.

The story is divided into little sections, as if the broken shape of the story reflects the brokenheartedness of the characters. Incidents have been reduced to a minimum, though the characters are care-fully and artfully depicted, mostly through what they think and what they say and the art they create. All the same, the story constantly wants to re-direct our attention away from what the characters are doing. It wants us to perceive and to know the historical forces be-hind the characters, and what has been mostly invisible to them. The question seems to be, not "What is to be done?" but "What's going away?" Lucien, thinking about Nathaniel, imagines that "his nephew's is the last generation that will remember what it had once felt like to blithely assume there would be a future—at least a future like the one that had been implied by the past they'd all been famil-iar with." No, the future they will actually have "had been prepared for a long, long time, though it had been prepared behind a curtain."

For its last nine pages, "Twilight of the Superheroes" is as much an essay as a piece of fiction, and its observations about power out-ages, and stolen pension funds, and bogus patriotism, and spiking levels of unemployment should feed the reality hunger of the most Shieldsian of readers. "One was sick," the story notes prophetically, "of trying to get a solid handle on the stream of pronouncements."

Bit by bit, detail by detail, as one piece of evidence follows an-other, Eisenberg's story charts how life in New York City changed after 9/11, but to do that, the story has to remember how things were, and to imagine "a pure, wholehearted, shining love. It hangs around him [Nathaniel] still, floating through the air out on the terrace—fragrant, shimmering, fading."

"Twilight of the Superheroes" is the greatest story by someone of my generation about the world we have recently lost.

At the moment, I am re-reading and revising this essay in 2021. The "things about to disappear" are growing in number. The music critic for the New Yorker, Alex Ross, several issues ago referred to clas-sical music concerts as subject to a "looming extinction event." My friends are now worried about the disappearance of restaurants—the pandemic has closed them—and retail outlets (people are afraid to go into stores), and dance concerts (dancers are broke and one whom I know has gone into tech support) and movie theaters, and we may be losing good nutrition and jobs for non-college-educated workers, and offices and places where people go dancing and . . . this is a list that anyone can fill out.

13.

In Edward P. Jones's story "Gospel" (collected in his book *Lost in the City*, published in 1992) the central character is Vivian, a member of a gospel group, the Gospelteers, whose members sing at the House of the Solitary Savior Church in Washington, D.C. The story opens with the four women gathering together, collecting themselves in a car, to go there to sing. The time is the early 1960s. When they arrive, they find that the church has burned down during the night. It's not, however, the loss of the church over which Vivian grieves. Churches can be re-built, after all, and the Gospelteers perform later that day, to great acclaim, at another church, the Holy Tabernacle.

What happens later is a small episode that, to most readers, will seem to be of small significance, but for Vivian its meaning enlarges and expands to fill up every available emotional space. On their way home, Vivian's friend and fellow Gospelteer, Diane, asks Vivian to stop at the corner of Fourteenth and Fairmount. Diane gets out of the car, crosses the street, and "in a few steps she was at the passenger side of a car that was waiting with its motor on. When she opened the door, the light came on, and in that instant, Vivian could see a bit of the driver, a man who took off his hat. It took her breath away to see him do that."

The rest of the story tracks Vivian's reaction to that small gesture, a man taking off his hat in deference to the arrival of a woman in his presence. As the story tells us, "she had not seen a man take off his hat in that old-fashioned way in a long, long time. It was a respectful gesture out of a country time when a little girl would watch dark young men tall as trees stand respectfully close to young women and say things that made the women put their hands to their mouths to stifle a giggle." A page later in the story, "She could still see him. . . . How much more grandness, beyond the gesture with the hat, was there to him? Her heart ached to know." And then: "She did not want to think that God did not make such men anymore. And that if he still did, he should waste them all upon women like Diane McCollough."

The loss of personal norms can feel like an erasure of a recognizable code of conduct. The gesture can be as small as the doffing of a hat. What bothers Vivian is that the gesture is a courtly one that she hasn't seen in a long time, and when she does finally see it, it is not for her, but for her friend Diane, who, by the way, is already married. This gesture is one of respect, a small courtesy, swept away by other norms, those of informality and equality between the genders, but the story *preserves* that gesture from a lost world, glowing, as if inside a piece of amber. But the gesture wouldn't be in the story if Edward P. Jones hadn't noticed that men rarely, or never, tipped their hats to women anymore. As a gesture, it was about to disappear. But it didn't disappear. Edward P. Jones saved it.

We might find a tip of the hat an offensive custom, but that's not how Vivian or Diane reads it, within the historical context that the author has created.

In the *MacDo* book, I was told that when a man is with a woman on a date, he should stand behind her chair at the dinner table and pull the chair out before she is about to sit down and then gently push it in as she descends. On the sidewalk, the man should always stand on the outside, next to the street. He should take off his hat or cap when he goes indoors. I was informed that these courtesies were norms. But they weren't norms at all; they were cultural conventions of their time, and they're gone, all of them, including the hetero-normative and binary man and woman.

14.

One of the most beautiful passages of music ever written in the state of Iowa is the Lento from Antonín Dvořák's String Quartet no. 12, the so-called "American" string quartet.

This is the kind of music Dvořák heard when he lived in America, in Spillville, Iowa, during the summer of 1893. When he heard Americans singing, this is the sort of music he heard. Others may hear something else when they hear this music, but when I hear this famous passage from Dvořák's American string quartet, all I hear is massive, inconsolable sadness, the sadness of total, catastrophic loss. You would call this music schmaltzy only if you had never felt a loss that great.

15.

Things that have gone away sometimes come back. You just have to be in the right moment of history to feel something that others have felt before, and to recognize that their words, or their music, express something that was gone for a while but has unexpectedly returned.

After the November 2016 election, I noticed that, on the internet and on Facebook, people were quoting Matthew Arnold's poem "Dover Beach." In my generation, it was cool to make fun of that poem. Anthony Hecht did so in his poem "The Dover Bitch." But the poem's belief that we are surrounded by ignorant armies, by stupid leaders and dumb wars, and that all we have is our love for each other—all this seemed, suddenly, correct, and Arnold's earnestness was the right tone for our new historical moment.

Call it vinylism. Vinyl records disappeared, then, slowly but surely, they came back. I know people who prefer landlines to cell phones because people sound more like themselves on landlines.

16.

In James Wright's "Two Poems about President Harding," we have the following stanza:

America goes on, goes on
Laughing, and Harding was a fool.
Even his big pretentious stone
Lays him bare to ridicule.
I know it. But don't look at me.
By God, I didn't start this mess.
Whatever moon and rain may be,
The hearts of men are merciless.

The phrase I want to call to your attention is "But don't look at me." It's a phrase from my childhood, when my friends and I wanted to shift the blame for some household misdeed. Something had been broken in the living room; some appointment had been missed; some pet in our care had run away, something else had been smashed, someone had been injured. What did I say when my parents accused me of these domestic crimes? I said, "Don't look at me." It was one of my favorite phrases. James Wright, who loved American idioms, loved it, too. And he saved it and located it in his poem, where you would hardly notice it. His book *Two Citizens* (1973) is a collection of American verbal idioms that he loved. When was the last time you heard the phrase "Don't look at me"?

All of us are the curators of words and language. If we don't re-member the phrases and words that are about to disappear, no one else will. Think back to the words that you used to hear but don't hear all that often anymore. When I was a kid, my parents would ask me if I felt "peppy." Peppy! What a word! *Weary.* Now there's a word you don't hear much anymore. Do people never feel weary? Are they always tired, instead? And what about *sorrow*? Are people who feel sorrow always depressed? No. They're not depressed, they're sorrowful. George Saunders brings back the word *sorrow* with great emphasis in his novel *Lincoln in the Bardo.* And what about *rectitude*? *Forbearance. Mercy. Tenderness.* Everyone can make their own list of antique words and put them back into use. The British novelist Rachel Cusk loves the word *costive.* My stepfather loved to describe men he didn't like as "four-flushers."

17.

Remembering, in certain historical epochs, can be a form of resistance. Remembering can even be subversive. It is not conservative so much as conservationist. You hold on to those features of behavior and those figures of speech that have been erased from the centers of commercial, consumptive culture. You become indifferent to the latest fashions. You use words that everyone else has forgotten. You remember how people behaved, and you use it, because you are the walking, living memory of your own time, and you are writing it all down.

This is the singular advantage that we have on Leo Tolstoy: he never knew what it was like to be alive in our era, and we do.

Captain Happen:
Some Notes on Narrative Urgency

For Matt Burgess

Some years ago at a writers' conference, in one of the most beautiful and placid locales where I had ever found myself, I was teaching a fiction workshop while a friend, an author of many fine novels, was teaching the other fiction workshop in a classroom adjacent to mine. My students and I would hear through the walls her voice rising and ringing with comic impatience, as she briskly ordered her students—encouraged them, really—to make more of their stories and to increase the voltage. "Something has to happen!" she would say in her mild but authoritative southern accent. "Something *more* has to happen!"

In the middle of the week, I had lunch with her. I asked her what she was saying to her students—that is, why she was emphasizing the events of the stories that she and her class were critiquing. "Ah," she said. "I just get so bored with *situations*, where the characters are *kinda* unhappy about something, and the whole contraption is decorated with pretty sentences, and then it's over. I just get so bored I could scream!" She looked around furtively. "But you can't say that to them!"

A year or so later, the fiction editor of the *Atlantic*, C. Michael Curtis, came to Ann Arbor, where I was then teaching. During a question-and-answer session, Curtis was asked what he thought was required of a story to be accepted by the *Atlantic*. Looking out owlishly at the student audience, Curtis leaned back and said, "Something . . . has . . . to . . . happen."

This particular coincidence has always stayed in my memory, mostly because I also believe that usually something does indeed have to happen (usually, but not always), but the trouble is that once you've made the claim that "something has to happen," you haven't really said very much. If I travel from my home in Minneapolis to visit New York City and see some friends and drop in at a couple of museums and use up all the credit on my MetroCard, something has happened, all right, and my friends will have to listen to me when I tell them about my trip to New York and what I thought of what I saw and did, but my story has very little or no urgency, and my friends will have to listen to this story only because they're my friends and have to pretend to be interested. No one was hurt, and nothing weird happened. Which is a bit like having to read a story to the end in the worksheets just because you're in the workshop.

If, however, I had been pushed onto the subway tracks and had somehow escaped with my life, the little details that led up to the assault would have increased in significance and importance.

Most would-be novelists know how to talk about characterization and motivation and even setting and voice, scene and exposition. What we rarely—or never—know how to talk about is the urgency or the lack of it in a story. Of course, we're dealing with subjective values: what may seem urgent to one reader will be rather dull and predictable to another. But the institution of the workshop itself tends to ban all discussions of urgency; you can't, for example, say that any particular story is well written but boring. I used to know a novelist and memoirist who would write the word *boring* all over her students' worksheets in large letters. This pedagogical tool was not admired by her students because there seemed to be no remedy. How do you unbore a story? After all, things about to disappear may bore many readers, as you can see from readers' reviews on amazon.com.

The sad truth is that many of the stories we write and read are unspeakably boring, yawn-inducing, mostly because they have avoided shaping their plots in a skillful way and because their concerns are too mild or too small and therefore lightweight, or because the pressure on the language is too slight.

Young writers tend to hate plots. They don't want to think about them; they claim they don't like them, and instead they want to give their characters, to quote Grace Paley, "the open destiny of life," but then these same students sit down and watch TV and movies and they talk about how good these shows are. But in a good series, not everyone has the open destiny of life. People get trapped. Some are afflicted with addictions. Situations go from bad to worse. The characters are visited by bad luck and horrible catastrophes, to the delight of the viewer.

Plots, as they're commonly understood, usually involve a chain of cause-and-effect circumstances set into motion by a desire or a fear that may encounter a conflict of some sort. The character often has a goal to reach. That's an abstraction of little practical use. To clarify what I mean about narrative urgency, I'll list a handful of questions that may help out the fledgling storyteller. Asking these questions and finding an answer for them do not necessarily guarantee that a story will be well made, but they may help to increase the voltage in a narrative.

Question number one: *Where's Captain Happen?*

I have named Captain Happen after a character in John Leonard's comic novel *Crybaby of the Western World* (1969). Think of Captain

Happen, your story's protagonist or antagonist, as a narrative enabler: Captain Happens, plural, *make things happen*. They are both a cause of trouble for themselves and also a cause of trouble for others. Captain Happen, often a transgressor, is the person in your story who is unstable and impolite, a source of disruption, and who blurts things out, who takes action when no one else does. The Captain is the sort of character who bravely acts on her desires, or, even better, her impulses or obsessions. She sets things into motion by telling lies, or setting out on a long dangerous journey, or stirring up a lot of mayhem, including crimes. Captain Happen is volatile. Think of Lady Macbeth, who is criminally ambitious: "Give me the daggers," she says at one point. She does not have to be likable, but she needs to be complex enough to be interesting. In fictional characters, interest and bad outcomes trump charm. Forget likable: Dostoyevsky's and Shakespeare's characters are often deeply unpleasant, but they are fascinating to watch, and the stories in which they appear are full of Captain Happens dominating the stage. Literary portraiture should have nothing to do with a character's popularity, which is a concept that belongs in high school.

Captain Happens can often be your story's sparkplugs and focusing agents, and it helps if they are slightly unstable or, as in Dostoevsky's novels, on the verge of hysteria or in the grip of an obsession. Captain Happen is a dropout from charm school, and the title is not gender specific. They may well be fuck-ups, cheats, liars, creeps—or greedy, sly, adventurous, opposed to domesticity in all its forms, mean-spirited, nasty, cruel, careless, drunk, and conniving. Captain Happen arrives at the party wearing the wrong outfit, swears at the hostess, drinks too much, tells the bridegroom to go fuck himself, and creates a scene. Perfect! That's what we want! We want someone who will create a scene, because then we'll all watch. Captain Happen is bad news, and bad news for the characters is good news for the story.

Good stories often require a good antagonist, especially when the protagonist is passive or nice. Kindness and tact and niceness are fine in real life but are toxic and lethal in fiction unless some contrast is provided. As the writer Susan Neville has pointed out in her essay "Where's Iago?" just as Othello's story doesn't really become his story until Iago appears in it, once he *does* appear in it, he becomes that story's focusing agent. Until Iago's appearance in *Othello*, Othello's life was all about military victories and his rise to glory. Okay, fine, but who cares? But once Iago appears in Shakespeare's play, the story quickly becomes a tragedy about jealousy and trust and the impossibility of proof. Once you've lost trust, you cannot get it back, and jealousy feels and behaves like a cancer. Without Iago's villainy, there's no story. He compels our attention by telling Othello a series of lies about Desdemona. Without the lies, we would go nowhere. Iago, set against Othello, becomes Captain Happen. Iago may not be an *interesting* character—W. H. Auden claims that Iago never says anything remarkable, which is often the case with villains—but he's *necessary* to the unfolding of the drama.

We are all interested in misdeeds. Criminals are the friends of fiction. My former neighborhood in Minneapolis had a resident criminal, and we all talked about him. He was quite charming and very handsome, and before he went to the workhouse he slept in the beds of many single women. In her short but quite interesting little book *Plotting and Writing Suspense Fiction* (1966), Patricia Highsmith, author of *Strangers on a Train* and *The Talented Mr. Ripley*, observes that "criminals are dramatically interesting, because for a time at least they are active, free in spirit, and they do not knuckle down to anyone." She goes on to say, "I find the public passion for justice quite boring and artificial, for neither life nor nature cares if justice is ever done or not. The public wants to see the law triumph, or at least the general public does, though at the same time the public likes brutality." Patricia Highsmith was not particularly likable herself if the biographies are to be believed (she could be quite scary), and her indifference to the "public passion for justice" is somewhat unnerving and repellent. Nevertheless, she is making a claim about why bad people earn the attention of readers. I despise her character Tom Ripley, but he compels my attention because he is a bit of an archetype: he is *telling*—he shows me how some social climbers behave and what sorts of crimes they are ready to commit.

Here's question number two: *Where's the one-way gate?*

By one-way gate, I mean an action that you cannot go back on. Once a character performs a one-way gate action, she cannot get back to the place where she started from because the action changes the fundamental situation. Furthermore, a one-way gate is often a definitive action: having performed it, you are the person who did that thing. A person who commits a murder is, forever after that, a murderer. Obviously, a murder is an action that cannot be undone. Once a person has been murdered, that person stays dead, and the murderer has walked through a one-way gate and has performed a definitive action.

But of course not all definitive actions are as extreme as a murder. Sometimes these consequences will be comical: situation comedy depends upon someone saying something that is not quite true and then having to face up to the consequences of that mis-statement. Sometimes forgiveness is the end of the one-way gate. Forgiveness can lead to forgetting. Forgiveness is the enemy of plot.

But most one-way gates depend upon an action that cannot be forgiven or forgotten. In Paula Fox's novel *The Widow's Children*, one of the characters, Laura Maldonado Clapper, learns that her mother has died, but she then refuses to tell her own daughter or her brothers. Once the truth comes out, Laura becomes the person who hoarded this information all day—while drinking, eating, and gossiping—without revealing what she knows about what has just happened. That is, a one-way gate can also be an inaction, a refusal, a doing-nothing at a moment that requires some action.

One of the features of stories with a large amount of narrative urgency is that the plots within them have a very distinct feature produced by the one-way gate. If you can't get back to where you started from, you have to move forward, pushed by events that have already been set powerfully into motion. Many stories with a certain amount of narrative urgency are about the way that characters are overtaken by events. They light the fuse, but then they can't put it out. The events become larger than the characters themselves. The events are no longer under the character's control. In Annie Proulx's "Brokeback Mountain," the love of the two men for each other sets into motion a series of events that they themselves are powerless to stop, given the historical period and the social milieu that surrounds them. This is sometimes called "the snowball effect," or "snowball plots."

Let's suppose that a company manufactures defective screws. These screws are purchased by a defense contractor, and they are used in the gyroscopes of fighter aircraft that are deployed in Vietnam. Because the screws are defective, the gimbals in the airplanes' gyroscopes are faulty, and the navigation systems of the planes are also faulty, and pilots are killed when their planes go off course. Two people are sent to Vietnam to investigate these mishaps, and these two characters serve as major dramatic characters in Joan Silber's novel The Size of the World (2008). A one-way gate can be produced by an object as small as a cheap defective screw. The tendency in stories of this kind is for the consequences to get larger and larger as the story goes on, like that snowball rolling down a hill. A person cannot be un-murdered, and the snowball cannot be stopped until its energy is dissipated.

Question number three: *Where's the clock?*

By asking question number three, I'm asking a particular question of a story. How long do these characters have to do what they need to do? If they have all the time in the world, there may be a fatal lack of urgency in the story.

The sense of a clock ticking somewhere in the background of a story is a device that is probably overused by every hack writer. We all have seen an artificial deadline set up in a movie to create suspense, or some outer space thriller in which the spaceship is going to self-destruct in T-minus two minutes, while the hero, let's say that other Ripley, in *Alien*, tries to get herself inside the escape pod before she's blown to smithereens or the alien eats her.

But if the artificial deadline has become an old narrative cliché, the clock itself and the sense of time running out have not. They're always with us as a fact of life shaded by mortality. The sense of a clock ticking is the oldest human truth. We're all going to die, and we do *not* have all the time in the world. One of the oldest forms of poetry is the carpe diem poem, the one that ends by advising us to seize the day. If you're going to make your move, make it now. If you don't make your move now, you may lose everything.

While I was in the first drafts of a book of mine called *The Feast of Love*, I found that I had written a succession of episodes concerning lovelorn characters who were mis-matched with various other characters. The episodes were seriocomic, but they had very little weight, and no urgency at all. I was in despair. I had a varied set of characters, a traditional theme, and a tone that seemed to be working adequately, and yet I didn't have a book. I just had a series of episodes. Somehow I kept writing through my despair until one morning I had one of my characters, Chloé, put her head down on her boyfriend's chest, at which point she heard the boyfriend's bad heart. At this point I realized that the boyfriend was going to die and that my book was saved. I actually shouted aloud with happiness. Nobody else's death has ever filled me with such joy.

The girlfriend, Chloé, who loves this guy madly, goes to a psychic to have her dire suspicions about her boyfriend confirmed. Once they are confirmed, she then takes action: she proposes marriage to the boy, he agrees, and they're soon married, and she quickly becomes pregnant before the boyfriend's untimely demise, which I had carefully planned. Once the boyfriend dies, all the characters gather around her in a kind of community of shared concern.

Her bad news saved my novel.

If the spaceship that's going to self-destruct in T-minus two minutes is the vulgar version of the ticking clock, one of the greatest versions can be found in Anton Chekhov's story "The Lady with the Dog." The story's protagonist is Gurov, a middle-aged womanizer, who on a vacation at Yalta has what he initially thinks of as a passing affair with Anna Sergeyevna, the lady with the pet dog. When the affair is over and he has to return to Moscow, the story says, "There was an autumnal feeling in the air." Gurov eventually goes to the provincial town where Anna Sergeyevna lives. Near the end of the story, Gurov embraces Anna near a mirror. Then we have this paragraph:

His hair was already beginning to turn gray. It struck him as strange that he should have aged so much in the last few years. The shoulders on which his hands lay were warm and quivering. He felt a pity for this life, still so warm and exquisite, but probably soon to fade and droop like his own. Why did she love him so? Women had always believed him different from what he really was, had loved in him not himself but the man their imagination pictured him, a man they had sought for eagerly all their lives. . . .

And only now, when he was gray-haired, had he fallen in love properly, thoroughly, for the first time in his life.

Although Chekhov does not make the point explicitly, Gurov has fallen in love, in part, because he has become conscious of his own aging, his own frailty, and he can see that frailty in others and feel compassion for them. Anna Sergeyevna's beauty initially draws him in, but her vulnerability (to time, to aging) inspires his real love—to his surprise. In Chekhov's hands, the ticking clock is a cause of the deepest emotions generated out of a sense of urgency, of something that has to be done as if your life depended on it.

A man who has all the time in the world will procrastinate, make up excuses, delay, and do nothing. All this is okay in dramatic writing if we know that the clock is ticking, but the clock can go on ticking forever unless we have a question number four, which is related to our previous question.

Question number four is: *Where's the time bomb?*

Our time bomb is a humble cliché that simply indicates that something is going to happen in the near or distant future that will alter things as they are. The time bomb does not have to be violent. But it has to have enough importance, once it explodes, to change the way the characters look at their lives. The time bomb opens the one-way gate.

A former student of mine at Minnesota, Matt Burgess, wrote a novel as his thesis manuscript, and the novel was called *Dogfight*, which was published by Doubleday in 2010. The book is about two Hispanic brothers—Alfredo, who lives in Queens, and his older brother, Tariq, who on the day of the novel is getting out of prison. Alfredo wants to welcome his brother home first by scoring some major drugs for him, and second by having a celebratory dogfight that evening in the basement of a Queens candy store. But neither of these events constitutes the novel's time bomb.

What Tariq does not know, and what we, the readers of the novel, *do* know is that Isabel, Tariq's girlfriend during the time before he went into prison, has become Alfredo's girlfriend during the two years that Tariq has been locked up. Not only that: what's worse is that Alfredo has gotten Isabel pregnant, and when the novel opens on the day that Tariq gets out of prison, Isabel is in her eighth month. We know that Isabel is pregnant because the narrative tells us that she is from the moment she enters the story in chapter two. But Tariq does not know that his brother has gotten his former girlfriend pregnant, and so we wait in suspense to find out what this violent man will do when he sees his now-pregnant former girlfriend.

Alfred Hitchcock, in his interviews, always made the distinction between suspense and surprise. There is suspense, Hitchcock observed, if you tell the audience a crucial piece of information that the characters may not know. If the audience knows that there's a bomb ticking away here in the room where we sit, but we in the room don't know that, that's suspense.

Where in the story do you put the time bomb? In Matt Burgess' novel, it's exactly halfway through. One time bomb often explodes before the story's climactic moment. We wait to see what Tariq will do when he finally sees Isabel, and then, for the second half of the book, we watch him as he slowly grows angrier and angrier as the day goes on. In the evening, Tariq explodes, and that's the second time bomb.

Let me offer up a smaller example of a time bomb that in certain respects violates everything I've been saying about the nature of these events, from Evelyn Waugh's A *Handful of Dust* (1934). One of the novel's central characters is Brenda Last, who has been carrying on an affair with the contemptible John Beaver. Meanwhile, back at her estate, her little son, also named John, is killed when he's thrown from his pony. Of course the reader wonders how John's mother, Brenda, will take this news—she is off in London pursuing her affair with John Beaver. The author forces us to wait for fifteen pages (in my Everyman's Library edition) before we have the scene in which Brenda is told about her son's death. She's given the news by a family friend, Jock, who tells her that John has died. Brenda thinks he's referring to her lover, John Beaver, and when she realizes that it's her *son* who has died and *not* her lover, she blurts out, "Oh thank God."

What can you say about this moment except that it's both a time bomb and a one-way gate? A little while later, ashamed of herself, and completely exposed, Brenda says, "I didn't say anything, did I?" to which Jock responds, "You know what you said." What can Brenda claim in her own defense? She can't deny saying what she said, so she says, "Yes, I know . . . I didn't mean . . . I don't think it's any good trying to explain."

Absolutely right. When you blurt something out, you can't take it back. Because of her statement, Brenda has altered forever the way that Jock thinks of her and the way that she thinks about herself. She will never be the same person. Blurting out one's actual thoughts is dangerous and often impolite, but it's powerful fuel for stories.

The blurt, at its greatest, is a leap of thought. The problem of narrative urgency in our time has often been misdirected in popular entertainment by purely mechanical means: the artificial deadline, in particular, and the crazed maniac—the vulgar version of Captain Happen—who's going to blow up the entire city of Centerville by eight o'clock tonight unless Jack Bauer tortures the guy enough to find out where the creep has hidden the A-bomb inside the suitcase. This sort of plot unfortunately seems to encourage and to support the utility of torture.

But narrative urgency cannot be degraded by its misuse(s). We need to be conscious of the problem of urgency because all fiction and all poetry want to assert a claim upon our attention even if they deny that desire for the sake of a higher goal, such as "art" or "subtlety" or "the sublime." The claim upon our attention is based upon the truth that for all of us, time eventually runs out.

Sometimes we just let our narratives simmer when in fact their materials need to be heated up in order to cook properly. Even Chekhov, the master of the low-temperature situation, allows things to boil over in the last act of *Uncle Vanya* and the last third of his great story "In the Ravine."

Moderate unhappiness is not, in itself, a story. It's a *condition*. A low-level irritation at your partner is not, in itself, a story either. It's a given. Irritation is a condition, but *rage* is a story. Rage is more singular than irritation, which is as common as dirt. Rage produces action and pushes events through a one-way gate. Irritation pushes nothing much of anywhere.

For this reason and for many others, writers—who are often mild-mannered types, observant and orderly and kind in their daily lives—tend to be afraid of rage. It's like handling a highly combustible explosive. It lays waste to the landscape and often burns the person who handles it. But rage has one great advantage over irritation: irritation is nearly always meaningless, and rage . . . well, rage is nearly always meaningful. As James Wright observes about Aunt Agnes in his poem "Ars Poetica: Some Recent Criticism": "She didn't weep. / She got mad. / Mad means something."

This essay was set into motion by the author of *Dogfight*, who complained to me that we rarely talk about urgency in our classes and workshops. He and I had been comparing notes about some writers we both admired—Walter Mosley, Patricia Highsmith, Iris Murdoch, Richard Price, Daphne du Maurier in her short stories—who are often condescended to and described as plot-driven writers. But the artistry of these writers' books is absolutely genuine. Highsmith's *The Talented Mr. Ripley*, for example, is possibly one of the great American novels about American-style social climbing and the murderous rage that accompanies it.

Or consider Mosley's Easy Rawlins novels, the first of which was *Devil in a Blue Dress* (1990). This book is set in post–World War II Los Angeles. I won't go into the plot of this book so as not to spoil it, but what particularly interests me about this novel and the other Easy Rawlins novels is not Easy himself, but his sidekick and friend, Raymond Alexander, "a small, rodent-faced man" known through-out the novel as Mouse. Mouse is a murderous little guy who heats up the narrative by several degrees whenever he enters it, so much so that the reader is tempted to page ahead to find out when Mouse will show up again to create his typical mayhem. It's an example of a minor character who almost overshadows the protagonist. Mouse is violent and loyal to Easy and is homicidal and crazy, a Captain Happen character whose great virtue—the virtue of all great villains—is that he's afraid of nothing, even death. Confronted with death, what does he say? "I tole'im that I had a man beat me four ways from sundown my whole life and I sent him t'hell. I say, 'I sent his son after'im, so Satan stay wit' me and I whip yo' ass too.'" He's a brave sociopath.

"Mouse didn't ever feel bad about anything he'd done," Easy ob-serves about his gun-toting friend. When Mouse disappears from the narrative, the reader speeds ahead until he reappears in full late-1940s regalia:

Frank did as he was told and there was Mouse, beautiful as he could be. His smile glittered. Some of the teeth were rimmed with gold and some were capped. One tooth had a gold rim with a blue jewel in it. He wore a plaid zoot suit with Broadway sus-penders down the front of his shirt. He had spats on over his patent leather shoes and the biggest pistol I had ever seen held loosely in his left hand.

Broadway suspenders: things about to disappear. Frank, who has been giving Easy some trouble, is no match for Mouse. But Easy worries about how much blood spatter there may be: "I don't want him [Frank] killed in my house," Easy says. "I thought maybe Mouse would sympathize with keeping blood off the furniture."

An honorable and sizable part of our literature is concerned not with the ticking clock and Captain Happen characters like Mouse, but with stopping the clock, with creating texts that have little or no urgency and that substitute for that urgency the arts of meditation and the transcendence of time. The arts of meditation allow a luminousness to become visible, and they can only do so by saying, "Wait a minute. Stop. Think for a minute. Get yourself out of the river of consequence." Things-about-to-disappear are often incompatible with a sense of urgency. This preservation of the moment is a much more difficult task for fiction writers than it is for poets, but the examples of V. S. Naipaul's *The Enigma of Arrival*, or Virginia Woolf's *The Waves*, or part two of *The Sound and the Fury*, and the grandparent of them all, James Joyce's *Ulysses*, among others including the Wright Morris examples I've given in the previous essay, prove that it can be managed. In such books all the pressure is on the sentences and on the quality of thought and feeling. Some books are apples; others are oranges. There's no point in comparing *The Waves* to *Devil in a Blue Dress*. They have different ambitions, that's all.

Years ago, when I was at that conference at Aspen, where I thought everything was beautiful and calm, I encountered on the last day of the conference the poet Robert Pinsky. We were in a gondola going up a mountain. So, Bob, I said, *How do you like it here in Aspen?* "I hate it," he said, overenunciating as he often does. But what about the Rockies? I asked. Aren't the mountains glorious? "They look like wallpaper to me," he said. But the town! Aspen! I said, Don't you like it? "No. In this town, I feel like the only Jew," Pinsky said.

In this little encounter, who's Captain Happen, Pinsky or me? Who, of the two of us, is the more interesting character, and why? These are not difficult questions.

Lush Life

Lush. The word sounds wet, lazy, supine, and it conjures up images of boring, loquacious drunks who grab you and exhale their poisonous fumes in your face. No one wants to be a lush, and no one wants it as a style. Even the sound of the word is bad: to say it, you have to breathe out and end with a damp outward rush of voiceless air like the *shh* you use to silence somebody. Most writers aren't interested in *any* of the lush styles, at all, ever—they're usually condemned as uncool or sentimental. Lushness has mostly departed from our scene. A hot and often extravagant style, it is taboo unless someone famous and above suspicion employs it, like Gabriel García Márquez or Toni Morrison. Otherwise it is typically vetoed or sneered at.

Furthermore, the matter is complicated: you can be lush in some designated areas but not others: Cormac McCarthy's novels are extravagantly rich in their descriptions of violence but laconic in their depiction of the more intimate emotions.

The climate of postmodernism has encouraged the cooler end of the emotional spectrum, which values understatement, irony, toughness, and skepticism. Most of us are well versed in such aesthetics by now; they are, for the most part, the aesthetics of suspicion. The conventional wisdom is that it is good to be cool because of all the fraudsters who are trying to put one over on us. Lushness is contaminated, everyone thinks, by its association with mindless emotion and the worst of romanticism; furthermore, because lushness is typically a "hot" style, Mediterranean, it can seem sweaty, violent, sexy, weepy, and naked—in a word, *embarrassing*. And because of its reliance on rhetoric, it can also seem manipulative and therefore sentimental. It puts all the emotions out there, like underwear hanging on a clothesline. To switch metaphors, it grabs you by the collar and breathes on your neck. It seems to want something from you. But every style wants something from you. However, if you want to be cool, detached, analytical, the conventional wisdom is that you can't be lush. You can be one or the other but not both.

So, to get at the problem of lushness, an anecdote about drinking at a bar: I happened to be in an airport bar a few years ago when Sarah Vaughan's cover of the great Billy Strayhorn hit "Lush Life" came on. It was recorded in 1956, I have since discovered. The song is a classic of what I'd call the it's-two-a.m.-and-I'm-alone-and-I'm-totally-desolate feeling. Anyway, Sarah Vaughan came on the background loudspeaker, singing "Lush Life," and I just sailed upward. I loved the song. I loved its classy despair.

The song does not feel as if it's of our time. It has the tone of an almost vanished era, the 1940s, and it expresses a despondent solitude that has temporarily calmed down into lyric eloquence. You can't imagine any of today's pop singers singing it straight, though to be fair, Queen Latifah has made a good shot at it.

According to David Hajdu, Strayhorn's biographer, the composer was seventeen years old when he wrote this song, an almost unbelievable feat of imaginative projection. The piece was first recorded in 1948 by Nat "King" Cole, in an upbeat rendition that Strayhorn hated.

The lyrics clue us in to three features of lush life. First, this emotion works out of a fever, not out of a chill, while "you" are still "burning inside my brain." Second, a lush style has, because of its large gestures, a component of unstable self-dramatization. But most importantly, lushness has a very particular sense of time: lushness refuses to give up the past and instead tries to superimpose the past on the present. The only way it can manage this superimposition is through lyric expansion.

Lush styles tend to be heated and even bloated by their efforts to compress two time frames together, to unite the past, the present, and the future. Whenever you find two time frames superimposed on top of one another, you may possibly find a lush style. Lushness is usually backward-looking, and it is the signature style of a present-past. You will find it in authors I've already mentioned and in Vladimir Nabokov, particularly *Lolita*. It is very much in evidence in Raven Leilani's contemporary novel *Luster* (2020), a searingly eloquent book with many extremely long, "hot" paragraphs that I will examine later in this essay.

But first I have to say a few words about paragraphing.

Gertrude Stein once claimed that the paragraph is the unit of emotion in prose fiction. She claimed that, of all the writers of his generation, F. Scott Fitzgerald took the highest honors for his expertise with paragraphs.

But what about extended paragraphs—long floods of prose that may go on for a page or two (or more)—what do such paragraphs signal to the reader? Many readers dread such paragraphs because of the effort they require; there are no stopping points, no resting places, no benches where you can sit down and think about what's just happened. My former editor always complained about them whenever I used them and said that no one would finish reading them, because they signaled mania, or an obsession that has displaced common sense. They can be hectoring. That is: they're just plain hard to read.

When moderation gives way to mania, the resulting long paragraphs, in their compulsive, trauma-ridden breathlessness, are like messengers who have come from a great distance and have much to say and insist on telling it all at once. Ordinarily, when you come to the end of a paragraph, you can stop. The paragraph relents. But when the paragraph doesn't end, when it *refuses* to end—as I noted earlier about Jamaica Kincaid's "Girl"—you can't breathe, as if the sheer intensity or obsessional content of the paragraph defies plain reason and is forced to rip away the mask of calm. These relentless paragraphs wish to dominate the reader and force that reader into a kind of submission. Certain German and Austrian writers—Thomas Mann, Thomas Bernhard, Wolfgang Koeppen—load down their long paragraphs with brilliant erudition laid out with cold, insistent feverishness. This is also true of the so-called "boom" writers of Latin America: José Donoso, García Márquez, Alejo Carpentier, and many others.

Most of the time, a long paragraph will raise the temperature of the prose. Speaking of Raven Leilani's *Luster*, the novelist Dean Bakopoulos noted the following, in a lecture for the Warren Wilson MFA program:

> But to my mind the beauty of *Luster* is that it captures the emotional condition of being perpetually insecure, perpetually in search of distraction, perpetually in search of reasons not to hate oneself, perpetually in search of the right beauty that will sustain us or the right joke that will distract us. To my mind, much of *Luster*'s charm and magnetism comes from the feverish run-on sentences and swing for the fences metaphors that [one critic] derides as undisciplined, but that I find beautifully evocative of a true mental health crisis.

As we shall see, Raven Leilani does not employ run-on sentences at all, just long paragraphs and the full resources of syntax in the service of a condition that cannot be managed otherwise—an intense feeling of compounded subjects sustained over an extended period. The run-ons in her prose are not the grammatical constructions but the time frames, reflecting a formal condition that is true to the experience of panic states.

But now, having started with Strayhorn's "Lush Life," I want to offer one other musical example. This one is a distant corollary to Nabokov's *Lolita*. In this musical example, we have a Russian, self-exiled from his mother country by the revolution. Like Nabokov (with whom he was acquainted), our composer finds himself in the New World, where, as a musician, he works tirelessly, giving concerts and traveling everywhere in order to support his family. He takes every job his agent offers him. He is known for his terrible melancholy and for a killing nostalgia related to his lost prerevolutionary Russia. He also carries with him a nostalgia for a set of musical styles that he has clearly outlived. He is very tall, and someone—actually, Igor Stravinsky—has described him as "a six-and-a-half-foot scowl." Sometimes at night the composer travels into New York City, where he hears and admires Art Tatum playing jazz piano in Harlem, and where, most tellingly, the old composer hears African American jazz musicians playing the blues.

Nearing the end of his life, this old Russian composer, whose name is Sergey Vasilievich Rachmaninoff, is inspired to write one last orchestral composition, which he calls *Symphonic Dances*. Among other things, the piece is a set of musical elegies to various period styles, and in the first movement, Rachmaninoff writes a melody that sounds like a lamentation from nineteenth-century Russia or before, and more specifically like a folk song or, slowed down, a Slavic church melody.

But now comes the odd part of the story. In a great fit of daring, Rachmaninoff assigns his great melancholic tune in the orchestra to the E-flat alto saxophone, an instrument he must have heard in America playing the blues. Rachmaninoff has never scored anything for saxophone before, so he consults with saxophone players. He is determined to play the blues in his own way in this last piece, on a borrowed instrument, the alto sax. By writing this tune, and giving it to the alto sax, Rachmaninoff combines two time frames, the old (his lost Russia) and the new (his adopted country, America).

The result? Every classically trained alto saxophone player knows this solo by heart.

In the lead-in, the transition to the tune, the sax is coaxed out of hiding by two other woodwinds, the oboe and the clarinet, both sounding like forest birds. This brings on the great tune, a real *earworm*: a melody that takes up residence in your head and stays there.

This melody is lush, emotionally quite naked, and lushness is a quality often criticized in Rachmaninoff. He is typically condemned for breaking the rules of good taste. But here he is simply combining two time frames, the old and the new, into his one solo. The effect is hot and lush and sorrowful but not overripe.

Rachmaninoff then inflates the sorrow. In music, as in literature, there is such a thing as overstatement. Instead of allowing his great tune to fade away, he has the tune re-stated by the violins and the cellos. It's as if he can't help himself. He wants to repeat the melody and give it more of a boost, to make it more emphatic than it already is. But if Rachmaninoff's melody has been about anything, *if it can be said to have a subject*, then that subject has been loneliness and solitude and nostalgia. But you can't give a melody that expresses loneliness and solitude to the entire string section. Or, rather, you *can*, but the result may sound wrong. A single alto saxophone can say, "I have never been so lonely." If you give the same melody to all the strings and turn up the volume, the effect is like saying, "We are all lonely, in exactly the same way." What is wrong here is not *what* is being said, but the *way* it is being said. Something that is already hot has been overheated.

Imagine the Frank Sinatra song "One for My Baby" as sung by an entire chorus, perhaps a glee club or the Mormon Tabernacle Choir, and you'll have a sense of the incongruity of this melody when it's played by the string section, with goopy embellishments by the piano and the harp.

In Rachmaninoff's first statement of the theme, we find those two time frames combined, and the emotion is displayed but not *sold*. In the slowly descending melody, a feeling is not being insisted upon, but merely stated. In the recapitulation of the theme in the string section, the emotion is being *recolorized and reinforced*, and a claim is being made that everyone should join in, that everyone should believe this melody. This is where lushness turns to the overripe, what Nabokov called *poshlost*, a Russian word—when the claim is being made that *everyone must believe or feel a particular emotion, and we are all agreed about that*. The result is not poetry but rhetoric, and it is typically the place where lushness meets the overripe, and it is why so many professional musicians once despised Rachmaninoff's orchestral music, and some still do.

Cool styles can descend into emotional frigidity, prideful stoicism, a kind of hipster zombie-ism. Hot styles lean toward overemphasis, coercion, and fraudulence.

Suppose we find ourselves in a common writerly situation: we are trying to combine two time frames, that of a character who is bored or preoccupied and is thinking of something else as she moves in and out of the present-time situation she's in.

Such paragraphs often start with what's going on at a particular narrative moment. They then shift through a transition marked by the verb *thought* ("Sitting back in her uncomfortable chair, Ramona thought of wild horses . . .") and go into the content of a memory, which may be salted with nostalgia or curiosity or lust or remorse. But notice that present narrative time is set aside in the process of evoking the memory. Essentially we go from one temporal plane to the other, moving back and forth, but not superimposing or combining them within the same sentence. With such flashbacks, there's a whiplash effect, or what a friend of mine calls "an expository pothole."

But many writers have been intrigued by the possibility of side-stepping flashbacks and using superimposed temporal planes by jamming together various images from different periods of time. The problem of combining present and past narratives became an imperative in the early part of the twentieth century, when many writers and artists felt that time was beginning to move too fast across all aspects of the culture. What these writers and artists wanted to do was to slow time down narratively or to stop it entirely. William Faulkner famously said, "The past is never dead. It's not even past." In his work, particularly *Absalom, Absalom!* the past exists within and not apart from the present moment. If the past lies somewhere dormant but still alive and nested *within* the present, as many twentieth-century writers thought it was, the writer's task is to express that simultaneity—and it is here, in the effort to combine time frames, that lush styles come to the rescue.

How can you possibly hold two or even three time frames in the same sentence or paragraph? In Malcolm Lowry's novel *Under the Volcano*, published in 1947, Yvonne, one of the novel's four central characters, has previously arrived in Mexico at the port of Acapulco. In a present-time scene, she stands at the entrance to the bar where her ex-husband, Geoffrey, a lush, by the way, sits on a barstool:

> So the bar, open all night for the occasion, was evidently full.
> Ashamed, numb with nostalgia and anxiety, reluctant to enter
> the crowded bar, though equally reluctant to have the taxi-driver
> go in for her, Yvonne, her consciousness so lashed by wind and
> air and voyage she still seemed to be traveling, still sailing into

Acapulco harbour yesterday evening through a hurricane of immense and gorgeous butterflies swooping seaward to greet the *Pennsylvania*—at first it was as though fountains of multicolored stationery were being swept out of the saloon lounge—glanced defensively round the square, really tranquil in the midst of this commotion, of the butterflies still zigzagging overhead or past the heavy open ports, endlessly vanishing astern, *their* square, motionless and brilliant in the seven o'clock morning sunlight, silent yet somehow poised, expectant, with one eye half open already, the merry-go-rounds, the Ferris wheel, lightly dreaming, looking forward to the *fiesta* later—the ranged rugged taxis too that were looking forward to something else, a taxi strike that afternoon, she'd be confidentially informed.

As a baroque construction, this sentence is a bit of a challenge, but you can find similar sentences in the work of many other modernist and contemporary authors. Compared to some of Faulkner's sentences, this one is easy. Standing at the doorway, Yvonne is experiencing three time periods simultaneously: *yesterday*, when her boat docked in Acapulco and she was surrounded by butterflies in the harbor; *today*, as she gazes into the bar where her ex-husband sits drinking (behind her is the town square); and *tomorrow*, which might include a strike by the taxi drivers. Each time frame is introduced by a physical prop. The past is marked by butterflies. The present is marked by the bar and the town square behind her. The future is marked by those taxicabs. In these instances, every time frame is not abstract but is marked with a concrete object. Time is concrete here and is marked by things that are proper to it.

At least two other features of the paragraph are worth noting. The first is that Yvonne is literally at an entryway; she is having a threshold experience. What is true spatially is also true temporally. She can't back away, but she doesn't want to move forward, either.

Thus, the time framing is a kind of double for her dramatic situation. Time is flowing in and through her.

The second feature to notice about this long sentence is the manner in which Malcolm Lowry uses the art of syntax. He has managed to separate the sentence's subject (*Yvonne*) and verb (*glanced*) by qualifiers and apposite phrases that tell us that Yvonne's mind is still in the past even though she stands before us here in the present. She's like anyone who's just gotten off a bumpy ride on a commuter airplane and isn't quite in the present, not yet. It's as if, physically shaken, you're still on that plane or that boat. The sentence, by extending itself in this way, seems to be putting the reader into a state of temporal and grammatical suspension: we can't see where the sentence is going to end, or where we'll meet up with the predicate, and though we're trying to keep Yvonne of the here and now in our minds, the sentence wants us to go back in time, not forward, to the previous day when she saw all those butterflies upon her departure from that ship; and, by putting both these elements into the same lush sentence, Lowry manages to subtly reduce Yvonne's here-and-nowness, and, I might add, her physicality. Yvonne is in two, maybe three, places at once. One effect that long sentences like this one have is that they force the reader to give up simple linearity: this no longer leads to that, followed by a period. Something has disrupted cause and effect. Past, present, and future are all in one spot. We don't know where Lowry's sentence is going to end, but we do notice how we're slightly lost within it, lost both spatially *and* temporally and perhaps even causally.

A final observation about this sentence. You can argue that its form is baroque—that is, it contains elaborations, qualifications, and decorations. But you cannot say that it is ironic or cool. Its emotional temperature is warm to the touch, as Yvonne shyly imagines her reconciliation with her ex-husband. Even the imagery is romantic—all those butterflies. It is probably a separate question whether people feel emotions like this anymore—whether anybody, that is, still feels as if love can transform the self and whether butterflies will ever surround you like a cloud of mist when you're in love. But Lowry felt that way, and he believed that his characters did, too. The sentence is still alive, still formally inventive, and its heart is still beating.

These "hot" styles are about fullness; they thrive when your heart is full, when you are feeling expansive, when your emotions are overflowing and unprotected. Transformative love is often a feeling of joy. We may also feel a negative fullness in panic states. And this fullness stands against what many of us feel these days most of the time, which is emptiness and skepticism. Irony and flat assertions are the signal tonalities of emptiness. A feeling combining cold removal, withdrawal, suspicion, and barely suppressed anger is this style's magnetic north. Irony is a form of protection, and it's possible that we're now all overprotected.

There is an even longer sentence in *Under the Volcano*, and it goes on for three pages midway in chapter twelve. In this sentence, Yvonne's ex-husband, Geoffrey, has sex with a prostitute. The sentence is too long for me to include here, but I recommend that you find this book and try reading it aloud, not ironically but with feeling. This sentence, in which Geoffrey is falling down to hell rather than rising up to heaven, is not merely hot; it is boiling. In the sentence, Geoffrey's downward tumble is replicated by a sentence that is dizzy, vertiginous, and boiling.

Let me turn now to another example, from Marilynne Robinson's 1980 novel, *Housekeeping*:

> Say that water lapped over the gunwales, and I swelled and swelled until I burst Sylvie's coat. Say that the water and I bore the rowboat down to the bottom, and I, miraculously, monstrously, drank water into all my pores until the last black cranny of my

brain was a trickle, a spillet. And given that it is in the nature of water to fill and force to repletion and bursting, my skull would bulge preposterously and my back would hunch against the sky and my vastness would press my cheek hard and immovably against my knee. Then, presumably, would come parturition in some form, though my first birth had hardly deserved that name, and why should I hope for more from the second? The only true birth would be a final one, which would free us from watery darkness and the thought of watery darkness, but could such a birth be imagined? What is thought, after all, what is dreaming, but swim and flow, and the images they seem to animate? The images are the worst of it. It would be terrible to stand outside in the dark and watch a woman in a lighted room studying her face in a window, and to throw a stone at her, shattering the glass, and then to watch the window knit itself up again and the bright bits of lip and throat and hair piece themselves seamlessly again into that unknown, indifferent woman. . . . I think it must have been my mother's plan to rupture this bright surface, to sail beneath it into very blackness, but here she was, wherever my eyes fell . . . a thousand images of one gesture, never dispelled but rising always, inevitably, like a drowned woman.

In this paragraph, which I have edited down from its much lengthier printed version, we may notice certain features of lush styles that I've mentioned: first, Ruth, the narrator, has a sense of fullness (in this case, leading to a metaphorical second birth); second, we're given a superimposition of two time frames: the narrator's current time in a rowboat with her aunt Sylvie, and past time, with the death of her mother. We are also in what I'd call hypothetical time, the time of possibilities and of the imagination. But lushness here also allows itself a considerable degree of freedom, a transfiguration out of the here and now. Ruth presents her thoughts as conjectural, introduced by the word *say*. A conjecture brings us a possible world. Interesting that she does not say "imagine" but "say." To be in it, you have to say it. The conjectural is also marked with an elevation of diction, with the use of words like *spillet, repletion,* and *parturition*. These sentences are cranked up rhetorically. They are starting to sail away from their usual earthy usages. Finally, something else marks this paragraph. In it, Ruth's thoughts—which by any measure are unrealistic—simply take the place of reality. It's almost impossible to find any solid reality in that rowboat. What time is it? Who knows? Who *cares*? It's like asking what time it is on the moon. This lush style, whose temperature is lower than that found in *Under the Volcano*, has simply vanquished reality for the sake of a powerful hypothetical reverie.

Notice how bravely the sentences shun the task of linear story-telling. Notice also how metaphors here have become, in effect, the reality that they have displaced.

Housekeeping has a kind of metaphysical project. The book wishes to loosen its narrator, Ruth, from what it understands to be the bondage of the flesh and the bondage of the physical world alto-gether, and, to a certain degree, it succeeds. In its closing pages, the reader cannot know whether the narrator is still physically alive. She seems to have turned into pure spirit, a wandering ghost. Whenever I've taught the book, my students are divided on whether Ruth is still alive or is speaking from beyond the grave in the last chap-ter. Such a transformation probably cannot be managed without a lush style, which enters *Housekeeping* around its eighth chapter and never lets up after that. The style creates an alternative world, build-ing that world out of words. But that world is a lonely one, inhab-ited by only two people, Ruth and her aunt Sylvie. And, just possibly, the reader.

Baroque styles can be used for unbelief and skepticism, but once they stake a claim for feelings of fullness, they start to slow down time and become lush. Lushness, though it can be destructive, can also be demanding; the reader has to keep both the present and the past in mind simultaneously. The past begins to live *in* the present, and the self moves into a realm of thought and belief and love that the sentences have created for it.

Now let's return, by contrast, to Raven Leilani's *Luster*. The protagonist and narrator of this novel is Edie, in her twenties and insecurely employed in New York City. She starts up a relationship with Eric, a suburban guy in an apparently open marriage. Eventually, through a cascading set of circumstances, Edie meets and befriends, in a manner of speaking, Eric's wife, Rebecca. She then starts to live temporarily in Eric and Rebecca's house, where, along with other tasks, she mentors Eric and Rebecca's adopted daughter, Akila.

But no summary can accurately convey the complex textures of this novel: observant, sensual, panic-stricken, ironic. Only a lengthy quotation can begin to give a sense of the tonal range and the eloquent desperation of its narrator, whose intelligence (witty, without exactly being funny or comic) keeps managing to connect one thing to another in an associational stream. Lush styles communicate an important cultural truth: *Everything is connected. Nothing is merely itself—it becomes itself by its temporal and associational connection to other things.* Conversations open up into histories that are then closed up immediately after one or two glimpses:

> I was not popular and I was not unpopular. To invite admiration or ridicule, you first have to be seen. So the story of the cell that once divided inside me and its subsequent obliteration is also the story of the first man who saw me. The man who owned

the gun shop, Clay, a metalhead who was pathological in the maintenance of his teeth. He was the seventh black person I'd met in Latham. Mixed-race, a riotous Punnett square of dominant Korean and Nigerian genes, so ethnically ambiguous that under different kinds of light he appeared to be different men. The first day we met, he was smoking a cigarette on the DDR machine outside the shuttered movie theater. He told me that he was in debt and that he and his brother were no longer speaking and there was something so easy about his immediate familiarity that I told him how my mother died. How I found her with one shoe still on. How I kept painting this moment and found no format suitable. How it had only been five months since her death and my father was already seeing someone. This was the contradiction that would define me for years, my attempt to secure undiluted solitude and my swift betrayal of this effort once in the spotlight of an interested man. I was pretending not to worry about the consequences of my isolation. But whenever I talked to anyone, I found myself overcompensating for the atrophy of my social muscles.

A Punnett square (in case you don't know, and I didn't) is, to quote the internet, a "graphical representation of the possible genotypes from a particular cross or breeding event," and a DDR machine is a Dance Dance Revolution arcade machine, and these objects have been placed next to Edie's unwanted pregnancy, and to a secondary character, Clay, and Clay's estrangement from his brother, and his own shape-shifting form, and all this is placed next to the death of Edie's mother, and Edie's discovery of her body, with that memorable one shoe, all of which leads back to current narrative time and Edie's "attempt to secure undiluted solitude" and her eagerness to leave it behind, along with her (in this case) failed efforts as a painter.

In this paragraph, the past is embedded in the present and is not re-located into a stand-alone flashback. There are several parallel sentences here, all of them beginning with "How . . ." The past is still alive and squirming in this paragraph.

I want to conclude with a couple of sentences that I would characterize as postmodern baroque, which is what remains of a lush style when the heat is taken out of it and skepticism, irony, and emptiness set up their brokerage house in its place. The passage is from David Foster Wallace's story "Good Old Neon," included in his book of stories *Oblivion* (2004):

> But with the real truth here being how quickly I went from being someone who was there because he wanted to wake up and stop being a fraud to being somebody who was so anxious to impress the congregation with how devoted and active I was that I volunteered to help take the collection, and never missed one study group the whole time, and was on two different committees for coordinating fund-raising for the new aquarial altar and deciding exactly what kind of equipment and fish would be used for the crossbeam. Plus often being the one in the front row whose voice in the responses was loudest and who waved both hands in the air the most enthusiastically to show that the Spirit had entered me, and speaking in tongues—mostly consisting of *d*'s and *g*'s—except not really, of course, because in fact I was really just pretending to speak in tongues because all the parishioners around me were speaking in tongues and had the Spirit, so in a kind of fever of excitement I was able to hoodwink even myself into thinking that I really had the Spirit moving through me and was speaking in tongues when in reality I was just shouting 'Dugga muggle ergle dergle' over and over.

The subject moves from being "someone" to "I" and back again to "someone." And the passage has certain features of the baroque in its elaborations and qualifications. But it's not lush by any definition. The goal of these sentences is not to slow down time but to replicate the overcharged and overheated rhythms of manic desperation. There's a variety of speed-freak word production here. The speaker is riffing himself to death. The passage I have quoted manages to be both funny and heartbreaking, since the project is not to transfigure reality here but to rip it, and oneself, into small pieces. The style is a vast destruction machine, a buzzsaw of rhetoric. Skepticism here moves to the most unlikely places, a revivalist Christian church, and then goes to work on the false self in its multiple false positions. The speaker puts himself into that locale of belief where he *admires* the believers. He then tries to become a believer himself. He cannot. So he *pretends* to be a believer, imitating what they do and often doing it better than they can. The sentences replicate a latent hysteria in this situation—a person trying to become someone he isn't, and never can be.

In Wallace's fiction, there are no safe places free from a corrosive irony. His sentences have the great virtue of sounding contemporary, but they do not exhibit what is considered precious or what is hoped for. If everything can be seen through, nothing can remain precious. In a story like "Mr. Squishy," the style reaches heights of mock eloquence by duplicating the advertising and marketing bullshit that surrounds all of us. Like Alexander Pope in the *Dunciad*, the Wallace narrator expends massive quantities of brilliance and energy on people and things he can see through.

What is considered precious and what is hoped for typically never arrive in this fiction because the aesthetics of suspicion cannot permit it, with the possible exception of Wallace's *The Pale King*. Almost everything wilts under this particular gaze. One is always a

spectator, a visitor, in the revivalist church, where the experience of
faith can be imitated but not inhabited. Drugs help, but not for long.
The zombie feeling permeates everything. You finish his books in a
state of heartbroken agony.

Why do we now distrust lush styles? Partly because we are all being
lied to, all the time, by politicians and commercial interests. We have
been lied to so often under so many different circumstances that skepticism simply seems to be the only survival mechanism in a trashy, du-
plicitous culture.

But the styles of skepticism can become stiff and gestural, just as
lush styles can sometimes seem nostalgic. If irony has become a mere
reflex, a gesture, then it has become a default style, and often, as a
consequence, lazy and unfeeling.

A final cause of our mistrust—apart from the Kierkegaardian leap
of faith required for a lush style, that is, the necessity that one must
believe in *something* in order to write in a securely lush manner—is
that most elements in our culture encourage us to believe that speed,
in and of itself, is just great and totally fabulous. Anything that slows
us down is bad, and a lush style, it has to be said, typically slows us
down. Lush styles require slow reading and focused attention. The
complete opposite of a lush style is a text message, and text messages
are . . . well, I don't have to characterize them.

In talking about styles—ironic styles, lush styles, styles of any kind or
description—I seem to be arguing that a style can be *imposed* upon
any given set of materials, or, for that matter, any given vision of the
world. But style, in my understanding of it, does not precede a vision:
it is, instead, an integral part of that vision. A vision of life gives rise
to a style that gives voice to it.

Nevertheless, I want to re-assert this argument: namely, that we
are often in two places at once, temporally; we are in the *here and*

now, but we are also in the *back then*. Fiction writing is of course a linear art, moving from one sentence to another across the page, but in our efforts to get the past into the present, the flashbacks we usually employ constitute a singularly crude means of importing the *what was then* into the *what is now*. Writers once perceived that the simultaneity of past and present experiences could be amalgamated within single sentences, and they deployed every resource of syntax, subordination, relative clauses, and apposite phrases, along with every resource of diction, in order to give a linguistic body to that vision of the world.

Two Interludes

What Happens in Hell

"Sir, I am wondering—have you considered lately what happens in Hell?"

No, I hadn't, but I liked that "lately." We were on our way from the San Francisco airport to Palo Alto, and the driver for Bay Area Limo, Niazi, was glancing repeatedly in the rearview mirror to check me out. After all, there I was, a privileged person—a hegemon of some sort—in the back seat of the Lincoln Town Car, cushioned by the camel-colored leather as I swigged my bottled water. Like other Americans of my class, I know the importance of staying hydrated. And there he was, up front, behind the wheel on a late sunny Saturday afternoon, speeding down US route 101, missing (he had informed me almost as soon as I got into the car) the prayer service and sermon at his Bay Area mosque. The subject of the sermon would be Islamic inheritance laws—a subject that had led quite naturally to questions of death and the afterlife.

I don't really enjoy sitting in the back seat of Lincoln Town Cars. I don't like being treated as some sort of important personage. I'm a midwesterner by location and temperament and don't even cotton to being called "sir." So I try to be polite ("Just call me Charlie") and take my shoes off, so to speak, in deference to foreign customs, as Mrs. Moore does in A Passage to India.

"No," I said, "I haven't. What happens in Hell?" I asked.

"Well," Niazi said, warming up and stroking his beard, "there is no forgiveness over there. There is forgiveness here but not there. The God does not listen to you on the other side."

"He doesn't?"

"No. The God does not care what you say and he does not forgive you once you are on that side after you die. By then it is over."

"Interesting," I said, nondirectively.

"It is all in the Holy Book," Niazi went on. "And your skin, sir. Do you know what the God does with your skin?"

"No, I don't," I said. "Tell me." Actually I was most interested in the definite article. Why was the deity referred to as *the* God? Are there still other lesser gods, minor subsidiary deities, set aside somewhere, who must be differentiated from the major god? I drank some more water as I considered this problem.

"It is very interesting, what happens with the skin," Niazi said, as we pulled off the Bayshore Freeway onto University Avenue. "Every day the skin is burned off."

"Yes?"

"Yes. This is known. And then, each day, the God gives you new skin. This new skin is like a sheath."

"Ah." I noticed the repeated use of the word *you.*

"And every day the *new* skin is burned off." He said this sentence with a certain degree of excitement. "It is very painful as you can imagine. And the pain is always *fresh* pain."

Meanwhile, we were proceeding through downtown Palo Alto. On the outskirts of town I had noticed the absence of pickup trucks and rusting American cars; everywhere I looked, I saw Priuses and Saabs and Lexuses and BMWs and Volvos and Mercedes-Benzes and a few Teslas here and there. The mix didn't include convertible Bentleys or Maybachs, the brand names that flash past you on Ocean

Boulevard in Santa Monica. Here, ostentation was out; professional-managerial modesty was in. Here the drivers were engaged in Right Thinking and were uncommonly courteous: complete stops at stop signs were the norm, and ditto at the mere sight of a pedestrian at a crosswalk. No one seemed to be in a hurry. There was plenty of time for everything, as if Siddhartha himself were directing traffic.

And the pedestrians! Fit, smiling, upright, well tended, with not a morbidly obese fellow citizen in sight, the evening crowd on University Avenue appeared to be living in an earlier America era, one lacking desperation, hysteria, and Fox News. Somehow Palo Alto had remained immune to what one of my students has referred to as "the Great Decline." In this city, the businesses were thriving under blue skies and polished sunshine. I couldn't spot a single boarded-up front window. Although I saw plenty of panhandlers, no one looked shabby or lower middle class. I noted, as an outsider would, the lines outside the luxe restaurants—Bella Luna, Lavanda, and the others—everyone laughing and smiling. The happiness struck me as stagy. What phonies these people were! Having come from Minneapolis, where we have boarded-up businesses in bulk, I felt like—what is the expression?—an ape hanging on to the fence of Heaven watching the gods play.

"You burn forever," Niazi said, drawing me out of my reverie. "And, yes, here we are at your hotel."

Sir and *Hell*: the two words belong together. After arguing with the hotel desk clerk, who claimed (until I showed him my confirmation number) that I didn't have a reservation and therefore didn't belong there, I went up to my room past a gaggle of beautiful leggy young men and women, track stars, in town for a meet at Stanford University, where I'd been hired to teach as a visiting writer. They were flirting with each other and tenderly comparing relay batons.

Off in the bar on the other side of the lobby, drugstore cowboys were whooping it up, throwing back draft beers while the voice of Faith Hill warbled on the jukebox. Nothing is so dispiriting as the sight of strangers getting boisterously, forcefully happy. It makes you feel like a stepchild, a poor relation. Having checked in, I sat in my room immobilized, unable for a moment even to open my suitcase, puzzled by the persistence of Hell and why I had just been forced to endure a lecture about it.

Rattled, I stared out the window. A soft Bay Area rain was falling, little dribs and drabs dropping harmlessly, impressionistically, out of the sky. A mass-produced motel version of an Audubon bird—how I hate those Audubon birds—was trapped and framed in a picture above the TV.

I am usually an outsider everywhere. I don't mind being one—you're a writer, you choose a certain fate—but the condition is harder to bear in a self-confident city where everyone is playing a role successfully and no one else is glancing furtively for the EXIT signs.

In his writings and his clinical practice, the French psychoanalyst Jacques Lacan liked to ask why any particular person would *want* to believe any given set of ideas. He initially asked the question of behavioral psychologists with their experiments with mice and pigeons, but, inspired by Lacan, you can ask it of anyone. Why do you *desire* to believe the ideas that you hold dear, the cornerstones of your faith? Why do you clutch tightly to the ideas that appear to be particularly repellent and cruel? Why would anyone *want* to suppose that an untold multitude of human souls burn in extreme agony for eternity? Having left a marriage, and now living and working alone, I found myself in that hotel room experiencing the peculiar vacuum of self that arises when you go on working without a clear belief in what (or whom) you're working *for*.

The idea of Hell has a transcendently stupefying ugliness akin to that of torture chambers. This particular ugliness is fueled by

the rage and sadism of the believer who enjoys imagining his enemies writhing perpetually down there in the fiery pit. How many of
us relish the fairy tale of endless suffering! Nietzsche claimed that
all such relishers are in the grip of *ressentiment*, whereby frustra-
tion against the rulers, and anger at oneself, are transformed into
a morality. *Ressentiment* is what happens to resentment once it goes
Continental and becomes a metaphysical category. After Marx, injustice no longer seemed part of a natural order. And if injustice *isn't*
part of a natural order, then *ressentiment* will naturally arise, the rage
of the have-nots against the haves, the losers against the winners.
Sometimes the rage is constructive, sometimes not. For Nietzsche,
the unequal distribution of power is simply a condition of things as
they are:

> It is not surprising that the lambs should bear a grudge against
> the great birds of prey, but that is no reason for blaming the great
> birds of prey for taking the little lambs. And when the lambs say
> among themselves, "These birds of prey are evil, and he who least
> resembles a bird of prey, who is rather its opposite, a lamb,—
> should he not be good?"
> —*On the Genealogy of Morality*

If you're a loser, you might as well get used to your loserdom and
sanctify it. Thus Nietzsche. The eagles will come down sooner or
later and grab you and eat you. It's how nature works. But if you, the
lamb, claim a superior virtue to the eagle, and you band together
with other lambs and consign the eagles to a sadistically picturesque
Hell, you will, in another life, find yourself behind the wheel working for Bay Area Limo instructing the hapless pale-skinned customer
from Minnesota about the manner in which some will find themselves scorched forever on the other side, forever and forever, oh, and
by the way, here we are at your hotel.

In one of Alice Munro's stories, a character observes that the Irish treat all authority with abject servility followed by savage, sneering mockery. *Ressentiment* has its comic side, after all.

After washing up, I went back downstairs through the lobby—more beautiful track stars, more flirting, and a micro-portion of *ressentiment* on my part against their beauty and youth and sexiness—and ambled to the Poolside Grille, where I ordered the *specialité de la maison*, blackened red snapper (California cuisine: black beans, jasmine rice, salsa fresca, lime sour cream), the snapper itself an endangered species. I hastily gulped down my chardonnay and like a starving peasant devoured the fish without tasting it. Gulping and chewing and swallowing, I watched the athletes in their skimpy garb promenading around the hotel, as graceful as swans. Ned Rorem on youth: "We admire them for their beauty, and they want us to admire them for their minds, the little shits." All the while Niazi's voice was in my head: "Every day the God gives you a new skin, so that he can burn it away." I paid the bill and returned to my room. *Fresh pain!* What a phrase. I couldn't read, so I watched TV: *CSI: Crime Scene Investigation*, Captain Jim Brass confessing to human failings, played very well by Paul Guilfoyle. Or did I watch another show, some pre-packaged drama interchangeable with that one? I can't remember. I do remember that I drifted off to sleep in my street clothes. There was no one around to tell me not to.

I didn't see Niazi again for another four weeks. On a Wednesday morning in April, he was to meet me in front of my Stanford apartment at 9:30 to take me to the San Francisco airport. At 9:25 I stood out in front with my suitcase beside me, waiting for him. I saw his black Lincoln Town Car in the visitors' parking lot. He honked, pulled up, and rushed out to put my suitcase in the trunk.

"Good morning, sir," he said. "How are you?" His eyes, I noticed, were heavy-lidded and puffy.

"Fine," I said, settling into the back seat and snapping on the lap-and-shoulder belt. "How about you?" I looked around for a bottle of water. There were two little ones.

"Very tired," he said, checking his watch before flopping in behind the wheel. "I could not sleep last night. I have been in this parking lot since eight-thirty."

"You should have called me," I said. "We could've left early."

"No no no," Niazi corrected me. "I have been trying to take the nap."

"Are you still drowsy?" I asked, noting again his use of definite articles.

"A little, somewhat," he told me. "But when I am that way, I think of the Holy Book."

"Ah."

He drove us up to Interstate 280, back in the hills, an alternative route to the airport. Here the rain was falling harder, and I noticed that Niazi didn't bother to turn on the car's windshield wipers. The rain spattered violently against the glass in an almost midwestern manner. I felt right at home. Stroking his beard, Niazi gazed out at the highway, and after about ten minutes, I saw that, with his eyes half-closed, he was turning his head back and forth, shaking it slowly, as if . . . *was this possible? Was I actually seeing what I was seeing?* He was driving the limo, with me in it, while sleeping.

My brother Tom used to get drowsy behind the wheel and one winter night in 1961 almost killed himself outside Delano, Minnesota, when he dozed off. Another irony: Delano's major business in those days was the engraving of cemetery monuments, and the town's motto was DRIVE CAREFULLY. WE CAN WAIT. Unable to walk away from his accident, his car in the ditch, my brother had to drag himself on all fours out of the wreck across a snowy field to a farm-house. As a boy, I was quite accustomed to my brother's sleepiness behind the wheel and would keep him entertained and awake with bright patter, for which I have a gift. So: "Niazi!" I said. "Do you have many jobs today? I'll bet you do!"

"Oh, yes, sir," he said dispiritedly. "Many. Two this afternoon." Maybe he wasn't asleep after all.

The rain fell harder, unusually hard for Northern California. I looked around at the interior of the Lincoln Town Car, thinking, *We're going to crash. But at least this limo is a very solid car.* With the irony of which life is so fond, I thought of two lines of a creepy song I had heard a few months before, by the group Concrete Blonde. The song was "Tomorrow, Wendy," and two lines serve as the song's refrain:

> Hey, hey, goodbye
> Tomorrow Wendy's going to die.

And just about then the car began to fishtail. When a car fish-tails, you take your foot off the accelerator and tap the brake pedal. Fishtailing occurs often in icy conditions (think: Minnesota winter), less often in rain. But California drivers aren't used to precipitation, so when the car began to lose control, Niazi woke up and slammed on the brakes, throwing the Lincoln into a sideways skid, and when the rear-wheel-drive tires acquired traction again, they pushed us off the freeway, onto the shoulder, and then, very rapidly, down a hill, where the car flipped over sideways and began to roll, turning over and over and over, until it reached the bottom of the hill, right side up. From the moment the car began to lose control until it came to rest, Niazi was screaming. All during the time we turned over down that hill, he continued to scream.

Reader, this essay is about that scream. Please do your best to imagine it.

Men don't scream, as a rule; they bellow or roar with fright or anger, but male screaming is an exceptionally rare phenomenon, and the sound makes your flesh crawl. A woman's scream calls you to protective action. A man's scream provokes horror.

Inside that car, I was holding on to the door's hand rest, clutching it, and I was as quiet as the tomb. I wasn't particularly scared, although things were flying around the car—my cell phone had escaped from my coat pocket and was airborne in front of me, as were various other items from the car, including those free little bottles of water and a clipboard from the front seat—and I heard the sound of crunching or of some huge animal chewing up the car. I thought: *Let this be over soon.* And then it was. They say everything slows down during an accident, but no, not always, and this accident didn't slow down my sense of time until we were at rest and I heard Niazi moaning, and more than anything else I wanted to get out of that car before the gas tank exploded, but my door wouldn't open—the right rear door—but the left rear door did, after I pushed my shoulder against it.

Around and inside the car was a terrible smell of wreckage, oil and burnt rubber, and another smell, which I am tempted to describe as sulfurous.

"Niazi," I said, "are you okay?"

"Oh oh oh oh," he said, "yes, I am okay" (he clearly wasn't), "and you, Mr. Baxter, sir, are you okay?"

"Yes." Where was I? Without a transition, I seemed to be standing in the rain outside the car, and Niazi, making the sounds that precede speech in human history, was trying to get himself off the ground, blood streaming down his face; and his shoes, I noticed, were off, which is one of the signs of a high-velocity accident. Amid the wreckage, he was barefoot, and blood was dripping onto his feet. I reached out for him.

Suddenly witnesses surrounded us. "You turned over four times!" an Asian American man said, clutching my arm. His face was transfixed by shock. "I saw it. I was behind you. Are you all right? How could you possibly be all right? Surely you are not all right?" He opened his umbrella and lifted it over my head, a perfect gesture of kindness.

"I don't know," I said. I looked down at my Levi's. The belt loops had snapped off. How was that possible? I stared in wonderment at the broken belt loops. I looked at the man. "Am I all right?" I didn't know.

He simply stared at me as if I had suffered through a resurrection.

The usual confusion followed: EMT guys, California Highway Patrol guys, witness reports. An off-duty cop from San Marino, another witness to the accident, said he couldn't believe I was standing up. He touched my arm with a tender gesture as if I might break. Someone asked me to sign a document, and I did, my hand shaking so violently that my signature looked like that of a third grader. And what was I worried about? My *laptop*. Had it been damaged? Furthermore, I thought, *I'm going to be late for my airplane flight!* In shock, we lose all sense of proportion. My signature on another official document looked like someone else's, not mine. And now Niazi was standing up, still bloodily barefoot, talking. He appeared to be in stable condition though they were putting a head brace on him and then lowering him onto a wooden stretcher, as if he had been smashed up. The witness who saw our car turn over four times asked me where I was going, and I said, "To the airport."

"I will take you," he said. "Just put your suitcase in the back seat. We will have to drop off my father-in-law in Millbrae. Do you mind?"

"No," I said. "Thank you."

The driver and his father-in-law spoke Mandarin all the way to Millbrae, the driver politely interpreting for me so that I wouldn't be left out of the conversation. "My father-in-law thinks you must be badly injured," the driver said. "I told him that you said you were fine." Thanks to this gentleman, I arrived at the San Francisco airport in time for my flight. My ribs hurt, and my back hurt, and I gave off an odd panic-stricken body odor, but all I wanted to do was to get home. All the same, I was still disoriented. Near the entrance to Terminal One, I noticed, was a sign with a name on it: NOSMO KING. It appeared to me as graffiti on behalf of a deposed potentate. Who was this oddly named Nosmo King? King of what? We were in Northern California! No kings here! Not until I was seated on the airplane did I calm down and realize that I had misread the sign and that, like other public places, the San Francisco airport did not tolerate lighting up or puffing on cigarettes.

My back still hurts sometimes, especially on long flights. Niazi called me at home a few days later and left a message on my answering machine. His voice was expressive of deep despair combined with physical pain. "Mr. Baxter, sir, I am worried about you. I am . . . I am not all right, but I am lying down, recovering. Would you please call me?"

No. I would not call him, and I did not. I couldn't. In Hell there is no forgiveness. I heard from someone else that he had broken his back. Guiltily, shamefully, I left him uncalled, and my inability to dial his number and to ask him how he was recovering surely serves as a sign of a human failing, a personalized resentment that will not be appeased. But all I could think of, then and now, was *That expert on Hell almost got me killed.*

The insurance company has promised to send me five hundred dollars to compensate me for my pain and suffering.

In another version of the accident, the one I sometimes told myself compulsively, I sit silently while Niazi screams and the car rolls over down the hill. But I didn't just tell myself this story; I told everybody. The accident turned me into a tiresome raconteur. A repetition compulsion had me in its tight narrative grip. I had become like a character in one of my own stories, the sort of madcap who buttonholes an innocent bystander to relieve himself of an obsession. Some stories present themselves as a gift, to be handed on to others as a second gift. But some more dire stories have a certain difficult to define taint. They give off an odd smell. They have infected the person who possesses them, and that person peevishly passes on the infection to others. In the story in which I am the victim, I am not an artist, but a garrulous ancient mariner who has come ashore long after his boat has been set adrift and long after his rescue, which does not feel like a rescue but an abandonment.

From the airport I called my wife, from whom I was separated, to give her the news. She met me at the airport, and we hugged each other for the first time in months. Near-death trumps marital discord but does not heal it. Then she took me back to my apartment, where she dropped me off.

I sat alone in the apartment for a few days, trying to read, but mostly writing emails. At night, I would fall asleep to the remembered sound of Niazi's screams. I announced my accident on Facebook, curious whether any of my FB friends would press the Like button. A few did. I picked up the phone and started calling people. "Let me tell you what happened to me," I would say. I had become strangely interesting to myself. One friend has called my compulsion to talk about the accident a form of "vocational imperialism," though I think he means *avocational* imperialism. After all, I am a mere tourist in the landscape of Islam. As an unsteady humanist, I don't believe in much, and the virtues that I do believe in—goodness, charity, bravery— abandoned me in the moments after that accident. Because, really all I thought as we tumbled down that hill, as I have said, was the hope that this awfulness would be over soon. We die alone even if someone else is dying beside us. And—this was my fleeting wish in the back seat of that Lincoln Town Car, in a wondrously dark clarity of thought, as the plastic bottles of water were flying around my head and my cell phone twirled in the air in front of me—I prayed that the car would land right side up, or, if this was to be the moment of my death, that it be quick.

All the Dark Nights—a Letter

I am writing this from a cabin north of Duluth, Minnesota, on Lake Superior. On my left are high windows that face southeast, toward the ledge rock down by the water. I'm typing at the dining room table, and I've positioned myself so that I can gaze out through the windows on the west side of the room. I can see several poplars, a stand of scrubby pines, and, between them and me, the snow that's been falling most of the morning. In the distance I can hear waves breaking on the rocks, and from inside the house, the sound of the water heater clicking on and off.

This time around, I had to travel a day and a half to get to this place, and I lost a pair of reading glasses along the way. Being farsighted, I can't at this moment see clearly the words that I am writing and that are displayed on the laptop. They're almost completely blurred. I'm not even trying to read them. Instead, I am watching the pines and the snow while I type. It's a kind of daydreaming, soul-satisfying and extremely pleasant, like having the gift to be able to write music without having to hear it, except internally.

When I told a friend that I planned to come up here—to this cabin, on the lake, near the woods—for four days just to write, she said, with a pleasant laugh, "That's great. I envy you."

I don't find it curious that some people should envy writers, but for the most part I think that people don't actually envy them very much (when they think about writers at all), and they probably envy them less now than they used to a few decades ago. People who have to do difficult or meaningless work often envy, with good reason, the life of the artist. Such a life can appear to be fulfilling and, in its way, luxurious. It can also look suspiciously like an escape from reality. As a compensating punishment, outsiders like to imagine the artist being plagued by poverty and unworldliness, a diet of ketchup sandwiches, which is what artists often have, and get.

Young musicians still starve, fledgling painters starve, writers starve. If they don't starve, they don't always eat well or buy brand-new BMWs. The idea that they're being self-indulgent and narcissistic is a common accusation leveled against would-be artists by friends, lovers, spouses, and family members. You don't often hear investment bankers being accused of self-indulgence, although, as a group, they are often noteworthy for that quality, living in houses that could be mistaken for hotels, but their indulgences sometimes make money, thereby exonerating them. The artist who fails, furthermore, has not beaten the odds, because the odds always favor failure and frequently justify the predictions. Fiction writers may have a gift, but they also have an affliction, and this affliction is not often noticed and not much discussed.

I don't really believe in most wisdom: not my own wisdom or anyone else's. What passes for wisdom is usually somebody's personal prejudice masquerading as truth. With good reason, young people often distrust wisdom from the old. They see the effort to justify past mistakes by replicating them in the young. Lars Gustafsson: "We take steps whose only function is to give meaning to the steps we have already taken. Obstinately, we stay on at the bad hotel in order to give meaning to the fact that we were once stupid enough to check in there."

Most young people can't get away from this scene fast enough. True wisdom is somewhat private, while public wisdom tends to be irrelevant: Wisdom from the middle-aged and the old has a tendency nearly always to miss its mark, to strike the wrong tone (usually one of smug self-importance) and to become fatuous. The fraudulently wise are figures of comedy and menace.

I keep starting this letter and throwing it away (though, without my reading glasses, I can't find the trash icon). It's a problem in tone. I think writers should make their own mistakes, the way that I made mine. Why should anyone try to avoid failure, mistakes, heartbreak, sorrow, drunkenness, sexual confusion, and apathy? I couldn't avoid them, you probably won't, and they will end up serving as resources for your writing. I managed to live through them, though I expect to see those bad friends again, someday.

I myself was both arrogant and insecure as a young writer; I think I must have been insufferable, thanks to my ignorance and knowingness—a dangerous combination, and quite inflammatory, though not all that unusual. Before William Faulkner became the William Faulkner we know, he was of course a young unfamous man, a "writer-to-be," to use Walter Abish's wonderful phrase. And what did the people in Faulkner's hometown call this young unknown man with great writerly ambitions, who affected to stroll around town with a walking stick, like an aristocrat, or a count? "Count No 'Count" was the name they found for him.

They were the first harbingers of the Fraud Police, who will dog your heels for much of your life—more about those sinister patrol officers later.

Advice is almost as bad as wisdom, especially when it hasn't been asked for. If you've read Rilke's *Letters to a Young Poet*, you'll notice that Rilke takes his young writer-friend very seriously, so seriously, in fact, that Rilke's book achieves a kind of weird and creepy grandeur, as if poetry and genius could be learned from a conduct manual. At the same time, Rilke's book is almost entirely impractical. It teaches you nothing except how Rilke felt about being himself. He is explaining to an ordinary person with an ambition to be a poet what it's like to be a genius, and he is pretending for appearance's sake that anyone can aspire to genius. Of course anyone can, but it'll wreck your life if you don't have the capacity for it, and it may wreck your life even if you do. But a life, Rilke might have said, may be a small price to pay for great poems. If you can give up your life for your country, why shouldn't you give it up for poetry? It's like a saint explaining to a house painter the steps to becoming a saint. It's not that the saint is wrong. He is, after all, a saint. (Rilke, after all, is Rilke.) The real problem is that only Rilke could be Rilke. Others have tried to be him and have failed.

The curse that the Great (like Rilke) leave behind is the curse of their absolutely unfollowable example. Their lives and their work cannot be replicated and they create a bizarre perspective when they seek to offer advice.

Like many other European artists of the early part of the twentieth century, Rilke thought of poetry as a calling, and of art generally as a redemptive spiritual project, though his poetry is never scrupulously clear about what form this redemption would actually take. Still, his message is straightforward: Poetry can save you. You must change your life. But how? Americans, who are at heart pragmatic, have rarely believed that art can solve much of anything or redeem anyone. If you tell them "Poetry can save you," they are likely to say "From what?" But they do like to buy how-to books, and, in a general way, they like to be told how to do something. Because fiction is even less transcendent than poetry is and is more remunerative, Americans, at least, seem to respect it, or used to. There are many how-to-write manuals on the bookstore shelves, most of them quite un-Rilkean and extremely practical. All the same, for fifty years, few people have seriously thought that the writing or reading of fiction is a sacred activity, or even much of an occupation, using the conventional yardsticks.

Nevertheless: here I am in this quiet house. I don't care if I am in
a minority. I am writing these words as I watch the snow fall, happy
to think of myself as a writer, someone who has found a calling, and
wondering: What can I say that will be of any use?

The first and last thing to say is, "I am happy, despite all my failures." And more: I am almost unbelievably lucky. But the point is not
me at all. The point has to do with an art, and a condition.

The condition first.

Probably you are a great or a good noticer. You may well be the
one in your family who paid attention to your family members more
than the others did. You sometimes knew what they would say before they actually said it. When they were out of the room, their
voices sounded in your inner ear. Quite possibly, you were good at
imitating all of them. Sometimes, you felt like a spy: you were spying
on the whole of life itself. This condition has its own kind of excitement and pathos, but it very clearly carries a feeling of tension and
estrangement. Without quite knowing how, you fell just a bit outside
the groups of which you were a member.

And if you were like me, you often sat in the back of the class near
the window, daydreaming. Much of the time, while you were observing the world, you yourself were in a fog. You *were* that fog. You
were capable of befogging others. You hardly knew who you were.
Sometimes you felt like everybody. You may have been very good at
telling jokes and stories, keeping the other kids amused or interested
for hours, but some part of you watched all this and watched how
others were reacting to you. I'm not very good at telling jokes, but
I do like to tell stories, and sometimes, in school, when I did so, my
friends would say, "Baxter, you're full of it."

Writers also have an early tendency toward funny and malicious gos-
sip, but in this they are not particularly different from anyone else.

In the later years of adolescence, writers, as a group, begin to feel a particular affliction, which is also a gift (similarly, a musical gift is often accompanied by the maddening experience of constantly hearing music in one's head, a gift that can also feel like an affliction). This feeling, which I think is peculiar to writers and more specifically to fiction writers, is that of feeling as if you are carrying a whole landscape of people around inside you. In one of Thomas Pynchon's novels this condition is described as "coming on like a whole roomful of people." You may not know who you are (my first book was titled *Chameleon*), but you often do know who these internalized people are, whose tantalizing stories are beginning to press out on you like something growing from the inside out, something extruded. You are full of it; you are full of them.

You are full of the possibility of characters and narrative.

I have not seen this condition described accurately anywhere. Kierkegaard, in *Repetition*, remarks on how quickly and how often young men, after falling in love with a woman, draw back slightly and find themselves becoming addicted to the experience they have just had of falling in love, which requires, not the continuation of love itself, but the repetition of the experience of falling in love, thus turning the object of love, the loved one, into a pretext, and the lover into a sort of addict. (Don Juan is an addict.) A sign of this, Kierkegaard says, is writing—usually love poems. Writers of fiction are a bit like that. They have fallen into the characters whom they have observed and imagined and loved. And the only way to get out of that feeling is to tell the story of that character. But it's not enough to tell one story. Because there are so many characters buried within the self, the only sensible activity is, to use Gertrude Stein's phrase, "tell[ing] it again and again." There is something in this process that resembles the dynamics of addiction. The practice of most arts is very hard to give up once you've started, and few people ever manage to stop doing it.

The young fiction writer lugs around something that seems to be part of being alive, but the only way to express it—almost literally, to bring it out—is to write it. What "it" is, in this case, is a piling up of selves, of beings, and of stories that are being experienced from the inside. What is it like to be you, to be me? You can't answer that question by answering it discursively. You can only answer it by telling a story. That's not therapy. You're probably not sick. You're just a certain kind of human being. It's like the necessity the musician has in humming a tune or playing a piano, or the necessity an artist has in doodling and sketching and drawing and painting. It's almost involuntary. Something needs to get out: not expressed but extruded. As the composer Camille Saint-Saëns remarked, "I write music the way an apple tree produces apples."

You would feel this necessity even if the novel died, even if there were no audience for fiction (but there always will be), even if it seemed that you might never be published. You would feel the press of stories and characters outward from yourself toward the world, no matter what the conditions of publication and distribution might be. Other literature has simply inspired and inflamed you. It's as if you've been given instructions: get it all down. The real question is what to do about it, this gift and affliction, how to organize your life so that the conditions of that life don't shape up as a full-fledged disaster. The size of a life disaster is often proportional to the size of the ambition. Just because you hear the call doesn't mean that you are saved.

Women and men who have decided to be fiction writers have a certain fanaticism. Sometimes this fanaticism is well concealed, but more often it isn't. They—you—need it, to get you through the bad times and the long apprenticeship. Learning any craft alters the conditions of your being. Poets, like mathematicians, ripen early, but fiction writers tend to take longer to get their world on paper because that world has to be observed in predatory detail and because the subtleties of plot, setting, tone, and dialogue are difficult to master. Fanaticism ignores current conditions (i.e., you are living in a garage, surviving on peanut butter sandwiches, and writing a Great Novel that no one, so far, has read, or wants to) in the hope of some condition that may arrive at a distant point in the future. Fanaticism and dedication and doggedness and stubbornness are your angels. They keep the demon of discouragement at bay. But, given the demands of the craft, it is no wonder that so many of its practitioners come out at the other end of the process as drunks, bullies, windbags, and assholes. The wonder is that any of them come out as decent human beings. But some do.

A writer's life is tricky to sustain. The debased romanticism that is sometimes associated with it—the sordid glamour of living in an attic, the ketchup sandwiches, being a drunken oaf or a bully, getting into fistfights à la Bukowski—needs to be discarded, and in the age of the internet, it probably has been.

I was a late starter, a painfully slow learner. I remember having a great idea for a story while riding a Minneapolis city bus at the age of thirteen. I was on fire with it. The idea was: an inmate of a mental hospital who thinks he is Christ *actually is Christ*! I thought this idea was so good that I was terrified that someone would steal it. I wanted to register this idea in the United States copyright office, though I didn't know how. I kept having ideas like this for years and would walk around in public with a sly, secretive smile on my face.

I first tried to write a novel at the age of twenty-two. I had only taken one creative writing class (insecurity, arrogance), and the single scene of this novel I can remember writing was one in which a man throws himself out of a window of a high-rise building. The man's fall is described in phantasmagoric detail. Everything in my writing was apocalyptic and cataclysmic.

Four years later, armed with an advanced degree and a job, I sat down in my free hours to write my first completed novel, *Ground Zero*, which you will never read because it has never been published and never will be. I think—I hope—no copy of it exists anymore. It was about a world in which everyone starts lying about everything all the time. Remember—in my defense—that this was the era of Johnson and Nixon and the war in Vietnam. I wrote this novel in a state of high excitement. I was exhilarated by almost every one of my sentences. I suspected I was a genius but was careful to keep this stupendous secret to myself. Angels and devils, truth and lying, ultimate realities all found their way into this book. A few people read it, most were mystified by it (I was mystified by their mystification—how could they not see how astoundingly good this book was?), and it found its way to a few editors, all of whom said it was interesting but that it was "not for us."

Undeterred, and now, by a set of bizarre circumstances, armed with an agent, I sat down and for the next two years wrote my second novel, *Media Event*, which you have not read because it has never been published and never will be. It was about . . . oh, never mind. I wrote this book in a state of high excitement—once again, I was exhilarated by my sentences and by my visionary power. I sent it to the agent I had acquired by writing *Ground Zero* and waited for her excited, blubberingly enthusiastic phone call.

I waited and waited. Finally I decided to call her myself. It was a summer afternoon. In Minnesota, my mother was dying of emphysema and heart failure. I was hoping that I might have some good news for her. At home, my wife was pregnant, and we were, despite my job, flat broke. I had spent the last five years of my life trying to become a fiction writer, to get a foothold. That afternoon, I was in the bedroom, sitting on the bed—a mattress on the floor—and the sun was shining through the west-facing windows, and I was getting up my courage.

After I dialed the agency's number, my then-agent, Julia, answered. I identified myself, and she said hi. There was a brief pause, an expressive air pocket of dead silence. I explained to her that a friend, a writer who was a visiting professor at my university, had read my new novel manuscript and had said that it might be snapped up at Alfred A. Knopf, his own publisher. I asked what she thought its chances were there.

"Charlie," she said. "Don't you want to know what I think of your new novel? The one you just sent me?"

"Yes, Julie, of course I do."

There was another pause, and I heard her taking a breath. "I hate it," she said, with what seemed to be an odd satisfaction expressed with deadening calm.

"You hate it?" My mouth had turned instantly to cotton.

"Yes, I hate it. Isn't that puzzling? I can't figure it out. How strange. Tell me why I hate it."

"What?"

"Tell me why I hate your novel."

"Julie," I said, trying to hold my head up while the room started to spin, "I have no idea why you hate my novel."

"Of course you do. Oh, sure, you must. You wrote it. Tell me why I hate it."

"I don't know," I said.

"Oh, you must. Please. Give it a try. Help me out here. Tell me why I hate your novel. Is it the characters? Is it the plot? I just don't get it. I don't get any of it. So," she said, cheerfully, "is that it? The whole thing? Is that why I hate your novel?"

That, almost word for word, is what she said to me up to that point, but I don't remember the rest of the conversation, except for the news that naturally she no longer wanted to represent me. I went into a sort of shock and can remember nothing else from the rest of the day.

Somewhat deterred by now, but still, after my recovery, brimming with guarded enthusiasm, I subsequently sat down, during those brief moments between child care and class preparations, to write my third novel, *In Hibernation*, which you have never read because . . . etc. Thanks to a new set of bizarre circumstances, I had acquired a different agent. When I finished *In Hibernation*, I gave it to my wife, who seemed unable to finish it. Nevertheless, I bravely sent it to my new agent, who called and told me with great tact and kindness, this time, that no one at the agency thought it was marketable; in other words, they would not be sending it out. I mailed a copy of the manuscript to a literary-minded friend on the West Coast—he's now a book reviewer there—who said to me over the phone a couple of weeks later, "Charlie, maybe your imagination is poisoned right at the source."

The condition into which I fell seemed to have no bottom layer. I just kept falling. I believed that I knew what I wanted to do with my life. However, I would not be allowed to do it in the way that I had imagined. People seemed to dislike what I produced and could not be persuaded to like it. I carried around within me stories that had, I thought, an aura to them. But these stories struck no chords in anyone else. No one heard the chords, and no one saw the aura. I thought I was reasonably smart. At least: smart enough. And reasonably talented. But none of it was working. I felt as if my nerves had moved out to the surface of my skin; I felt humiliated and exposed. At this point in my life, only my wife and my child and my job kept me anchored to the world of the living.

I was close to being a menace to myself. I decided, among other resolutions, that I would never write another novel.

I also decided that I would never be a writer, in the sense in which that word is commonly used. What I thought was my calling probably wasn't my calling after all—that in fact I didn't have a calling except to be a decent human being, a teacher, a husband, and a father, if indeed I could manage those categories. I was in my early thirties by this time and felt that I had become an expert on failure and the day-to-day management of despair. I found that I had a new streak of verbal cruelty that I could not always control. I decided to write one last piece, on my particular subject, about a young man who fails to be a good musician and who becomes a critic instead. It was a story called "Harmony of the World," and I sent it to a local journal, *Michigan Quarterly Review*, expecting the usual rejection and scathing comments to which I was now becoming accustomed.

A few weeks later I was watching TV in the basement when the phone rang. It was the editor of *Michigan Quarterly Review*, Laurence Goldstein. He told me that he had read my story; he was quite enthusiastic about it. And then he asked me a question. I sometimes remind him of this moment, because it struck me then as one of the kindest questions anyone has ever asked me, and because it suggested ever so slightly that I might be somebody, rather than the nobody I had resigned myself to being.

"Who are you?" he inquired.

For the next five years I wrote about failure. It had become my subject, my koan, my home base, my infinitely renewable resource. The abyss turned into a mine shaft. My first book, a collection of stories titled with nasty irony *Harmony of the World*, appeared in 1984. The book deals with the failure of characters to do successfully what they have set out to do. It's an interesting subject, though slightly un-American. By the time the book appeared, I was thirty-seven. After my sister-in-law read it, she asked me, over cocktails, "Why do you write about characters with such pathetic little lives?"

Because I know them, I said, or wanted to say. Besides, who are *your* people? These are my people. They're telling. In the title story, there is a character named Luther Stecker who asks the narrator, a pianist, why his playing makes him—Stecker—sick. Why, he asks, do I hate your playing? Tell me. Be courageous. Tell me why I hate your playing. (What I, as a writer, was doing in this story might be called "taking my demons out of the unemployment line and putting them to work.") Thank you, Julie, wherever you are, for your cruelty to me. Now I am an expert on cruelty. Couldn't have done it without you.

In my next book of stories, called *Through the Safety Net*, there is a story called "Media Event," and another story, called "Gryphon," in which an atmosphere of constant lying is created in a classroom, very much as it was in *Ground Zero*, and there is another story called "The Eleventh Floor," in which remnants of *In Hibernation* are visible. As my aunt used to say, "Nothing is ever gained or lost in the universe," and I suppose I had learned that lesson. *Through the Safety Net* is, in part, a massive salvage operation, in which a few moments are retrieved from my personal sunken scrap heap of failures.

It seems a shame to say so, but the hardest part of being a writer is learning how to survive the dark nights of the soul. There are many such nights, far too many, as you will discover.

Part of the deal of having a soul at all includes the requirement that you go through several dark nights. No soul, no dark nights. But when they come, they have a surprisingly creepy power, and almost no one tells you how to deal with them. You can do illegal drugs or take psychoactive pills, you can have affairs or masturbate, you can watch movies 'til dawn, but that only produces what doctors call symptomatic relief. In these nights you confront your own doubts, lack of self-confidence, the futility of what you are doing, and the various ways in which you fail to measure up. Feelings of inadequacy are the black lung disease of writing. These are the nights during which the Fraud Police come to knock on your door.

Psychologists have their own name for this set of feelings. (They have clinical names for most of our emotions by now.) They call it imposter syndrome. Imposter syndrome is endemic to the art of writing because gifts—the clear evidence of talent—are not so clearly associated with writing as they are with music and graphic art. Not everyone has perfect pitch, not everyone can carry a tune, not everyone can draw or create an interesting representation of something on canvas. But almost every goddamn moron can write prose.

Furthermore, anyone's apprenticeship in the writing of fiction has several stages, at least one of which involves an imposture. To be a novelist or a short story writer, you first have to pretend to be a novelist or a short story writer. By great imaginative daring, you start out as Count No 'Count. Everyone does. Everyone starts as a mere scribbler. Proust got his start as a pesky dandified social layabout with no recognizable talents except for making conversation and noticing everybody. So what do *you* do? You sit down and pretend to write a novel by actually trying to write one without knowing how to do it. It is clearly not a rule-governed activity; there are only rules of thumb that sometimes work. As you pretend to write your novel, you learn, if you're lucky, actually how to do it. You learn this intuitively. After you've learned how to do it, you proceed to write another novel, and, if you're lucky, it turns out to be a real novel.

The first stage—of pretending to be a writer—never quite disappears. And there is, in this art, no ultimate validation, again because it's not a rule-governed activity. The ultimate verdict never comes in. God tends to be silent in matters of art and literary criticism. Reviewers and editors who pretend to be God make fools of themselves. Besides, what's the yardstick? It's hard to make a lot of money from writing, and even if you did make a lot of money, what then? You might be labeled as a hack. No one asked you to do what you're doing, so you can't satisfy that person by doing it. You don't find out until much later that you may have helped some people who have read your work. Reviews may eventually come, and they're good (or bad), and there are prizes, and you get them (or don't). When one of my novels was published, one reviewer said it was destined to be a classic, and another reviewer—Michael Upchurch (how could I forget?)—said the book was a clear sign of my total incompetence as a novelist. Someone is always doing better than you are, some-one is always being loved a little more, someone is always telling you that the work is not up to snuff, or that it shows incompetence or a decline.

You may often wake up at night and feel like a fraud. That prob-ably happens to you now, before anyone has said your work is any good, and it will continue to happen, once you are published and are reviewed. The fraud feeling is very mysterious and, for most of us, never quite goes away. Prozac and Xanax are sometimes prescribed to banish it. By contrast, bracing self-confidence among writers is a rare commodity and often a sign of psychic instability.

I once saw Toni Morrison on national television. In front of a large audience, she was asked if she thought she was a great writer, whereupon she smiled and laughed, then nodded, and said, well, yes, but she had *always* thought that she was a great writer. Her laughter made the admission appear to be part of an outburst of great good humor, even gaiety, that the audience could share, as in an inter-view with a good-natured someone who admits that, yes, she won the lottery. It's just a fact. Toni Morrison was admitting that, indeed, yes, she was Toni Morrison and was lucky and talented and a hard worker, and indeed a great writer, just as, in *Letters to a Young Poet*, Rilke eventually gets around to admitting that he is, indeed, Rilke. This feeling of artistic power—aesthetic triumphalism—seems to me to be increasingly rare in our time, but Toni Morrison had it, and it blazed out in her work.

Not in mine. The result of my early failures is that I find writing to be almost unimaginably difficult. I always suspect that I am about to make a terrible set of mistakes. Therefore, the writing comes slowly, when it comes at all. I'm not by any stretch of the imagina-tion, *my* imagination, prolific. It's good to be confident, but a lack of self-confidence can be turned to your own purposes if it helps you to take pains, to take care, to avoid glibness.

Thomas Mann said, "A writer is someone for whom writing is more difficult than it is for other people."

Native Americans thought that you couldn't own land, because land wasn't yours to own. Any talent, any gift, any art, can leave you. I've done my best to learn a craft, which is like acquiring a set of tools. And what power anyone can acquire, anyone can lose. Fiction writers don't necessarily get better as they get older. Frequently, they get worse.

You do what you can. You wait, in readiness. You try to be modest. You try not to destroy yourself with drugs and drink and sex and selfishness. You are grateful for what you get, knowing that it could be much worse.

It's still very quiet here, and it's still snowing, of course, and the waves are higher, and it's the next day, and as you know perfectly well, I lied to you: I have a second pair of glasses, and I have been watching these words, each letter and phrase, as they appeared on the screen, and I've been changing them and correcting them minute by minute, hour by hour, day by day, year after year, because that is who I am, and that is what I do.

Charisma and Fictional Authority—
Nine Fragments toward an Essay

1.

After long delays, the person we have waited for stands *up there*, elevated above everyone else. From moment to moment, the speaker's face is solemn, mocking, knowing, scornful, *radiant*. The audience members—and there must always be an audience—lean forward toward the person addressing them, and from their expectant expressions, you can tell that they're transfixed by the words that are somehow running parallel alongside the charismatic figure's physical presence. You had questions? Here at last are the answers, but the words—this is strange—are less important than the presence.

Toward the end, the listeners applaud and stomp their feet; they nod; they roar their approval. They are lifted up. In our time, they raise their iPhones to snap pictures. Many audience members are dressed in clothes that somehow imitate their leader's clothing, and some of their hats and shirts contain quotations from speeches that the speaker has uttered. They are branded with the speaker's brand. They may have tattoos of the speaker's face or initials on their flesh. The speaker, who has certain powers denied to everyone else, is saying that they, the ones in the room, are *in a special group, consisting of us,* and those who oppose us are *not important* and can be classed as unenlightened nobodies—or enemies. The outsiders may comprise the terrible, unknowing, and malevolently contemptible *others* beyond the group, and—don't forget—these others should be ignored or converted or healed, at best, and, at worst, well, *use your imagination.*

The atmosphere in the room is electric with rage, devotion, excitement, and permission giving. It is epiphany time. Ordinary day-to-day meaninglessness has been replaced by meaning, great gobs of it, almost too much meaning, an overflow of meaning that answers all doubts and will lead to *action.* There are goals that, given great communal sacrifice and sometimes big monetary donations, *will* be met. Or else.

The arrow goes into the string of the bow and is pulled back. The speaker is often absent once the arrow reaches its target.

2.

In the wake of the Trump presidency, I feel compelled to write an essay on charisma, a topic I previously thought to be impossibly large. Where do I start, where does *anyone* start? The first hurdle one has to jump over has to do with definitions. The word has morphed from the early Christian era, when in the Pauline epistles *charisma* referred to a variety of grace that had everything to do with the divine presence. It was thought to be conferred by the Holy Spirit through the gift of Christ's divinity, and all good things flowed through it; those who received it were blessed. "Charismatic Christianity" still holds on to this definition.

When the social theorist Max Weber brought the word back into common use in the early part of the twentieth century, however, he applied the term to a certain kind of political authority: the charismatic figure is assumed to have supernatural, superhuman, or godlike powers that the rest of us lack. (A friend of mine, speaking of a charismatic teacher and mentor of hers, said to me, "He can summon angels.") In Weber's terms, this charismatic power is neither good nor bad, although it certainly can be misused. It requires the audience's belief or faith, without which it disappears. Charisma answers to—and responds to—chronic neediness and creates a kind of feedback loop in which an appetite is fed, providing a brief satisfaction that in turn increases the appetite. Weber does not, to my knowledge, take up the related problem of meaning at any length, nor does he discuss the techniques that the charismatic leader uses to fill in the emptiness of daily secular life, but a feeling of emptiness serves as a catalytic entry point into the circuitry and the jolt of electricity provided by the Weberian charismatic figure.

A second theory of charisma (in fiction and elsewhere) arrives at politics through the back door: in René Girard's version of it in *Deceit, Desire, and the Novel* (1965), charisma arises when two conditions meet: the person, usually male, is physically striking or beautiful *and* also seems to love no one and to need nobody. This is the where's-my-mirror narcissism of the stupendously beautiful or of the supremely confident and self-absorbed. Girard's charismatic figures may not have an agenda, but people go out of their heads when they're near them, and violence is often in the air—people don't look at such stars; they *stare* at them and want to crowd up close to get inside the aura. Think of the immobile and indifferent Andy Warhol and the mayhem surrounding him. Everyone want to get ahold of *that*, but it's maddeningly hard to get ahold of *that* when the Fortunate One doesn't give anything back and doesn't even seem to care that other people exist.

Girard's exemplary fictional character for this version of charisma is Stavrogin in Dostoevsky's *Demons* (1872), and there's a brilliant and witty reading of Girard's theory, and of Dostoevsky's novel and narcissistic autonomy, and of life as a graduate student in Elif Batuman's nonfiction memoir *The Possessed* (2010). Girard's theory could equally be applied to Djuna Barnes' novel *Nightwood* (1936),

as it happens, and its female protagonist. *Nightwood*'s central figure
is the enigmatic and almost silent Robin Vote, whom everyone in
the novel—Felix, Nora, and Jenny—would like to possess or get a
piece of, but Robin is the sort of person who doesn't notice you when
you're in the room, who often doesn't listen when spoken to, who
would rather play with her dolls. She's beautiful, of course (Barnes is
cagey on this point), but she sleepwalks through life, and just when
you think you've got her attention, she wanders away, muttering half-
intelligible statements on her way to the nearest back-alley bar. When
the person you love doesn't seem to remember your name or notice
you enough to recall what you look like, you either give up or go a
little crazy. Your love may *intensify*. You should know better, but in
matters of love, who knows better? Despair and crazy eloquence at
its outer limit are the two poles of the battery in *Nightwood*.

Max Weber's theory of charisma is closely related to a variety of
demagoguery, which amounts to rhetorical control over an audience,
whereas Girard's theory has nothing to do with demagoguery, although the audience is still under a kind of spell. Both theories lean
toward what happens when there's the creation of a spellbound cult
around the charismatic figure. In my own thinking about charisma,
I'd emphasize the spellbinding: how we get there, and what we're
like when we're under a spell, the way that we're bound, tied up, and
stuck in a web of fixation. The charismatic figure is best understood
by observing not the figure, but the audience. This is an important
point for fiction writers who are crafting characters who compel our
attention. Most of the time, we pay attention to fictional characters
because of what they *do*. With charismatic fictional characters, we
pay attention because of what they *are*.

For example, here's Elif Batuman on the subject of a fellow graduate student at Stanford, whose name was Matej. He was from Croatia
and thus was exotic at Stanford. She notes that, like Dostoevsky's fictional character Stavrogin, the real-life Matej had a certain masklike

beauty: "narrow glinting eyes, high cheekbones, too-black hair—with a long-limbed, perfectly proportioned physical elegance, such that his body always looked at once extravagantly casual and perfectly composed." If the reader should happen to think that what's being described is an instance of standard-issue physical attraction by the bedazzled author in response to stone-cold male beauty, Batuman is quick to set to set us straight:

> But the more time I spent around Matej, the more vividly I realized that I was for the first time in the presence of pure charisma, the real thing. It was an elemental power, like weather or electricity. Recognizing it had no effect on your physical response.

Notice the switch from "I" to "your" in this paragraph. Soul and body take a vacation from the mind and rational judgment when Matej is around. But now another problem has arisen. Batuman has made a claim about Matej's charisma, but, simply by using words, *she cannot prove it.* The charisma experience is hers alone. All writing distances, filters, and mediates charisma so that it loses its initial force and becomes just another reaction between two people. One of those people cannot be the reader because all of us are positioned too far away from the charisma to feel its voltage. We can only note its presence in the text and its effect on others. Batuman may think that Matej's charisma is like weather or electricity, but we, her readers, register her reactions and not the electricity. Words are there instead, and mere words can't reproduce what someone's physical presence can do to you. Something about writing adds distance and dimension to physical life and experience, making it referential. In fiction, a beautiful or charismatic character has to be beautiful or ugly *to someone in the story* if it is to have any dramatic force.

Therefore: charisma in writing can only be asserted, even in romance writing and pornography, and its effects can only be shown through the behavior of those who are clustered around the charismatic figure. It's the same with beauty. You can say a character is beautiful by writing about that person, but you can't substantiate that beauty—*eye of the beholder*, and all that.

Movies are opposed to written fiction in this respect. The eye of the beholder is fixed on the screen, and suddenly a big star, let's say, shows up. The big star's appearance is proof or disproof about claims that may have been made about her/him/them. The viewer is free to decide if the actor on screen is beautiful and whether it matters. The star's appearance is more than an assertion of a claim; it is the evidence of the claim. An actor's appearance in a film may even convey the force of charisma to the viewer. I don't happen to find movie actors charismatic, but many people do—and they may feel similarly about some rock stars, politicians, and religious leaders. The word we have for this awed fascination is *starstruck*. But it's complicated: years ago, when I was in my thirties, I met an unfamous writer whose work I admired, and I was so starstruck that I could hardly speak. Years later, I met Morgan Freeman and thought he was a polite, courtly old gentleman from the South who had been in pictures. There he was—no charisma. The unfamous writer had once met Elvis Presley on a movie set. The movie was based on the unfamous writer's first novel. What was the writer's reaction? "Elvis? Oh, well. He was a polite young man with very good manners." To the unfamous writer, Elvis was just another guy. This, I think, is one definition of sanity—the ability to keep things in perspective.

When charisma fades, you are disenchanted and are living in the dreaded realm of sobriety. It may feel like a hangover, but that disenchantment is a very important spiritual and psychological condition, a cold-hillside sanity realm whose great poets are Keats and Coleridge. The secret word of admission to this realm is *forlorn*. Coleridge names the lime-tree bower as his prison, a place of terrible gravity. Keats' knight at arms wakes up on a cold hillside after his encounter with *la belle dame sans merci*. In the nightingale ode, the last stanza begins with a bell ringing out the word *forlorn*.

3.

In the only undergraduate creative writing class I ever took, the instructor was at pains to encourage us to make our characters "lively" and "colorful." The idea was that colorful characters were good for the story and helped to make it memorable. He also said that we should write our characters so that they became "real *characters*," by which he meant standout weirdos. The example he used was that of a small-town crackpot. The result of his advice and suggestions was disconcerting. For several weeks, most of us in the class turned in stories about an array of zany relatives and friends: Old Uncle Torpash, who smoked tobaccy in his corncob pipe while taking a bath; Little Aunt Mildred, who went deaf when the whole town started talking about the affair she'd had with the mayor; Cousin Ralphie, who worked on his souped-up Chevrolet when not putting in paid hours at the garage, and who was, by the way, secretly gay; and a character named Borden Cow (I still remember that name), who was rewriting the Bible in his spare time, in hopes of making it more forgiving to sinners like him.

The stories were tedious and rarely went anywhere. You were supposed to be amused or appalled by the characters, and once the character had performed the signature actions the author had prepared, the story was over. Colorful characters are not charismatic, and their actions are usually inconsequential. What's interesting is to make them a part of a community, as David Rhodes does in his novel *Driftless* (2009). Once you give a colorful character a hazardous dramatic situation and a goal, you can ramp up a plot. Colorful characters freed of plot stop being entertaining rather quickly and sometimes seem to have walked out of the pages of the *Reader's Digest*, from their regular series My Most Unforgettable Character.

Charismatic characters are not merely colorful but have to be dynamic and transformative, and they appeal to people who want to be healed and who are hungry for meaning. According to Girard, such characters also seem to be autonomous in some way. They do not love anybody and have no friends but wallow in the love that others send in their direction.

4.

So how do we recognize a charismatic character in fiction (and maybe outside of it) even if we are not directly electrified by that person's force field? Here are eleven observations on the subject taken from my notebook from the election year 2020.

- *The charismatic character never tells the story.* Someone else has to tell it. Conan the Barbarian doesn't write his own history because he never feels the need to explain himself. There is no horse's mouth with charisma, only relatives and friends and witnesses who will testify about what the horse said and did. Often when the charismatic figure speaks, nonsensical blather comes out; you have to have been there. This is a problem for storytellers. Only Ishmael can tell us about Ahab and the whale; you need some distance and perspective to get the story down on paper.

- *In stories, the person afflicted with viewing or experiencing the charisma is at least as important as the charismatic figure.* In reading about the NXIVM cult or watching the HBO documentary about it, *The Vow*, you notice that the leader, Keith Raniere, is much less interesting than the people who have fallen under his spell. Raniere himself is a semihandsome con artist who utters nonstop platitudes from the literature of self-help and self-actualization, with heavily diluted wisdom sprinkles from the writings of Ralph Waldo Emerson and Werner Erhard. He can be boring, but his enthralled followers never are. Their need for him powers the narrative. When you watch them, you watch glamorous people being hypnotized, falling under a spell, and then waking up on the cold hillside as Raniere is sentenced and is led away to prison in handcuffs.

- *Charismatic figures are actors and performers.* They are always performing in the theater of themselves. They are most at home on a stage, even when you can't see the stage. The charismatic figure typically likes stages and will try to find a stage anywhere to stand on and cannot function very well without an audience.

- *Given their usual narcissism, charismatic figures love no one in particular. Instead of love, they have obsessions.* Most of them do not have friends, either. Their grandiosity precludes friendship.

- *Charismatic figures often stage-manage their first appearance from above:* Hitler, in Leni Riefenstahl's *Triumph of the Will*, descends from an airplane; Donald J. Trump comes down to us on an escalator. The deus ex machina effect is often engineered into the show right at the start.

- *For their followers, something about charismatic figures seems special, glittering, but only the circle of followers can feel that specialness.* For everyone else, the emperor is prancing around, naked.

- *When the charismatic figure is around, violence is in the air.* So are sudden healings and cures. Desperation and ecstasy are the bipolar moods in play. In this environment, sanity, balance, and cool judgment are discarded and often treated with contempt.

- *Although charismatic figures are sometimes capable of conversation, they prefer monologues, speeches, and arias.* Conversation breaks the single-minded spell they depend upon. This point is related to their taste for being onstage.

- *In some versions of this story, the charismatic figure may be obsessed by something to get, kill, or acquire: twenty Rolls-Royces (the Bhagwan Shree Rajneesh), the white whale (Ahab), an end to slavery (John Brown), a following (Jean Brodie), money and sex (Keith Raniere), fame and brand recognition (Trump) and, more distantly, enlightenment that will fill up the emptiness.*

- *Most of these characters are needy men impatient with ordinary life.* With such men, fascist thinking is not far off. But, given certain conditions, women can evoke it.

- *When the charismatic figure is a woman, as in* Nightwood *or* Anita Brookner's Look at Me *or* Toni Morrison's Sula, *and* Claire Messud's The Woman Upstairs, *or* Henry James' The Bostonians, *power arises from the force of indifference, which is established by the woman's lack of interest in or hostility to social norms and the usual social courtesies.* The assumption of transgressive authority leads to genuine authority.

5.

According to the novelist Stacey D'Erasmo, to whose ideas I am indebted in this section, narcissism has a tendency to split off into two forms, *light* and *dark*. Both forms, light narcissism and dark narcissism, depend on a division between *us* and *them*, the inner circle and the outer circle, but with light narcissism, everyone out there is invited in to the party—the more people, the better. The light narcissist is always telling jokes and throwing parties and having a good time, roping everyone within sight into the twenty-four-hour festivities. You may lose your job if you stay at the party, but the light narcissist doesn't care about your job or your social obligations or your fate. Falstaff and Gatsby and Dean Moriarty are light narcissists, and so, probably, is the god Dionysus; I will therefore use the masculine pronoun to describe them. Light narcissists give you laughing permission to ruin your life. They will laugh as you go down the drain. The light narcissist magnetizes followers by giving them permission not to go to work or into the army, and encourages them to stay out all day and all night smoking weed, drinking wine, taking off their clothes, having mindblowing sex, and applying hammer blows to the alarm clock. The light narcissist, charisma ablaze, torching the house of the self, can be seen at conventions surrounded by admirers at breakfast, as he tells jokes from his endless supply—for such a person, jokes and booze substitute for conversation. He is a lovable figure for many people, but the end point is drunkenness, madness, or frenzy—not his, but yours.

By contrast, the dark narcissist sits elsewhere, usually in the corner, eyes shifting around the room to see who's coming in through the door. This guy is not lovable. Dark suspicions are his passion. His opening line is, "You *do* realize what's going on, don't you? If not, I'll tell you." He holds on to dark, secret truths, but only the dark narcissist and his associates know what they are, although if you're lucky and are admitted into the inner sanctum, he'll share them with you and wise you up about who's in charge; what they're doing; who they claim to be; and the evil they're perpetrating. The dark narcissist leads his own conspiracy against other conspiracies, against *those people*. There are always *those people*, the enemy, and they are gaining ground, day by day, minute by minute, hatching their terrible plans. The dark narcissist is drunk not on wine, as the light narcissist is, but on conspiracies. You are privileged to be admitted into the dark narcissist's inner circle, but time is running out. Here, "Everything has meaning," to quote QAnon. What parties and jokes are to the light narcissist, crusades are to the dark narcissist, who has to lure you to follow him on his quest for the white whale or whatever the white whale happens to be this time. *We have to do something*, the dark narcissist says, or *evil will triumph*. The dark narcissist is obsessive and goal-oriented by nature and is close to being a flat character because of obsession's grip: he wants only one thing, which is typically unobtainable. Treated without respect, the dark narcissist, or the person in league with the dark narcissist, may become a semicomic character, heading for Washington, D.C.'s Comet Ping Pong pizzeria in search of a pedophile sex ring. The trouble is, he has a gun.

Funny story: the dark narcissist can be noble and heroic, given the right circumstances, when the darkness of his conspiracy theories matches the truth of the actual situation.

Both light and dark narcissists are larger than life when they're found in fiction; they are often rambling around in ego palaces of their own design. Orson Welles' films contain both dark and light narcissists: Charles Foster Kane starts as a light narcissist before turning into something else. Booth Tarkington's George Amberson Minafer is a dark narcissist who puts hobbles on his mother, and Falstaff is entirely a light one. Some of our greatest literary works contain both kinds of charisma, notably *Wuthering Heights* (Heathcliff) and *Jane Eyre* (Rochester). Count Dracula has gothic supercharisma, and he has an ever-enlarging retinue in thrall to him. But for writers, these sorts of characters are extremely dangerous to handle because the somewhat amorphous meanings they generate are larger than they are, and, having risen to a level high above everyone else, they have washed their hands of ordinary life and common sense and have therefore become, to a smaller or greater degree, monsters. You can't leave a monster alone; you either have to convert it or humble it or kill it. The monster, rather than the writer, directs the story.

As a consequence, both light and dark narcissists—bathed in the charisma granted to them by their observers—take up a great deal of space in everyone's consciousness. You are compelled to think about them—they are high-voltage soul magnets attracting the attention they seem to require. Those who surround them—the observers or fans or worshippers or followers—cannot stop discussing them, sometimes guiltily, as if there were some X factor in their makeup, a quality or substance that no one else has access to, and that makes them endlessly fascinating and disturbing, human mysteries that need to be solved.

The four years of the Trump presidency were notable not for discussion of policy but for endless discussions of Trump himself. Trump was a highly charged combination of light and dark narcissism, and as a permission giver, he was capable of producing a violent frenzy in his followers.

6.

At this late point in literary history, it is hard to say anything about Captain Ahab and *Moby-Dick* (1851) that hasn't been said several times already, but in thinking about charisma in a literary and an American context, I want to draw attention to a few small and (for me) telling details in Melville's novel, particularly Ahab's habit of referring to himself in the third person as the novel reaches its conclusion. This tendency of his becomes more pronounced as the whale approaches and becomes visible, and it follows the much-delayed introduction of Ahab himself, who stays belowdecks until his first appearance in chapter twenty-eight. Given his initial invisibility, the crew members are forced to speculate about him. Charisma undiscussed is like an unlit match. As I've noted before, charismatic figures are rarely on time: they often make you wait for them before they appear, the teasing, withholding strategy of rock-star gods, who can be as late as they want to be to demonstrate their power over you.

Ahab is talked about even before Ishmael and Queequeg have boarded the *Pequod*. In chapter nineteen, the dockside prophet Elijah shows up and begins to jabber about Ahab as if he's the only worthy subject of conversation, the source of all future significance on the voyage. Ahab's semisupernatural status is signaled by the biblical haze surrounding Elijah and by the warning Elijah gives Ishmael and Queequeg that their souls are in danger if they go on board under Ahab's command. Souls? "Oh, perhaps you hav'n't got any," Elijah says, quickly adding that Ahab has enough soul to take up the slack in the souls of his followers, "to make up for all deficiencies of that sort in other chaps."

At this point, before the ship has even left the harbor, the gods up there and the souls down here have been implicated in Ahab's behavior. This is not, to put the matter in the simplest possible terms, an ordinary voyage with plain old commonsensical meanings; the voyage has turned cosmic and supernatural before it's even started. The problem of bloated meaning in *Moby-Dick* has enlarged to such an extent that human beings seem inadequate to the task of handling or interpreting it—we are in a world governed not by humans but by forces said to be invisible to them. Nature itself is on trial for criminal behavior, and the problem of meaning in *Moby-Dick* is as outsized as the white whale himself, which is Exhibit A for nature's horror show. It's as if the novel is engaged in a life-or-death battle with the problem of what matters, and the holders of common sense—the *Pequod*'s crew, particularly Starbuck—have to be converted by Ahab to the fanatic cause of the pursuit of the white whale. It is not a reasonable quest, and Ahab is not a reasonable man, but a mesmerist.

The white whale is the MacGuffin in *Moby-Dick*—its blank, unreadable, perpetually mysterious unsignified signifier, and in order to enlist the crew into the cause of killing it, Ahab must become a charismatic performer: he must somehow convince his crew members that his personal injury, the loss of his leg, is also *their* injury. He does so through ritualistic initiation rites, including call-and-response in chapter thirty-six, "The Quarter-Deck." Ahab's wound enlarges to absorb everything surrounding it—the whole world and the totality of one's experiences comprise the wound. What the novel *Moby-Dick* teaches us is that in great literature, a personal injury, a grievance, can be converted into a communal grievance if the charismatic figure can universalize the source of his private pain and turn its perpetrator into an entity that menaces everybody. Communal grievances typically take on overt form in warfare, concluding with massive casualties that provide the narrative's climactic moments. Welcome to a collective death wish: "so Ahab's purpose now fixedly gleamed down upon the constant midnight of the gloomy crew" (chapter 130).

Moby-Dick as a novel, as several commentators have noted, comes close at times to comedy, some of it deliberate, and Ahab himself would be an almost comic figure if he didn't take the whole crew (except for Ishmael) down with him. The crazy theories of the mass murderer are often funny until the shooting starts and the innocent bystanders drop to the ground or sink into the ocean. The fanaticism of Ahab and his inability to get a grip are made manifest in his way of referring to himself as if he were subdivided into crazed actor on one side and a transfixed audience member on the other, who observes the performance and comments on it. "Is Ahab, Ahab?" he asks in chapter 132. "Is it I, God, or who, that lifts this arm?" A few pages later, he is still speaking in the third person, isolated: "Ahab," he says, apparently in awe of himself, "stands alone among the millions of the peopled earth." In chapter 134, Ahab refers to himself in the third person no less than four times.

The doomed Pequod sinks like an object out of a bad dream, a "fading phantom," its "pagan harpooneers" still standing in their lookouts as it goes down, a flapping bird, a "living part of heaven," nailed to its mast, all the overdetermined ingredients of a nightmare that no psychology can adequately interpret. One critic, Robert M. Adams, in Nil, has called it a "clogged allegory." Another commentator, Andrew Delbanco, in Melville, His World and His Work makes a connection between charisma and fascism and destruction: "In Captain Ahab," he writes, "Melville had invented a suicidal charismatic who denounces as a blasphemer anyone who would deflect him from his purpose—an invention that shows no sign of becoming obsolete anytime soon."

7.

Muriel Spark's novel *The Prime of Miss Jean Brodie* (1961) is indeed a comedy of manners and attitudes, though it is rarely funny, and reading it is a bit like watching laboratory mice jumping around after being given periodic shocks. The novel's last shock—administered to the reader—is the observation by Sandy, one of Miss Jean Brodie's former pupils, that "she's a born Fascist, have you thought of that?" But how can Jean Brodie be a person of fascist consequence? She's only a charismatic schoolteacher in Scotland. What harm could she possibly do?

I want to pause here for a moment to ask what domestic fascism might look like, what might be called the *fascism of ordinary life* as pictured in fiction. Spark's Miss Jean Brodie is a female Ahab in a schoolroom where she is shorn of the metaphysical and spiritual hubbub of Ahab's mania but is still self-obsessed to a fault. Her retinue, "the Brodie set," is reminded at every possible moment that they are the chosen few, and their future is in Miss Brodie's hands. "Give me a girl at an impressionable age, and she is mine for life," Miss Brodie says, the startling claim of an enchanter who's pleased to use her "suicidal enchantments" on her willing victims. Instead of hunting a white whale, Jean Brodie has more modest aims: she's merely the charismatic teacher who wants to make you into one of her own and then to claim ownership over you. She earnestly wants you to be in her set, to be special, to be branded as *hers*. Like many teachers and lovers, she wants to assert certain proprietary rights over you and to be the person who issues permissions and prohibitions. In Spark's novel, such assertions are not sexual, exactly, but they feel erotic all the same and use some of the language of Eros. "'It is because you are mine,' said Miss Brodie. 'I mean of my stamp and cut, and I am in my prime.'"

The novel in which she appears is largely nonlinear, with the result that there is no white whale, or anything else out there, to hunt down. There is simply the collective falling under a spell inspired by Miss Jean Brodie. The plot, such as it is, deals with the resulting collective disillusions of the young women who had once idolized her because she made them feel elevated above the rest and who wake up, one by one, into their adulthoods, when they realize, first, that they are nothing special, and second, that they were tricked. At least one of her students takes orders as a cloistered nun and, when we last see her, is behind bars.

The girls speculate about Miss Brodie's love life at considerable length, and she is betrayed (her favorite word) by a girl with "piggy" eyes. The arc of the novel is largely formed when it becomes apparent that teenagers in the Brodie set are more susceptible to pedagogical charisma than adults are and will eventually grow out of it. Spells, and spellbinding, it turns out, usually expire with maturity and age, and when they do, *if* they do, the audience wakes up and grows angry at the magician. (Benito Mussolini, much admired by Miss Jean Brodie, was eventually hung upside down and stripped in the public square.) But before that, "they had to admit, at last, and without doubt, that she was really an exciting woman as a woman."

Muriel Spark is at some pains to make sure that the almost humdrum situation of a classroom teacher and her pupils serves as a miniature replica of charismatic performances going on beyond the walls of the Marcia Blaine School for Girls, a locale presented in a tone of "amused and mannered irony," as the critic Frank Kermode describes it in his introduction to the Everyman's Library edition. "*Brodie*," he says, "is charmingly and always relevantly funny." Of course no one wants to be a dullard, left out and clueless about a charming joke concerning fascism and fascist interactions between an authority and her subjects. A plainspoken American reader, immune to charm, may be excused for being dour and unamused when, at the end of World War II, Miss Brodie observes that "Hitler *was* rather naughty." The whole enterprise has gone a bit beyond dramatic irony prior to that anyway when Miss Brodie, in the mid-1930s, goes on summer vacation to Nazi Germany, where Hitler, she says, "was become [sic] Chancellor, a prophet-like figure like Thomas Carlyle, and more reliable than Mussolini." After all, the typical charismatic figure is untroubled by doubts: "she let everyone know she was in no doubt, that God was on her side whatever her course."

For the charismatic leader, God is either an ally or an implacable enemy, and the Bible is held up high in the air, as proof of either point.

Frank Kermode's claim that this novel is charmingly and always relevantly funny probably holds true if a reader doesn't mind it when a person of authority takes malevolent and manipulative control over another human being. You're supposed to see the joke in that, the comic premise, the lighthearted entrapment. The literature of love stories, after all, is a collection of tales about one person, or many people, who fall under the spell of another. That's not about fascism, that particular story. It only becomes a story on that subject when the powerful and charismatic one in control, seeking an advantage, commands the spellbound lover to do his or her bidding and then, slowly but surely, reduces that person's liberty and increases the surveillance until the hapless victim is enclosed in a house or apartment and feels like a political prisoner in a police state. The request moment returns in such situations as a command moment, and woe to the person who does not, in this situation, follow the command of the leader. The primrose pathway trod by lovers in such stories leads by winding twists and turns to the place of confinement.

8.

At the risk of undermining my entire argument, I want to introduce as my final example of charismatic leadership the figure of John Brown in James McBride's 2013 novel, *The Good Lord Bird*, the National Book Award winner in fiction that year. Like other novels of its type, it is narrated by an observer-bystander, in this case the young Henry Shackleford, a slave in the Kansas Territory in 1856, who, disguised as a girl and named Little Onion, becomes John Brown's sidekick and good-luck charm.

McBride's novel does the seemingly impossible: its central character, John Brown, is righteous, fanatical, charismatic, noble, *and* weirdly comic. To have a protagonist who is both noble and comic, correct *and* maniacal, constitutes a balancing act that almost never succeeds in the literature of charisma, partly because a charismatic campaign typically ascribes meaning to objects that refuse it, such as the white whale, or to events that are empty of commonsense significance and become inflated with conspiratorial meanings. One theory of comedy asserts that the comic figure is mechanical, repetitive, and predictable—in a word, obsessive. Comic characters do the same thing every time, at any opportunity, and at length. *The Good Lord Bird*'s way of exploiting these patterns is to provide us with an antagonist—slavery itself—whose evil is as large and as significant as John Brown says it is. His fanaticism is entirely appropriate to the size and malignity of his opposition, and if he believes that God is on his side, and prays at predictable, tiresome length, who could possibly oppose him, and on what grounds?

In the struggle in which John Brown is engaged, reasonability and perspective and good liberal values are beside the point. With slavery, no middle ground exists where compromise would be the sensible alternative upon which all right-thinking people would agree. If there were any such ground, the Missouri Compromise would be noted in our nation's history as a triumphant act of diplomacy. In McBride's novel, it is as if mania and single-mindedness have finally met their heroic protagonist and their proper opponent, and charisma has finally been conferred on someone in whom the divine forces have installed an unshakable conviction in a just cause. He is a fanatic, a comic figure, and a holy man.

Above all, in McBride's portrait of him, John Brown is a scary guy whose fanaticism cannot be separated from his religious faith. In the Pottawatomie Massacre in Kansas, the five people killed were all slavery advocates who refused to renounce it. There are no mass murders involving slavery that need to be explained away, according to the novel. Still, there's no question that John Brown was a religious fanatic and is portrayed as one. "He got downright holy when it was killing time."

Henry Shackleford's perspective on John Brown's campaign has the down-to-earth sanity of a Sancho Panza who notices Don Quixote's mania but loves it and serves it anyway. Most of John Brown's followers, however, resemble sheep:

> They followed him like sheep, though. Smart as they was, nary a one of 'em challenged him on his orders or even knowed where we was going from day to day. The Old Man was stone-cold silent on his plans, and they trusted his word. Only thing he allowed was, "We going east, men. We are going east to fight the war against slavery."
>
> Well, there is a lot of east. And there is a lot of slavery. And it is one thing to say you is gonna fight slavery and ride east to do it and take the war all the way to Africa and so forth. It is another to keep riding day after day in the cold to do it.

In this novel, John Brown's conviction that he is on a mission from God relieves him of earthly concerns. Early in the novel, when he is asked whether he is indeed John Brown, he replies, "I'm the child of my Maker." Questioned again, he replies, "I'm whoever the Lord wants me to be." Having shed the clothing, the appearance, and the mundane concerns of ordinary secular life, John Brown (often referred to as "the Old Man," as Ahab is, in *Moby-Dick*) doesn't bother with any of the usual pleasantries. Smiling, for example, is not in his range of skills; he has no aptitude for it, as Little Onion notes. "The Old Man stretched his lips in a crazy fashion. It weren't a real smile, but as close as he could come. Never saw him out and out smile up to that point. It didn't fit his face."

If we know a bit of our history, we know how this story will end, with the raid on Harpers Ferry in 1859, John Brown's arrest, and his execution by hanging—witnessed, we learn, by Robert E. Lee and Stonewall Jackson, among many others. But immediately before his execution, he shares a scene in his jail cell with Henry Shackleford, our narrator, and he smiles again, a different smile from the one several hundred pages earlier. This time, Shackleford says, "It was the first time I ever saw him smile free. A true smile. It was like looking at the face of God. And I knowed then, for the first time, that him being the person to lead the colored to freedom weren't no lunacy. It was something he knowed true inside him."

This scene, possibly the most important one in the book, flips the story's entire point and creates a thematic reversal: *this* soldier in the army for truth is not crazy at all. We may have thought so, but our perspective, sitting in our armchairs and reading the book at a safe distance, was mistaken. John Brown's mania is more noble, and saner, than our moderation.

9.

Many readers are so accustomed to mad, villainous, charismatic preachers in literature, like Preacher Harry Powell in Davis Grubb's

1953 novel, *The Night of the Hunter*, or plain, homespun hypocritical evangelists like Sinclair Lewis' Elmer Gantry, that finding a charismatic figure who is on the right side of justice and of God tests a person's twenty-first-century skepticism. Someone who gives up common sense and leads a go-for-broke crusade has *got* to be wrong—this is the settled position of the ironist who sees through every blind faith. For such an ironist, however, there is no such thing as a hero, and no such thing as heroism. For the ironist, everybody sooner or later proves to be a hypocrite. Everyone traffics in fraud. *The Good Lord Bird* disproves this kind of thinking.

Philip Rieff's book *Charisma* (2007) denies that the charismatic divine power once bodied forth by Christ (in Rieff's formulation) is available to us in our present world. Most current examples, such as Susan Choi's sinister fictional character Mr. Kingsley, an acting teacher in the novel *Trust Exercise* (2019), can be seen as updated versions of Miss Jean Brodie, and would reinforce Rieff's theories on the subject. A more complicated example might be Jude, the wounded, charismatic center of Hanya Yanagihara's *A Little Life* (2015), a man whose brilliance and beauty cast a spell over those who surround him, a spell that, like a floodlight, shines out from his suffering, which the novel rather relentlessly and remorselessly contrives to intensify until it reaches its inevitable ghastly outcome.

I started this essay with a deep distrust of the dynamic power of charisma. When I see someone who wants me to dress up in a uniform for the next crusade, I quickly turn and head in the opposite direction—no Jerusalem for me; you can have your Jerusalem. In daily life I am more a skeptic than a believer. Confronted with believers and their charismatic leader, I usually think, "What's wrong with them? Look at how crazy they are! *Who* could believe that?"

My position, however, would make heroic action impossible in situations that require sacrifices for which people may have to give up their lives. When the innocent and downtrodden are being hurt, someone must try to rescue them. To watch and to do nothing is a failure of character. In our writing and our thinking, skepticism and irony are too easy, too close to philosophical and metaphysical clichés, unless they are well and truly absorbed. When we see a charismatic figure—and we have seen plenty of them—we often think, "It's a con job." In our literature, America is a breeding ground for confidence men. Everywhere you turn, a trickster is around the corner. But then someone like James McBride's character John Brown shows up, and suddenly it feels like cowardice not to take a stand. It seems small and mingy to deny the existence of heroic action and charisma that serve a good cause. To quote the title of the old Pete Seeger song, "Which side are you on?"

Wonderlands

For Sally Franson

1.

This is you.

Let's say that your life is in order, and your work is progressing. But because you are ambitious, or because you have fallen in love with somebody, or simply because you are bored or just happen to be in the wrong place at the wrong time, you cross a border that you may not have known was there. Once you have crossed that border, the world changes—not just the setting, but the world itself that includes you. In this world you have crossed into, the people, places, and things you encounter no longer have a temperature of 98.6 degrees Fahrenheit. They are all running a high fever, which is contagious and conducive to hallucinations.

On the other side in that strange territory, you may be in a city. In that city no one speaks your language, and the inhabitants look at you rudely. They stare at you *fixedly*, as if you were an interloper, or, worse, a criminal; maybe you have something they want. The city is filled with strange noises, which no one explains, and signs that cannot be decoded. It is as if everyone knows something important that they're not telling you. You go to a newspaper kiosk to buy today's paper, which you cannot read, and when you offer a coin to the vendor, who is wearing dark glasses, he laughs at you.

The strange place may be, however, a suburb inhabited by White people (if you are African American), or a small village in Vietnam (if you are in the American army), or Iraq, or Afghanistan.

Everywhere you go, you have a feeling of being unwelcome. *I don't belong here*, you think.

It gets worse. A few days into your visit, you see, or you *think* you see, a copy, a replica, a double, of yourself walking down the street toward you. Then you start to see doubles of yourself everywhere, walking around confidently, full of the purpose that you yourself lack. The local people continue to stare at you menacingly. Strange instructions written on dissolving paper are shoved under your hotel room door. You can't breathe. It occurs to you that everyone wants something from you, but they won't say what it is. There is no one to ask for help, and no one seems to be kind or thoughtful or to be in possession of common sense. Every building, every interior space, seems to be haunted by some cryptic intention. Things are out of proportion. Every location you enter is soaked in a particular kind of subjectivity. In the distance, barely visible, is some kind of violent horror in which you may be implicated. The logic of things here leads to menace falling out of the sky to tear you, or someone else, apart. Even children are not safe.

When you try to cross the border to get back to where you came from, you can't. The border has closed, and you can't get out. You can check in any time you want, but you can never leave unless you figure out how.

People here are under a spell. Soon you are spellbound, too.

Everything here seems to reflect back on you. Nothing about it is, or can be, objective. A feeling, usually of dread, rules the day.

Somehow, subjectivity has become bloated and has seeped into the environment. The day is bright but no sun shines in the sky.

Welcome to Wonderland, a small but important subcontinent of Literature.

2.

In 2011, all of us in my graduate seminar at the University of Minnesota were reading a series of seemingly haunted narratives, and we noticed something about these texts that we all tried to describe and to pinpoint. What we noticed—a psychological atmosphere mirrored in the settings—was complicated and multifarious, but gradually we started to call this phenomenon Wonderland, maybe in honor of *Alice in Wonderland.* Haruki Murakami's novel *1Q84* (2011) compelled considerable readerly attention that year; Murakami's narrator indeed calls his setting, a kind of alternative reality, a Wonderland, at least in the English translation from the Japanese. The name stuck.

One of the students in our class, Sally Franson, whose novel, *A Lady's Guide to Selling Out* (2018), was published by the Dial Press (and which is that rare thing, a seriocomic Wonderland), wrote to me two years later about what we were discussing:

> My overall memory is that an x factor needs to happen so that a metaphorical (or literal) door closes, whether in the mind or in the physical universe, and subsequently reality becomes destabilized. Both reader and character have trouble distinguishing what is "real" from what mysterious x factor is disrupting the mental or physical landscape. Obviously in *Macbeth*, I think, the witches play a key role in this, by encouraging Macbeth to enter a mythic plane where all is absolved for the sake of kingship.

Wonderlands, the way I see it, are extremely isolating by definition. Character or characters enter an unspoken agreement to indulge in their greatest fantasies, horrors, ambitions, and fears.

Another one of the students in our class observed that Wonderlands
contain extreme characters in extreme settings. Everything surrounding the characters is watching them, and breathing, and thinking.
The setting carries the burden of subjectivity, of interiority, and the
setting often feels irrational. The inside *becomes* the outside, given
the presence of fugitive subjectivity. In this way, the writer avoids
the dreaded verbs of consciousness—"she felt," "he thought," "she believed," "he perceived"—and you write, instead, "Clouds in the staring sky transmit to one another, by means of slow signs, incredibly
detailed information regarding him. His inmost thoughts are discussed at nightfall, in manual alphabet, by darkly gesticulating trees"
(Nabokov, "Signs and Symbols").

What dawned on us, collectively, was that the deployment of
Wonderlands was invaluable to all writers who are delving into psychological and psychic trouble, especially writers who wish to signal
an estrangement from a given reality, to express a feeling of not belonging, and of menace. It was valuable to writers whose characters
are indulging their greatest "ambitions, horrors, and fears." I finally
felt that I had to write about Wonderlands after seeing Jordan Peele's
movie *Get Out*, a perfect example of what all of us in that seminar
were trying to describe.

Wonderlands are caused by, or are expressive of, emotional instability, estrangement, fantasy, and solitude. Genuine love is the
antidote to any Wonderland. So is the feeling of belonging in a particular place. To repeat my previous point, the emotional instability
in a Wonderland story is both inside, in the mind, and outside, in the
setting. *There is no clear division between setting and consciousness.*
They bleed, if that's the verb, into each other. The estrangement one

feels in a Wonderland can occur, however, in ordinary life. We've all felt it.

My students and I even drew up an inventory:

- It's usually somewhat isolated or separated from mainstream life.
- People there are under a spell or are spellbound or somehow hypnotized.
- It's a closed system; the visitor doesn't know why anything happens in the way it does.
- The people in Wonderland look at you (or the protagonist) strangely, and often. They want you to "join" them somehow.
- Having gotten there, the visitor has trouble getting out (it's the "Hotel California" syndrome).
- A crime, or a set of crimes, underlies much of it.
- The interiors are haunted by something.
- There's an air of menace, danger, imminent violence.
- Subjectivity has leaked into virtually all the settings.
- It's impossible to get a sense of perspective there—no wise aunts or uncles ever show up to bring back common sense.
- Nature is out of kilter there.

3.

Wonderland may be entered by an innocent, or semi-innocent protagonist, such as Chris Washington, the Black photographer in the movie *Get Out* (2017), who has agreed to meet the family of his White girlfriend, Rose Armitage. The X factor here is a scheme of soul and mind theft by Rose's family and their circle of friends, aided by hypnosis, which gradually becomes apparent to the viewer and to Chris, who has felt, almost from the start, that something is wrong, and that he doesn't belong in this rich suburb with all these weird White people. In this movie, horror is the natural outcome; the horrible offspring, of racism. The only escape is through violence. I think that in this story Jordan Peele has found a metaphor for racism that actually expresses its horror. The horror isn't tacked on. The horror story that's being told is a perfectly adequate metaphor for its subject.

But the catalyst, the X factor, doesn't have to be racism. It can be anything.

To quote another creator of Wonderlands, William S. Burroughs, author of *Naked Lunch*: "A paranoid-schizophrenic is a guy who just found out what's going on."

4.

It is 1997, and we are in Berlin—my wife, my son, and I. None of us speaks adequate German. For some reason, we notice that people tend to stare at us, as Americans. At an intersection, midday in Berlin, the three of us cross against the traffic light, jaywalking like the good Americans we are, since there are no cars visible anywhere, and on the other side of the intersection a German man, a Berliner, watches us crossing against the light, and when we are almost at the other side, he sticks out his index finger and wags it back and forth at us.

As the day goes on I feel more and more oppressed over my inability to use my one strength, the one and only weapon that I possess to deal with the world: my English, my mother tongue, my home, my eloquence, my articulation. In Germany I don't have it. I don't belong here.

That night, in our hotel room, after my wife and son are asleep, I have the overpowering feeling that something awful is in the room. This something is malevolent. I don't know what it is, but I feel its presence. For much of the night, I stay awake, thinking that I must protect my wife and son from whatever is in the room. I am so sure that it's there that, in the morning, I ask my wife if she felt it. She doesn't know what I'm talking about. Nevertheless, I don't back down. Whatever it was, it was there. I felt it.

5.

In real life, we usually feel that our thoughts and feelings are in *here*, in our heads and our hearts, and our environment is out *there*, separated from us: the buildings and trees and grass and the sky and the clouds, the whole external world where we can take a walk. We are in concert with our environment.

But in the literature of fantasy and estrangement, no such separation is possible. The inner life and the outer world are conflated in stories and poems. They are all one thing, inseparable. The spiritual contents of a person's thoughts and feelings are typically smeared and extrapolated onto the fictional and poetic landscape, or the reverse: what the setting is feeling—its intentions—becomes the character's emotional life. Every setting becomes expressive of something. Wonderlands, as I'm defining them, tend to provoke violence, or are provoked by violence. Wonderlands are, by nature, violent. The cloudless and sunless bright day in Flannery O'Connor's "A Good Man Is Hard to Find" reflects the characters' knowledge that they have crossed a border into Hell, presided over by the Misfit, whose gang shoots everybody one by one. With each death, the forest in the background gives off "a satisfied insuck of breath." When a landscape becomes sentient, there is nowhere to hide. These are horror stories, and here are a few lines from a horror poem, one of the greatest in English— "The Rime of the Ancient Mariner," by Samuel Taylor Coleridge—in which a sailing ship is becalmed:

> Day after day, day after day,
> We stuck, nor breath nor motion;

> As idle as a painted ship
> Upon a painted ocean.

And later:

> I looked upon the rotting sea,
> And drew my eyes away;
> I looked upon the rotting deck,
> And there the dead men lay.

—

> An orphan's curse would drag to hell
> A spirit from on high;
> But oh! more horrible than that
> Is the curse in a dead man's eye!
> Seven days, seven nights, I saw that curse,
> And yet I could not die.

The ancient mariner has killed the albatross, and now the dead are looking at him on that "painted ocean." Is the mariner's thoughtless murder of the albatross the X factor that ushers him into this horror? Possibly. But it may have something to do with his professed inability to love, which may have preceded the killing; something has typically gone wrong with love in such stories, and the ancient mariner cannot get out of the prison of solitude he has created until he blesses the water snakes. The poet Frank Bidart once observed that the dead calm that the ancient mariner's ship falls into could be a representation of Coleridge's estrangement from his own desires brought on by his drug taking. When you don't know what you want, your ship is becalmed. No wind comes from anywhere.

Love may be the antidote to Wonderlands, just as lovelessness may be its starting point, but the thing about love is that it cannot be willed. It either flows naturally, or it has dried up, and there is a phrase in Coleridge's poem that points us to a condition that evokes a Wonderland: Life-in-Death. After all, there are times in our lives when many of us have felt a kind of ordinary, humdrum Life-in-Death. You drag yourself from one place to another; you can't remember what, or who, you ever loved; you can't get out of bed; the sun doesn't seem to be able to move in the sky; the nights bring no sleep; everybody else is calling the shots and you feel like an automaton; you are in a strange environment where no one cares about you or recognizes you or speaks to you and where the language is not your own; and nothing, absolutely nothing, seems like a blessing.

Welcome to Wonderland. How does anyone ever get out of here?

6.

Here is a brief inventory of Wonderlands in movies and books. Some of them are trashy and some are great art, and some are both trashy and great.

The last half of Toni Morrison's *Song of Solomon*. Jean Rhys' *Good Morning, Midnight*. Much of the fiction of Shirley Jackson. Most of Ralph Ellison's *Invisible Man*. James Hannaham's recent novel *Delicious Foods* (in which drugs speak and have a point of view). Jay McInerney's *Bright Lights, Big City*. Tim O'Brien's *In the Lake of the Woods*. Most of Murakami's fiction and much of Bolaño's. Flannery O'Connor's novel *The Violent Bear It Away*, which nobody ever reads because it's so twisted. Graham Greene's *The Third Man*. Nathanael West's *Miss Lonelyhearts* and *The Day of the Locust*. Daphne du Maurier's "The Birds" and "Don't Look Now." Lorrie Moore's story "Real Estate." Joyce Carol Oates' novel *Wonderland*, her story "How I Contemplated . . . ," and many of Joy Williams' short stories. Anita Brookner's *Look at Me*, and Jennifer Egan's novel of the same title.

Edward P. Jones' story "Young Lions" and a later story of his, "Root Worker." Nabokov's story "Signs and Symbols" and his novel *Bend Sinister*. Kafka's *The Trial*. Stanislaw Lem's *Solaris*. Stephen King's novel and Stanley Kubrick's movie of *The Shining*. Thomas Mann's *Doctor Faustus*. Lovecraft.

In movies, *Jacob's Ladder*, Hitchcock's *The Birds* (which is inferior to the Daphne du Maurier story it's based on), and Terrence Malick's *Days of Heaven*, the last third. Everything directed by David Lynch after *Blue Velvet*, notably *Twin Peaks*. A friend has suggested Donald Glover's FX series *Atlanta*, especially the second season. Several of Ingmar Bergman's films, including *The Hour of the Wolf*. Horror films generally. Sometimes a Wonderland is gendered: *Fight Club* creates a Wonderland for men; *Black Swan* creates one for women.

In poetry, Wonderlands are less common, because of the difficulty in constructing a Wonderland landscape in lyric form, but we can still find them here and there. They're there in Coleridge's "Christabel" and the "Ancient Mariner," in Ellen Bryant Voigt's *Kyrie*, Robert Frost's "The Witch of Coos," Frank Bidart's "Golden State," and quite explicitly in many of the wonderful poems of that shamefully almost forgotten American poet Vern Rutsala.

You know you've entered a Wonderland when someone says, "There's something bad and weird in the air," and when the landscape has more character than the characters who inhabit it.

7.

One of the features of the kind of fiction and poetry I'm describing is that the setting is as alive as the characters are, if not more so, and has as much presence as they do, or more. The House of Usher looks out at you as you approach it. When you think of Stephen King's or Stanley Kubrick's *The Shining*, you think of the Overlook Hotel, which has a mind of its own, as does Poe's House of Usher. When you read Graham Greene's *The Third Man* or see the movie, you think of post–World War II Vienna, both alive and dead. Louise Erdrich's fiction cannot be separated from the haunted tribal lands in which it occurs. Is Gabriel García Márquez's *One Hundred Years of Solitude* about the Buendía family or about the town of Macondo? It's a meaningless question. The two cannot be separated.

In psychically and psychologically supercharged narratives there is no sense of proper proportion and almost no one who has common sense. Everyone is in the grip of some mania. Alice eats a cake and becomes huge; then she drinks a potion and becomes small. In Wonderland, no one is ever the right size.

8.

In Wonderlands, a correspondence exists between mood and place, and the energy goes in both directions: a character's mood or condition may generate a setting; or the setting may generate an inescapable mood or emotion thanks to the X factor. Why, then, are pleasant or neutral settings, which reflect or produce a character's cheerfulness, not also Wonderlands? After all, most fiction and most poems have neutral settings.

I don't know the answer to this question, except to say that stories are not typically about happy people, and fiction is not about happiness. It is about trouble, and the trouble that characters get themselves into. High or extreme drama calls forth eccentric spaces full of a terrible, cryptic menace. Neutral settings do not affect the characters, and therefore they cannot affect the reader. A beautiful place is perfectly nice in life and in literature, but few remember it later. A neutral locale slips from the memory, whereas Wonderlands are like an indelible stain on the memory that spreads slowly outward. Here is the Bates Motel. Twelve cabins, twelve vacancies. Hitchcock's instructions to his set decorator: "Let's have lots of mirrors."

9.

In Daphne du Maurier's story "Don't Look Now," a bereaved couple, John and Laura, are on vacation in Venice, doing their best to recover from the death of their daughter from meningitis. At the beginning of the story, a blind woman, one of twin sisters, tells Laura that she has seen the ghost of their dead daughter sitting and smiling between John and Laura in a restaurant. The story itself begins with the two old sisters in the restaurant staring fixedly at John and Laura. "'Don't look now,' John said to his wife, 'but there are a couple of old girls two tables away who are trying to hypnotize me.'"

Not long after this scene, John and Laura go walking in Venice. It is twilight. Soon they are lost, and the city takes on the characteristic geometry of most Wonderland cities, that of a labyrinth:

> The canal was narrow, the houses on either side seemed to close in upon it, and in the daytime, with the sun's reflection on the water and the windows of the houses open, bedding upon the bal-conies, a canary singing in a cage, there had been an impression of warmth, of secluded shelter. Now, ill-lit, almost in darkness, the windows of the houses shuttered, the water dank, the scene appeared altogether different, neglected, poor, and the long nar-row boats moored to the slippery steps of cellar entrances looked like coffins.

The setting becomes more labyrinthian, more confusing, and more haunted. They hear a cry of some sort coming from behind the shutters. "Less like a drunk than someone being strangled, and the choking cry suppressed as the grip held firm."

And then there are the birds, in Daphne du Maurier's story "The Birds," which has a moodiness and austerity about the environment that Hitchcock's film completely lacks. As Patrick McGrath points out in his introduction to the *New York Review of Books* edition of Daphne du Maurier's stories, "The Birds" was "to anticipate an imminent large-scale ecological catastrophe. It can be seen as a starting point in the popularization of an entire genre devoted to environmental-disaster narratives. It could not be more timely, yet it was written more than forty years ago."

"The Birds" is written in black-and-white prose, not Technicolor, to fit the setting, which is Cornwall, the south of England, close to the sea:

The sky was hard and leaden, and the brown hills that had gleamed in the sun the day before looked dark and bare. The east wind, like a razor, stripped the trees, and the leaves, crackling and dry, shivered and scattered with the wind's blast. Nat stubbed the earth with his boot. It was frozen hard. He had never known a change so swift and sudden. Black winter had descended in a single night. . . .

When he reached the beach below the headland he could scarcely stand, the force of the east wind was so strong. It hurt to draw breath, and his bare hands were blue. Never had he known such cold, not in all the bad winters he could remember. It was low tide. He crunched his way over the shingle to the softer sand and then, his back to the wind, ground a pit in the sand with his heel. . . . As he opened up the sack the force of the wind carried [the dead birds], lifted them, as though in flight again, and they were blown away from him along the beach, tossed like feathers, spread and scattered, the bodies of the fifty frozen birds. There was something ugly in the sight. He did not like it. The dead birds were swept away from him by the wind.

10.

Early in Haruki Murakami's *1Q84*, an editor at a Japanese publishing house begins to describe a novel manuscript that has come to his attention, and what he says sounds like a preview of the book we are about to read:

> "You could pick it apart completely if you wanted to. But the story itself has real power: it draws you in. The overall plot is a fantasy, but the descriptive detail is incredibly real. The balance between the two is excellent. I don't know if words like 'originality' or 'inevitability' fit here, and I suppose I might agree if someone insisted it's not at that level, but finally, after you work your way through the thing, with all its faults, it leaves a real impression—it *gets* to you in some strange, inexplicable way that may be a little disturbing."

After arriving at page 928 of *1Q84*, the reader is likely to see an analogue. In this book, Murakami, who is nothing if not ambitious, has created a kind of alternative world, a mirror of ours, reversed. Even the book's design emphasizes that mirroring: as you turn the pages, the page numbers climb or drop in succession along the margins, with the sequential numerals on one side in normal display type but mirror-reversed on the facing page. At one point in the novel, a character argues against the existence of a parallel world, but the two main characters in *1Q84* (Q = "a world that bears a question") are absolutely convinced that they live in a replica world, not a parallel one, where they do not want to be. The world we had is gone, and all we have now is a simulacrum, a fake, of the world we once had. "*At some point in time,*" a character muses, "*the world I knew either vanished or withdrew, and another world came to take its place.*" (The italics are in the original.) This idea, which used to be the province of science fiction and French critical theory, is now absolutely mainstream, and it has created a new mode of fiction—Jonathan Lethem's *Chronic City* is another recent example—that I would call unrealism. Unrealism, the home of Wonderlands, reflects an entire generation's conviction that the world they have inherited is a crummy second-rate duplicate.

The word *realism* is a key descriptive term that readers often apply to certain works of literature without any general agreement about what the word actually means. After all, if we cannot agree about what reality is, then why should we agree about what realism is, either? Much of the time, we can talk about fiction without having to take a stand about what is real and what isn't, although we do sometimes say that this or that event or character is "implausible" or "fantastical," thereby rescuing truth-value for the plausible and the everyday.

Murakami's novels, stories, and nonfiction refuse to make such distinctions, or, rather, they showcase the pull of the unreal and the fantastical on ordinary citizens who, unable to bear the world they have been given, desperately wish to go somewhere else. In unrealism, characters join cults. They believe in the apocalypse and Armageddon and conspiracies, or they go down various rabbit holes. They long for the end times. They reject science. Not everyone wants to be in such a dislocated locale, and the novels are often about heroic efforts to get *out* of Wonderland, but it is a primary destination site, like Las Vegas. As one character in *1Q84* says, "Everybody needs *some* kind of fantasy to go on living, don't you think?"

1Q84 is a massive narrative inquiry into the fantasies that bind its characters to this world and the ones that loosen them from it. At its center are two figures—a young man, Tengo, a would-be novelist who by day teaches mathematics at a Tokyo cram school; and a young woman, Aomame ("green peas" in Japanese), a physical trainer and specialist in deep-tissue massage who is also a part-time assassin. We learn that at the age of ten the two of them met in grade school and joined hands and fell in love, and though they were separated soon after, they have somehow managed to continue to love each other, at a distance and sight unseen, over the course of two decades. The novel tracks their gradual coming together through a maze of trials in which monsters and devils figure prominently. This romance constitutes the core of the novel, as if Murakami had somehow hybridized *The Magic Flute* and Bulgakov's *The Master and Margarita* with a touch of *Rosemary's Baby* thrown in for good measure.

The other really inescapable presence behind *1Q84* is George Orwell's dystopia. The novel's events occur in 1984, but instead of a Stalinist police state where the clocks strike thirteen, Murakami conjures up a cult, Sakigake (or "Forerunner"), with a charismatic leader, Tamotsu Fukada, along with a legion of mesmerized followers. Tengo and Aomame fall out of the ordinary world into a counterworld, 1Q84, shadowed everywhere by Sakigake and its goons. Although religious cultism has taken the place of political cultism, the effects here are remarkably similar and may remind the reader of recent American political history. Within the Sakigake organization are thuggish enforcers and various forms of thought control. As if that weren't enough, Sakigake has under its command uncanny dark powers that threaten the novel's heroes and keep them in hiding, allowing the author to deploy various elements of the demonic. Just when you thought demons had been banished from serious fiction, Murakami has figured out a way to get them back in again.

"Their world," one character notes, speaking of the Takashima Academy where the young Fukada, aka "Leader," went after having dropped out of a university, "is like the one that George Orwell depicted in his novel. I'm sure you realize that there are plenty of people who are looking for exactly that kind of brain death. It makes life a whole lot easier. You don't have to think about difficult things, just shut up and do what your superiors tell you to do."

What complicates *1Q84* are the details of the alternative reality into which its two main characters have stumbled, mostly by accident. In this particular Wonderland, as in Orwell's, surveillance is everywhere; the innocent must hide; torture goes on in secret places; thugs rule. Who is to say that this unrealism isn't true to life?

The geography of *1Q84*'s Wonderland comprises Tokyo and its outskirts, along with recognizable cultural artifacts from the present and the past. The two protagonists are ushered into it to the strains of Leoš Janáček's *Sinfonietta*. But the locale also includes two moons, miniature angels or demons (it is hard to tell which they are) referred to as "Little People," ghosts knocking on the door demanding payment, insemination by proxy, and air chrysalises: cocoons created by the Little People in which pod-like human replicas, referred to as "dohta," are hatched. *1Q84* is a marathon novel. (Murakami himself is a marathon runner and has said that "most of what I know about writing I've learned through running every day.") The experience of reading this book is anything but a long-distance trial, however. For most of its length, *1Q84* is a weirdly gripping page-turner, and its tonal register—as if serving as an antidote to the unsettling world it presents—is consistently warm-hearted, secretly romantic, and really quite genial.

In *1Q84* the point of view strategy alternates between Aomame and Tengo until a compellingly pathetic monster, Ushikawa, enters the book two-thirds of the way through and gets his own narrative. In the first chapter, on her way to an assassination, Aomame finds herself in a taxi trapped in a Tokyo traffic jam. Getting out of the cab, she walks over to a freeway turnout underneath an Esso gasoline billboard. Having been warned by the cab driver that "things are not what they seem," she takes an emergency stairway from the turnout downward to ground level where she slips through an opening in a fence. Any experienced reader of Murakami's novels knows that from here on out, she's in for it. Soon enough she recognizes that "the world itself has already changed into something else."

The men Aomame periodically assassinates with an ice pick are sadistically abusive, and we are to understand that in some sense she serves as an agent of divine justice. Sexual assaults recur throughout the novel, shadowing both the male and female characters; these assaults serve as the novel's baseline of depravity. Such depravity is countered by true love, which both Aomame and the novel believe in, or at least remember—in her case, with Tengo. By various twists and turns enabled by a patron usually referred to as "the dowager" and the dowager's murderous gay bodyguard—a very lively character, by the way—Aomame eventually gains entry to the Leader's presence, under the pretext of giving him a therapeutic session of stretching exercises to relax his musculature. The Leader, as Aomame has been informed, has been having intercourse with preadolescent girls and is therefore worthy of execution, and her actual mission is to kill him. Here at the dead center of his novel in a dialogue between Aomame and the Leader, Murakami gives us, for several chapters, a twenty-first-century updated version of the Grand Inquisitor—a debate, that is, on the nature of the sacred.

Meanwhile, the other hero of the novel, Tengo, has taken on the task of anonymously revising a novel, *Air Chrysalis*, dictated by a young woman, Eriko Fukada, called Fuka-Eri throughout. Her novel at first seems to be a farrago of Jungian archetypes and fairy tales, but once you get to the bottom of it, you find doubles, *mazas* and *dohtas* as they are called, "receivers" and "perceivers," in a veiled allegory of her upbringing. The novel becomes a huge best seller, and Tengo finds himself in trouble for having collaborated with Fuka-Eri in giving away the esoteric truths and holy mysteries of Sakigake that comprise the core of her tale. Fuka-Eri, it turns out, is the Leader's daughter, or the daughter's replicant, and as a replicant she has several zombie features, including affectlessness, the inability to use rising inflections for questions, and the capacity to quote long passages of literature (which she may not comprehend) from memory. She is sexually active although her periods haven't started, and she serves—in an impossible-to-summarize manner—as a sexual surrogate. So: at the same time that Aomame is putting herself into jeopardy with her mission to kill the Leader, Tengo is finding himself equally endangered, simply for having ghostwritten a book. They both go into hiding, at which point the hideously repulsive hired gumshoe, Ushikawa, who is working for Sakigake, begins to track them down.

If my summary seems to suggest that some elements in *1Q84* are trashy, so be it. Murakami is a great democrat when it comes to subject matter and plot development. Digressions on the *St. Matthew Passion*, *The Brothers Karamazov*, and Chekhov's book on Sakhalin vie for air time with observations on, and citations from, Sonny and Cher and Harold Arlen. Despite its various digressions, however, all roads in *1Q84* lead back to the Leader's cult. The cult serves as the source, the electrical generator, of Wonderland and its spectacles, and cultism has the book's imagination tightly in its grip. Sakigake in effect converts the world Tengo and Aomame live in from 1984 to 1Q84. Cultism *rules* this world. Only love can defeat it. In this sense the book's redemptive structure could not be more traditional.

What's fascinating about *1Q84* is the narration's ambivalence about "the logic of reality" and its wish to plunge the reader into the "far greater power" of unreality's unlogic, which has the advantage of revolutionary fervor and reformism. Unrealism rejects what we have, or what the newspapers say we have, as uncongenial and loathsome and unsustainable, and offers up its own alternative. Within the subcultures it creates, almost all questions are answered; fantasies are enacted. Beauty is reinstalled as a category. Everyday objects take on magical properties and serve as fetishes. Fiction, as Murakami knows perfectly well, can and does serve as a mirror world itself. It can both evoke unrealism and collaborate with it, or it may deny it entirely. Fiction, then, can serve as both the poison and its antidote, though it is not scrupulously clear in *1Q84* whether Fuka-Eri's novel *Air Chrysalis* has functioned as a cultural anti-toxin or a hallucinogenic. Are novels good or bad for us? Tengo himself is not sure. Perhaps it is the wrong question.

The rogue power of unrealism finds itself evoked in the chapters devoted to the dialogues between Aomame and the Leader, who sometimes sounds like Sarastro in *The Magic Flute*—a sorcerer who is suffering and wise and extremely dangerous. He can cause objects to levitate. He hears voices and transmits them to others. He is capable of causing paralysis in those close to him. He can read thoughts. He has read *The Brothers Karamazov* and *The Golden Bough* and can provide learned commentary on both. In short, he is not a monster; monsters work *for* him. As a figure of ambiguous purpose, he also promises Aomame that he will save Tengo's life if only she carries out her assigned task. The Leader says that he himself, the Leader, must be killed, as it is written. Speaking to his personal assassin in order to persuade her to do her job, the Leader launches into a lecture on anthropology out of Sir James Frazer:

> Now, why did the king have to be killed? It was because in those days the king was the *one who listened to the voices*, as the representative of the people. Such a person would take it upon himself to become the circuit connecting "us" with "them." And slaughtering the *one who listened to the voices* was the indispensible task of the community in order to maintain a balance between the minds of those who lived on the earth and the power manifested by the Little People.

The reader will note that the Leader's explanation lets himself off the hook ethically for who he is and what he does. He isn't quite responsible for his actions, nor are his followers. He is simply listening to the voices and passing on what the voices say to those who believe in him. He serves as a transmitting station of mythic patterns and extrasensory truth. If he dies, the "Little People would lose one who listens to their voices."

And who are the Little People? The Little People, it appears, are unsignified signifiers. Almost everything in *1Q84*, the book and the mirror world it creates, depends on their identity and their actions. If there is anything wrong with Murakami's novel, it has to do with these figures, on whom the meanings of the counterworld absolutely depend and who are absolutely mystifying. It is as if the Seven Dwarfs had gradually made their presence known and their powers understood in a novel by James T. Farrell. What are we to make of them? Or of the hybrid novel in which they appear? Such are the perplexities, pleasures, and revelations of unrealism. The author himself seems somewhat undecided about who these creatures are—that is, what his imagination has created. The creation of the mirror world is essentially the doing of the Little People, but the Little People are accountable to nobody, and no one knows who or what they are.

Here is Murakami in an interview: "The Little People came suddenly. I don't know who they are. I don't know what it means. I was a prisoner of the story. I had no choice. They came, and I described it. That is my work."

As if to compensate for the Little People's enigmatic existence and behavior, we are given in the last third of 1Q84 a recognizable monster, Ushikawa, a hideously ugly outcast who listens to the Sibelius Violin Concerto while soaking in the bathtub. People cringe at his approach. Even his children avoid him. An entertainingly satanic figure, he sees it all; nothing escapes him, especially his own repulsiveness. "He felt like a twisted, ugly person. *So what?* he thought. *I really am twisted and ugly.*" He serves as the novel's diabolical antagonist, the enemy of love between Tengo and Aomame, and he is quite wonderful to contemplate, up to and including the unforgettable scene in which he meets his nemesis, the dowager's murderous gay bodyguard.

The whole of 1Q84 is closer to comedy than to tragedy, but it is a deeply obsessive book, and one of its obsessions is *Macbeth* and the problem of undoings. After saying that Banquo is dead and cannot come out of his grave, Lady Macbeth in act five observes that "What's done cannot be undone." Then she leaves the stage for the last time.

What the two major characters in *1Q84* desire above all else is to undo Wonderland and to get out of it and back to each other, but "gears that have turned forward never turn back," a phrase that is repeated with variations three times in the novel, as if the problem of a snowball narrative had to do with how to melt the snowball and escape the glittering and thrilling world that unrealism has created. *1Q84* seems to be about the undoing of a curse, so that the characters who believe that "the original world no longer exists" can somehow get back to that original world they no longer believe in. In a somewhat startling form of humanism and faith, Tengo and Aomame come to believe that what has been done *can* be undone.

That they do so by means of loyalty, prayers, and love is the most touching element of this book, and for some readers it will be the most problematical. Aomame, the novel's assassin, repeats to herself a prayer that Murakami quotes several times. This prayer is the novel's purest article of faith:

> O Lord in Heaven, may thy name be praised in utmost purity for ever and ever, and may Thy kingdom come to us. Please forgive our many sins, and bestow Thy blessings upon our humble pathways. Amen.

In our own somewhat unreal times, younger readers would have no trouble at all believing in the existence of Little People and replicants. I did, but they probably won't. What they may have trouble with is the novel's absolute faith in the transformative power of love.

11.

Almost anyone might benefit from a construction of a Wonderland inside the work if the psychology and psychic and spiritual content call it forth. It seems to me that all of us have had an experience of a

Wonderland, particularly in the last few years, and straightforward realism with neutral settings may no longer be up to the task of evoking what it's like to live in these times.

Alice puts the book aside. She's drowsy. A rabbit with a pocket watch runs past and goes down a rabbit hole. She follows him. We follow her. You—this is you—are on a path, and up ahead is a strange place, though maybe no stranger than the world we live in. Up ahead, the lights blink on and off and even the blind stare at you. But we must enter.

Toxic Narratives, and the Bad Workshop

For Chris Bram

Reader, do you remember that time when you were in your teens, or maybe your early twenties, when you did that thing that you never told anybody about? Possibly you did it *with* somebody else, and *that* person never told anybody, either. Maybe you talked about it with that person, or . . . maybe you didn't. I'm not referring to that event that happened *to* you, that someone else did to you. Those are trauma narratives, and they're not my subject now. No, I'm talking about that thing that *you* did, mostly because you wanted to. You owned that desire. And you never told anybody. You couldn't, or . . . anyway, you didn't tell anyone.

Maybe you were drunk, or high, or, better yet, maybe you were stone-cold sober. And maybe what you did was: you lied about something, and that lie put you on the up escalator leading to more lies, or . . . maybe that was the time when you slept with the wrong person or . . . *multiple* persons. Maybe you stole something, or you engaged in petty criminality, or maybe the criminality wasn't so petty. I had friends who broke into draft boards in the early 1970s and poured pigs' blood all over the office files. I knew them personally,

181

and I never reported them. One time in 1968, the FBI came to my door, and I lied to the agent who was inquiring about a friend of mine who was in a different kind of trouble. In my own case, the thing that *I* did back then wasn't exactly criminal, but it was something I really wanted to do, and I did it, and I didn't tell anybody for a while, and then, when I finally did tell someone, I lived to regret it, though I didn't regret the action itself; I regretted *saying* anything, and I've never told anybody else since then about what I did, and that story will go with me to my grave.

Every serious fiction writer needs to think about secrecy, the narrative power of the unsaid, unnarratable, unsayable, and the initially unreportable action.

Secrecy is narration's anti-matter, its force field of opposition, and its inspiration. Some incidents just don't want to be told; these are the stories that people are incapable of telling. They contain massive negative energy. Secrets oppose the basic impulse to narrate, to explain, and thus to reveal. These suppressed untold stories, these secrets, properly treated, are among the more valuable narratives we have, and one mission of any fiction writer is to open up that particular black box and to do an inventory of what's inside.

Any story wants to reveal a secret when it finds one. Stories can rarely keep a secret; it's against the whole logic of narration to hold a secret indefinitely. If you want a story, find a secret, then bring it to the surface. Secrecy conceals and corrodes and leads to cruelty, while narrative reveals and heals. The negative energy of secrecy should always attract the positive energy of narration.

So if secrets resist the entire narrative enterprise, they also *defy* and therefore empower it. A conflict is created—very much in the logic of narrative.

When we operate in secret, we may be doing so because we hope to gain an advantage over others who don't know what we're up to. Their ignorance is our freedom. These days, secrets have gone to the forefront of public policy discussions, what with the NSA and Edward Snowden & co., and WikiLeaks, and the rest of them.

Secrets hide our intimate darkness, which is the shadow of our best selves. The covert public policy of recent history—the dissembling, hiding of information, and the resulting dysfunctional narratives that they created—set the USA into multiple foreign adventures. An interesting discussion of this problem can be found in Timothy Melley's critical book *The Covert Sphere: Secrecy, Fiction, and the National Security State* (2012). Melley's idea is that strategies of secrecy in the political sphere echo strategies of secrecy and disclosure in contemporary fiction. Can an entire culture or nation or subculture harbor a secret? It can when collective shame is involved, and especially when the subject is massacres and lynchings.

The theoretical loss of shame and secrecy in our current lives as they are lived on the internet is a subject that's too large for an essay or even a book. You could argue that our generations are, as a massive spiritual and psychic project, trying to give up shame and privacy, just as governments and tech giants are, through stealth, trying to learn everything about you.

Some forms of secrecy are relatively innocent. Your friend tells you that she's in love with this guy, and she wants you to keep this knowledge in confidence. "What I've told you is between us," your friend says over coffee at Starbucks. She's grinning. You could call this form of secrecy "the confidential disclosure agreement." Confidences like this arise from joy and excitement. Your friend wants to hide her good fortune—she wants to hoard it, like money. Fine, wonderful. Or: A friend tells me that she's going to elope with her boyfriend, Al, but she says I can't tell anybody. Because why? Just because. Okay, I won't tell. I happen to think that she *should* elope with Al, that Al is a great guy: generous, sweet, hardworking, and handsome. I also have to add that *as a writer* (though not as a human being) I am totally indifferent to this kind of sweet sugary secrecy.

The harmless, sweet secret is the equivalent of a little white lie, and it has little or no narrative value because it has virtually no dramatic consequences. If my friend tells me that Al experiences flatulence during breakfast, that he farts while eating Cheerios, I stifle a yawn, because Al's flatulence is inconsequential except as comedy. Such knowledge is not really going to change my opinion of Al.

No, the secrecy that I'm interested in comes from the dark side of our imaginations, and it's *consequential:* the personal and shameful narrative secret creates a snowball effect, because hiding a secret has consequences, and consequences, the circumstantial chains of cause and effect, constitute a plot, and that's where we find solid dramatic structures. Secrets, it turns out, are the friends of writers. A secret (number one), its consequences (number two), and its revelation (number three)—these three naturally fall into three-act structures. Just ask Gurov, in Chekhov's "The Lady with the Dog." He falls in love with a married woman; he has a secret; he can't tell anyone; and then he realizes that his life has changed forever.

Everyone knows Truman Capote's *In Cold Blood* (1966). The story in that book concerns the murder of the Clutter family in Holcomb, Kansas, by two men, Richard Hickock and Perry Smith. It is also the story of their apprehension, trial, and executions. This is its well-known narrative.

What has become the secondary narrative, and perhaps, by now, equally well known, is the part of the story that was so toxic that Truman Capote could not tell it. Here is the French writer Emmanuel Carrère's take on the toxic part of the events, from a fall 2013 interview in the *Paris Review*:

> The whole last part of the book is about the years the two criminals spent in prison, and during those years, the one main person in their lives was Capote. Nevertheless, he erased himself from the book. And he did so for a simple reason, which was that what he had to say was completely unsayable—he had developed a friendship with the two men. He spent his time telling them

that he was going to get them the best lawyers, that he was working to get them a stay of execution, when in fact he was lighting candles in the church in the hopes that they would be hanged because he knew that was the only satisfactory ending to his book. It's a level of moral discomfort almost without equal in literature, and I don't think it is too psychologically far-fetched to say that the reason he never really wrote much else is related to the monstrous and justified guilt that his masterpiece inspired in him.

What makes a narrative toxic? Here's a partial formulation. Something is kept secret, and becomes toxic, when what people have done is in conflict with who or what those people believe themselves to be. You have stolen money, *but you don't believe that you are a thief.* There's the money on the table in front of you, and you have stolen it, but you tell yourself that you aren't the sort of person who would do that. The devil made you do it. In denying who you are, you go to war with yourself, and you are split into two persons: the one who knows and the one who denies, the Good and the Bad. As David, the narrator of James Baldwin's *Giovanni's Room*, says, "Judas and the Savior had met in me."

Cognitive dissonance in this case has two ingredients, idealism and cold fact, and these two ingredients mixed together create a form of toxicity that no one can live with for long. Toxic narratives don't exist in isolation; they are always poisonous to particular persons and their idea of who they are. Toxicity is about the harm one has done to others, a harm whose origin cannot be acknowledged. A toxic narrative is therefore difficult to tell effectively in a first-person narrative; that person is saying something about themselves that may not square with their self-image, or it may incriminate someone else; the psyche is amping up all kinds of resistance, which results not in an unreliable narrator but in an evasive one. This is particularly true in cultures and subcultures given to righteousness and hypocrisy.

Obviously this problem is at the center, the core, of self-narratives about drinking, drug use, sexual violence, or addictions of any kind.

If the story is about something the first-person narrator has done, that narrator may be unable to tell it to anybody else except the reader. Telling certain stories may change your view of who you are, and it will probably change the way other people view you.

Two examples of such stories might include Andre Dubus' "A Father's Story" and Alice Munro's "Child's Play," a story that I discuss elsewhere in this book. Both stories have first-person narrators; and what these first-person narrators tell us is a story that they will tell no one else. Dubus's narrator, Luke Ripley, can tell his story to God, although, as a Catholic, he cannot do so even in confession, only in his prayers (he does not want his priest—his friend—to know what he's done); but Munro's narrator, Marlene, will not even tell God, in whom she does not believe. Only the reader will ever hear their stories.

A toxic narrative like Alice Munro's poisons her character's high-minded and righteous view of who she might have believed herself to be; as I'm arguing, such narratives create a conflict between reality (what the person actually did) and idealism (how she imagines herself). Carrying this cognitive dissonance around can make a person really sick, but such cognitive dissonance often makes for a strong story about the effort to cure that sickness by narrating it, or at least its consequences in stories within stories (Raymond Carver's "Where I'm Calling From," which has approximately six stories, all of them surrogate narratives, embedded inside it).

The toxicity level of a story can usually be measured by how difficult it is to tell it, by how much inertia and resistance it puts up to being told, and by how sick it has made the person or the group that is carrying it around.

The Catholic Church and Sigmund Freud did not agree about much, but both are and were in total agreement that toxic narratives have to have a private, safe location where they can be told, such as the confessional box or the therapist's office. In both cases, you are not necessarily looking into the face of the person to whom you are telling your story. You don't tell a toxic narrative in front of the TV cameras to Dr. Phil. It must not be a performance for an audience—that would be false consciousness. If it's performative, it's already false and clearly not toxic. But if the stories *aren't* told, if they don't find a form of release, the carrier becomes progressively sicker from its side effects.

To return to Macbeth, as I have done throughout this book: Macbeth has initially committed a murder, that of Duncan. He's done it out of ambition. Also, his wife encouraged him. But he can't quite believe that he's done it, and he can't admit it to anyone except Lady Macbeth. He doesn't think he's a murderer, but he is, and his inward conflict makes him and the entire kingdom ill (the horses start eating each other), and the conflict between Macbeth's bravery and his criminality makes Lady Macbeth crazy. The first murder leads to several others in a snowball effect. Also, ghosts show up. Secrets are the eggs out of which ghosts will hatch. The toxicity level in *Macbeth* is extremely high, perhaps higher than in any other Shakespeare play, one factor that may have led to the superstitions about the play that actors carry around—*you mustn't speak the play's title aloud, it brings on bad luck.*

On the subject of toxicity, think of *Crime and Punishment,* whose subject goes beyond the murders that Raskolnikov commits early in the novel to the spiritual problem of hiding the secret of those very murders, and what hiding a secret does to the person who hides it, and to the world he inhabits.

To choose another example, this time from popular culture: there is a very strange book out there called *If I Did It* (2007), and its author, sort of, is the former football star O. J. Simpson, and its subject, sort of, is the double murder of Ron Goldman and Nicole Brown Simpson that O. J. Simpson committed in Brentwood, California, in

1994. In the book, written in a bizarre and schizoid style that might have interested Dostoevsky, the murders are all cast in an account that the author claims is hypothetical, including the bloody details of what he calls "the night in question." The entire account is in the form of *as if*, that is, hypothetical because the author can't admit to the public, much less to himself, that he did what he did. An audience is required for shame; no audience is required for guilt. In the immortal words of the blues singer Etta James, "It Ain't Always What You Do (It's Who You Let See You Do It)." When O. J. Simpson actually gets to the murders, he blanks out in selective inattention, can't remember exactly what he's done, and can only remember seeing the blood that somehow got all over his clothes and is pooling in the driveway where the bodies are.

As the commentator Morgan Meis has written about this strange book:

> First, O. J. wants to make it clear that he is not a man given to physically abusing women. He is not a violent man. He didn't hate his ex-wife, he wasn't jealous and he did not want her back. Those are the central points in his version of the story. It doesn't really matter how true they are. What matters is that O. J. absolutely believes these things to be true. Proving these "facts" has become, in a sense, the primary mission of O. J.'s life since the murders. At the very least, the people who believe he murdered Nicole and Ron should find it shocking that a man like O. J. could have done such a thing. This is how O. J. feels about himself, in any case. He can't believe he was capable of murder. And he can't understand why anyone else would believe such a thing. . . .
>
> Confessing to the killings, once the accusations were out, would have amounted to admitting that he is not who he believes himself to be. *It would have amounted to obliterating his identity.*
> (my emphasis)

Any narrative that obliterates a person's identity—that fragile concoction, that soap bubble, that meringue—is likely to be toxic to that person, and it will remain a secret, or toxic, until the person, or the group he or she is part of, is forced to acknowledge it by narrating it in a story. The meringue collapses, and that person stands revealed as someone you didn't know at all.

In Katherine Anne Porter's story "Noon Wine," the protagonist, Mr. Thompson, doesn't believe that he has committed a murder, although he has. He therefore goes around to his neighbors denying that he's done what he's done. He also enlists his wife in this project, forcing her to lie about what's happened. The neighbors don't believe him, and they pity his wife. Mr. Thompson cannot bear what he has become and puts an end to himself.

The toxicity level of a secret is therefore in exact proportion to its power to obliterate or change a person's understanding of who they are and what other people think they are. The person's friends and loved ones discover that the person they thought they knew is not the actual person who stands before them. Anna Sergeyevna in "The Lady with the Dog" does not consider herself an adulterer, and yet she is sleeping with Gurov and is in love with him. How does she live with herself? It's the sort of question Chekhov is interested in.

The telling of such a story is a one-way gate: you can't get back to where you were after you've told the story. You can no longer pretend to be someone you're not. The actions in the story are also one-way gates. You can't get back to where you were before the events occurred.

There is one other feature to toxic narratives that I want to touch on. Suppose a person carries around a secret within herself of an action she has perpetrated or has some knowledge of. That person is haunted by the memory of this action, as Macbeth is, for example. In literature, the hauntedness a person experiences in his mind and memory has the capacity of moving out of that mind into the world and the settings, which then become haunted too. Hauntedness is a contagion and can be passed on like an airborne virus—as in, for example, the hallucinatory St. Petersburg through which the characters wander in Andrei Bely's *Petersburg* (1913) and that Raskolnikov inhabits in *Crime and Punishment*. Haunted houses, haunted landscapes, all seem to want to say something that they can't say. The settings take on the burden of feeling that the characters themselves cannot bear. These settings turn into Wonderlands that someone's secret has set into motion, and a Wonderland is always in motion. Everyone in a Wonderland is under a spell. Even the animals are spellbound. Inanimate things start to look back at you. Your double shows up. Ghosts start to appear. Ghosts almost always seem to want to *say* something, but they occupy a realm that is somehow beyond language, like the shameful secret itself. They are frightening to us because they want something from us that's post- or pre-linguistic, like an imagistic emanation from the unconscious.

What can't be expressed becomes a form of fugitive subjectivity, enraged by its singularity, its loneliness, its heartbroken longing, its sense of waste and unwelcomeness, its homelessness, and its guilt; and the haunted landscape opens itself up to a homeless subjectivity that floats free into the settings, to occupy them and in some sense to become them.

Fugitive subjectivity is a mood you have, unspeakable and unarticulated, that's so powerful that it escapes you in literature if not in life. It infects everything surrounding you. It takes over the entire house of your being.

The literature of the secret is so large that it encompasses many novels, epic poems, narrative poems, and short stories. Literature returns to secrets the way birds return to their nests. Most of Faulkner's great novels have something secret or shameful at their core, and their majestic lunacy—the grave lunatic eloquence of *Absalom, Absalom!* for example—has its source in a kind of massive cultural and personal dissonance whose origin is Thomas Sutpen's hypocrisy and violence

and willfulness and subterfuge. Almost none of Toni Morrison's characters are what they first appear to be, and almost all of them harbor
terrible secrets, as is often the case in the stories of Louise Erdrich.
Paula Fox's *The Widow's Children* depends on a secret. Philip Roth's
novels, especially *Sabbath's Theater*, locate shame and its overcoming as central to the protagonist's understanding of a life. Nathaniel
Hawthorne's greatest works dealt with shame and secrecy and adul-
tery, and Joseph Conrad's *Lord Jim* is one of the greatest novels about
shame in the English language. Some of the great novels are about
overcoming shame and guilt, though sometimes the victory is pyr-
rhic, as in Vladimir Nabokov's *Lolita*.

In an age of Twitter and texting and internet porn and the iPhone,
is there any such thing as privacy and secrecy anymore among
twenty- and thirtysomethings? The ubiquity of twelve-step programs
suggests that there is. For the purposes of this essay, however, I will
retrieve, from the past, two works by authors of the same generation almost seventy years ago: John Cheever's story "The Country
Husband" and James Baldwin's novel *Giovanni's Room* (1956). The
American 1950s seem to have been a time in which the entire culture was infected by the toxicity of suppressed, unsayable narratives,
and characters who went around with their lips sealed against what
they really wanted to say or do. Cheever's story was published first
in 1954. Hemingway admired it. Its tone attempts a sunny eloquence
totally at odds with the terrible events going on in it. The story's protagonist, Francis Weed, is carrying around narratives of extreme poi-
sonousness, made worse because they have no outlet. For the sake
of discussion, let us briefly diagram the events of the story, reducing
them to eleven numbered entries:

1. Francis Weed, a suburbanite, is in an airplane that encounters
   turbulence and crash-lands in a field. He survives. He makes his
   way back home by bus, taxi, and commuter train.

2. When he returns home, his children are quarreling noisily. Francis tells everyone that he's been in a plane crash, but *no one pays any attention to him.* No one cares about his story. This gap creates what I would call fugitive subjectivity, which arises when you have a story that you can't tell, or which, when you tell it, no one hears.

3. The next night, Francis and his wife go to a dinner party. Francis, who was a soldier in World War II, recognizes a serving maid at the party as a woman who was publicly chastised and stripped naked in France at the end of the war for collaborating with the Germans. Francis saw her stripped naked. But "[h]e could not tell anyone." His fugitive subjectivity grows more acute.

4. Because his memory has been "opened," he now sees his family's babysitter, Anne Murchison, in a new way, as when "music breaks glass."

5. Because he is in this condition, when he takes Anne Murchison home, "he seemed . . . to have come into the deepest part of some submerged memory."

6. Because "he had been bitten gravely," he now feels he is in "a relationship to the world that was mysterious and enthralling."

7. Because of this new condition, he is irritable with his fellow commuters and creates a scene for which his wife chastises him.

8. The babysitter, Anne Murchison, has a boyfriend: her fiancé, Clayton Thomas. Discovering this, Francis Weed goes into a rage and eventually strikes his wife in the face after she asks him how he'd like to be "a social leper" for having fallen in love with the babysitter.

9. Because of this violence, Julia, Francis's wife, decides to leave Francis; nevertheless, despite what she says she's going to do, she stays. Francis conspires to prevent Clayton Thomas from getting a job the young man urgently needs.

10. Because of his recognition of his own shameful treachery and that he is "in trouble," Francis eventually goes to a psychiatrist. He sits down and "[says] hoarsely, with tears in his eyes, 'I'm in love, Dr. Herzog.'" This is the story's climax.

11. In a brief coda, we see Francis Weed back at home doing woodwork, and his household restored to its previous (dis)orderliness.

A plot summary is never art, and I don't pretend that this one is. Nevertheless, I need to point out certain features of this story's construction that might be useful to writers of fiction.

First, note the number of "because" structures: six of them, at least. These mark the existence of a chain of cause and effect running through the story. That's the plot. Events build up based on prior events. Things get set into motion. We have a series of one-way gates, along with a snowball effect, and a ticking clock, which is Francis Weed's sense of his own mortality: time is running out on him. Francis Weed is therefore a Captain Happen figure.

Second, there is a generosity of incident in the story. Events keep occurring (a plane crash, a public shaming, a suburban insult, a moment of treachery), and there are no stalemate effects, no dull moments. The strength and quantity of the incidents are such that they can support the almost overpowering weight of Francis Weed's overwrought but often suppressed emotions. Without the dramatic events to carry them, the story would collapse under the weight of the sky-is-falling emotions within it. If you want a story to support the weight of the characters' feelings, it helps to keep things moving and to have a multiplicity of other characters. Stories cannot always support emotions without the force of lyric language, but the problem of too much lyric language in a narrative is that, without contrast, it clots the atmosphere. In a narrative, dramatic actions and the everyday objects in the setting will support and cause emotions. Let the objects and the actions carry the feeling. If you want to make a child's sorrow dramatic, don't spend time laboriously describing his feelings about his grandmother. Just have someone run over his bicycle.

Third in our outline of Cheever's story, we have a morally craven and unlikable protagonist who nevertheless qualifies as the story's Captain Happen figure. Cheever has laid down a bet that your interest in Francis Weed, a morally compromised figure, will trump your disapproval of him. He has also laid down a related bet that if events in the story have sufficient urgency and momentum, you'll keep reading. (If you stop reading fiction because you don't like to read about morally compromised figures, you will have no fiction to read.) Furthermore, we have to pay attention to the man's past: Francis Weed (note the name) is oppressed by his war experiences, by his domestic life (his children are constantly fighting), by a routine existence that's transformed by his sudden, almost inexplicable love for the babysitter. He may be despicable, but we have the means to understand him if we choose to. Our real task *as writers*, however, is *not* to approve or disapprove of him, which is what ordinary readers do, but to understand how the story in which he appears has been constructed.

Fourth, the story contains within it three forms of the unheard or the unsayable: Francis has no listeners when he tries to tell the story of how he survived a plane crash; he cannot tell anyone that he recognizes the woman who was publicly chastised; and of course he cannot tell anybody that he's fallen in love with Anne Murchison, a situation that is truly toxic and shameful. His situation is like that of Gurov in Chekhov's "The Lady with the Dog," about whom Chekhov writes, "He could not speak of his love at home, and outside his home who was there for him to confide in?" Francis Weed's disgraceful secret life festers and then blossoms, beautifully, into narrative, as secrets will. Anyone who reads Cheever's story with any care will notice the spritely, elegant, winsome tone of the story, as if the narrator is taking great delight in this particular chronicle of degradation and woe. The story's prose just sparkles with schadenfreude-ish glee.

Finally, there's a ghost in John Cheever's story, perhaps not a literal ghost, but a ghost all the same, if you define "ghost" as a spectral presence from the past who does not speak and who carries some significance around with her. I refer, of course, to the woman who is serving food at the Farquarsons' dinner party and whom Francis Weed recognizes from his time in the army as the woman who was chastised at a crossroads in Europe during the war. She's not labeled as a ghost. She's supposed to be a real person at a real dinner party. But it doesn't feel that way when you read that scene. It feels as if this woman has come out of the past and can't possibly be related to current events. She's an ambassador from Wonderland. As the narrator says, "The people in the Farquarsons' living room seemed united in their tacit claim that there had been no past—that there was no danger or trouble in the world." This variety of baseline hypocrisy provides liquid fuel for the ensuing story.

Cheever knows, and keeps insisting in his short stories and novels, that much of what passes for polite social life in Connecticut or anywhere else is total bullshit, but if you have the nerve to call bullshit by its true name in public, you will be scorned. Therefore, Francis Weed says nothing. A polite dinner guest keeps his mouth shut. The story, however, does *not* keep its mouth shut. Like all good art, the story gives away everything that the characters themselves cannot acknowledge.

But notice what is happening in this scene. Planted in the middle of this story is a coincidence, the odds for which are several million to one. A woman whom Francis Weed saw in Europe, stripped bare and punished at a crossroads, has shown up serving drinks at a dinner party in suburban Connecticut. It's an impossible coincidence, straight out of the life of dreams. But it's narrated with such conviction that the implausibility of the entire scene probably doesn't occur to the average reader. Notice that the spectral servant is not just *anybody* that Francis Weed saw in Europe, but a woman who had something extraordinarily humiliating done to her following a moral crime she committed, and who may be a stand-in for our protagonist, and who for that reason is dramatically interesting as her suburban, high-functioning double. Her dramatic interest trumps her implausibility. It never occurs to you to think that what Cheever is putting before you is a virtual impossibility. Instead, you think, "That's really interesting." What you are responding to is the courage and nerve of the narrative, its disregard for its own safety, and the plausibility of this particular dream world.

Imagine a Bad Workshop where everyone has an opinion and wants to enforce conventional thinking. In the Bad Workshop, Cheever's story does not get a free pass. In the Bad Workshop, the respondents in the seminar room complain to Mr. Cheever that his story shouldn't start with the melodramatic crash landing of a passenger plane. The Bad Workshop finds Francis Weed to be unsympathetic and unlikable. The Bad Workshop notes that the servant woman's appearance at a dinner party in Connecticut is kind of implausible. The Bad Workshop members irritably note instances of sentimentality in the writing, particularly its corny metaphors, as witness the story's final line: "Then it is dark; it is a night where kings in golden suits ride elephants over the mountains." The Bad Workshop doesn't like that line. Mr. Cheever should revise or delete it. The Bad Workshop feels that Mr. Cheever has too many minor characters in his story, and his milieu consists of White suburban middle-class people who are of no interest to anybody anymore. This is the same Bad Workshop that complained a few weeks ago to a chastened Franz Kafka that the chapter excerpt from his novel *The Castle* was really confusing and monotonous and morbid, almost as bad as his failed novel *The Trial*, and, two weeks before that, the Bad Workshop complained to the bearded and stoop-shouldered Herman Melville that his novel about whaling, *Moby-Dick*, had too many wordy digressions and too many out-there bizarre characters, and besides, diffuse allegories are passé. The Bad Workshop got really, really upset at Virginia Woolf's habit of telling, not showing, in *The Waves*, and it told James Joyce that *Ulysses* was awfully hard to follow and sort of show-offy. Compared to James Joyce's novel, in fact, the Bad Workshop thinks Mr. Cheever's story is almost okay. It shows promise and readability. If only it could be revised to make Francis Weed more likable and its plot simpler! The Bad Workshop told Gertrude Stein to leave immediately and never come back. The Bad Workshop did not like *The Making of Americans* and never got past the first chapter. It did not like James Baldwin's *Giovanni's Room* for its ambivalent, ambiguous, self-lacerating melodramatic plotting as a consequence of the narrator's hypocritical behavior. David, the narrator, should have been more *positive*, more *upbeat*, about his gayness. He shouldn't have been so misogynistic in the episode of his self-loathing and sickened love-making to Sue, a woman he picks up midway in the novel. David's fiancée should *certainly not* have been named Hella, an icky name that isn't very subtle or very nice—too point-making. The book should be revised so that it is more optimistic and not so *morbid*.

Next week: Jane Austen will show her fiction to the Bad Workshop.

At this point, I need to return to Baldwin's *Giovanni's Room* as something of a final test case concerning toxicity, earnestness, and something I have to call timeliness. The author's mixed loathing *and* sympathy for his own narrator is intermittently visible in the book's clotted, quietly raging, self-correcting, anguished prose. Our narrator, David, is hardly admirable: he's a kind of container into which has been loaded everything that the author himself may have despised: David is White, a smiling, professionless American ex-pat in Paris in the 1950s—an alcoholic, a sponge, a betrayer, and a closeted gay man who is trying to fool everybody, including his father, and Hella, his fiancée, about what and who he is. Baldwin has created a narrative whose central character is kidding himself for much of the time, and whose only joy arises from those moments in which he is in the arms of the man he truly loves, Giovanni, in Giovanni's room. He cannot acknowledge that joy to anyone; he can barely make it visible to the reader.

The novelist and critic Christopher Bram has summarized the novel, in *Eminent Outlaws*, this way:

> The narrator, David (we never learn his last name), spends a long night alone in a rented house in the south of France, getting drunk and remembering the past year. In Paris, while his girl-friend Hella toured Spain, David met and became involved with an Italian bartender named Giovanni. The two men lived to-gether in a small room for several months until Hella returned and David needed to choose between his loves. He chose Hella and handled it badly. Giovanni fell apart, giving himself first to a man he didn't love, then to a hated boss who humiliated him. Giovanni murdered the boss. He is sentenced to die on the morning after the night we spend with David.

This summary is true to the facts of the plot, but it does not—cannot—detail the fevered emotional temperature of the novel. The story begins with the narrator almost literally self-divided: in a brilliant feat of writerly staging, Baldwin places his narrator in front of a window at night. David cannot see out to the countryside but instead sees his own reflection looking back at himself. In our first image of him, he is not one person, but two people.

Even the wording is curious. "I watch my reflection in the darkening gleam of the window pane. My reflection is tall, perhaps rather like an arrow, my blond hair gleams." A slow, careful reader will note that the narrator is watching his reflection as if his reflection is not a reflection of himself. And then there is that strange repetition of that word, the rarely used *gleam*. How does the windowpane cause a "darkening gleam" unless the narrator himself is growing dark? And then in the next sentence there is his blond hair, which "gleams"—my dictionary says that the word's definition refers to a sparkle, or glitter, or something that sends forth light. One part of David is darkening, and the other, the blond part, gleams. David is in two parts, one light, one dark. And employing the same word, once as a noun and then as a verb, in two consecutive sentences is an obvious editorial mistake unless the author wants the reader to register that very repetition, which in this case takes us right back to the national anthem: "What so proudly we hailed / At the twilight's last gleaming." What was so proudly hailed? The stars and stripes of the American flag, which has been implicitly superimposed on David's reflection by means of the author's word choice. David, in all his beauty *and* his hypocrisy, is a true American.

In the morning, David's ex-lover, Giovanni, will be guillotined, having been convicted of a murder that followed David's abandonment of him and Giovanni's subsequent psychic disintegration.

In a toxic narrative the splitting-off of the central character into the part that appears in public (a false-self system, to use R. D. Laing's terminology) and the part that goes unacknowledged (the true, hidden self) can threaten the narrator's very sanity. Such first-person narratives are not "unreliable." Unreliable narrators, those steadfast features of workshop discussions, are not interesting. Who cares if a narrator is unreliable? *Every* narrator is unreliable to one degree or another. Baldwin's narrator in *Giovanni's Room* is as reliable as he can stand to be, given his background and his circumstances and his inability to acknowledge who he is. He isn't unreliable but self-divided, almost literally on the path to madness.

Others have told David what's obvious. It's not as if he hasn't told himself. In Giovanni's room, David has undergone what he himself calls "a sea change." Using another metaphor, David observes that Giovanni has awakened a "beast" in him. The most damning accusations made against David are made by the man who loves him, and who hates in particular David's smiling American self, associated everywhere in the novel with our national characteristic—this was the 1950s—of apparent affability:

> "You are evil, you know [Giovanni says to David], and sometimes when you smiled at me, I hated you. I wanted to strike you. I wanted to make you bleed. You smiled at me the way you smiled at everyone, you told me what you told everyone—and you tell nothing but lies. What are you always hiding? And do you think I did not know when you made love to me, you were making love to no one? *No one!*"

Later in this same scene, Giovanni returns to David's terrible smile (nowhere else in literature is a smile more damning than it is in this book): "I can see you . . . looking at me and looking at all of us and tasting our wine and shitting on us with those empty smiles Americans wear everywhere and which you wear all the time." To close the case, Giovanni reports back to David what their mutual friend Jacques thinks of David: "He thinks you are a monster."

A first-person narrator who is labeled a monster, who feels, when he tries to be straight and enters the body of his fiancée, whom he does not love, that "I began to feel that I would never get out alive"—such a monster-narrator, contemptible and pitiable all at once, uncharming, unlikable, hypocritical, and broken—such a narrator requires an author who has great reserves of nerve and bravery, who is going to tell a truth as he sees it, and James Baldwin was certainly one of the bravest writers of his generation. The situation is not hopeless: at the end of the novel, David is hoping to reintegrate himself: "I long to crack that mirror and be free." Good luck with that.

In a great novel, the narrator need not be likable, charming, affable, companionable, virtuous, or fun to be around. A first-person narrator can be a monster to the benefit of the novel that contains him, but only if his monstrosity is important and telling and has been suffered through and if it tells us something about the culture that contains him. By contrast, if the monster-narrator is entertaining, and entertains us with his monstrosity and his crimes, the game is lost; it has given itself over to evil.

A second point about toxic narratives has to do with shame. It could be argued that America in our time has been stripped, high and low, of shame. My introduction to this essay, confabulating some shame on the part of every reader, may be a touching relic in a time when no one feels shame for anything. Has shame become a museum feeling, visible only in the documents of the past? Probably not. In *Eminent Outlaws: The Gay Writers Who Changed America* (2012), Christopher Bram notes about *Giovanni's Room*, "The plot has not become dated, sad to say, which is why the novel is still powerful for readers fifty years later. . . . Our poisonous fear of what other people think of us remains strong."

So finally I return to secrets and toxic narratives, the ones that risk the reader's disapproval and dislike of the characters and their actions. Something is going on in our society right now having to do with privacy and secrecy and revelations. This "something" is absolutely central to our understanding of ourselves. There are some writers, such as Patricia Lockwood, who seem intent on abolishing the distinction between private and public, who believe that such a distinction is meaningless. We now have many examples of autofiction. Such works are indeed loaded down with shame, oddly enough, and they depend, dramatically, on request moments, very often requests that others cannot fulfill.

The idea that we do not have secrets anymore is a massive delusion fueled by pop psychology. If distraction is at an all-time high, so is loneliness. And loneliness breeds secrecy. If we're writers, we need to ask what secrets our characters share, if indeed they do. What is poisonous in *that* group's secret, *those* lovers' secret hearts, what causes them shame? What is the worst thing you can say about those characters? The worst thing that you can say about them is what makes them most human and most interesting to us, because it will start all the alarm bells ringing. Maybe you're writing about a personal disaster. In literature, there are worse things than disaster: lassitude and boredom and self-pity, for starters. Literature *thrives* on disaster.

On the Plausibility of Dreams

for Mary Cappello

Let's say that one morning you wake up from uneasy dreams. Let's say that in the first dream you misplaced your car somewhere in Buffalo, New York. On that day, you're supposed to play the lead in a drama that'll premiere that night. The trouble is that you don't know any of the lines—not *one* of them. You don't even know *where* it's to be performed or what the play *is*. On that same day, you are also scheduled to perform a piano concerto with the Minnesota Orchestra. You are the soloist. And there you are, wearing formal clothes, a tuxedo, for the occasion. You are standing in the wings of the stage, about to go on. The orchestra's conductor is standing next to you. But there is a small problem. You say to the conductor, "Uh, I can't go out there." He asks why. You say, "I can't play the piano." The conductor says, "Oh, Charlie, you're so modest," and you say, "No, no, really. You don't get it. I *can't* play the piano. I don't know how," and he looks at his watch and says, *Well, it's time to go on*, so both of you go onstage, and there's applause while you sit down on the piano bench, and the conductor gives the downbeat, and the orchestra begins with the opening chords. You want to do a good job, you don't want to disappoint anybody, even though disappointment is inevitable, so when it's time for the pianist to start in—the piece is by Sergei Rachmaninoff—you begin to pound on the keys, any keys, just noise, like a toddler banging the keyboard with a fist, whereupon the other musicians and the members of the audience stare at you with horror and shock and cruel mockery, and in a great rush of terrible shame, you awaken, if you're me.

When I had a dream like this one a few months ago, my first waking thought was *That's very odd: I believed that dream while I was having it.* No matter what the content of my dreams is, I never seem to disbelieve them while I'm having them. As long as I'm dreaming, the dream is plausible. But the real question is why. Why, while we're dreaming, do we believe the dream's content, and what implications does this have for the making and reading of fiction, and, in some cases, of poetry?

The problem of plausibility often comes up in workshop discussions of fiction and reviews of novels and almost never arises when people are talking about poetry. Why is *that?* Maybe reading itself, in certain cases, is a form of controlled reverie induced deliberately by sentences meant to get us out of the real world and into a replica world composed partially of dream content. I am going to call such sentences "transit sentences," though there probably is a better phrase. In some such stories, the characters may become aware that they're dreaming, but in most cases, they aren't. They can't be.

For the sake of argument, my claims here about the plausibility problem are applicable only to realist or semirealist fiction, on a spectrum leading to irrealism or unrealism. Not all transit sentences lead to Wonderlands, but *without* a small amount of dream content, fiction may go flat, like someone telling you a story not because it's interesting but simply because it happened to her, or to him. Fiction can be true to life and *still* lack a certain voltage; in that case, we may not get attached it. We forget it soon after we read it. Purely realist fiction full of factoid sentences might be capable of telling us what it was like at a certain time and place and thus can be a valuable and honorable record of life, but that may be all it can do. Just because it's true doesn't make it art. Just because it's true doesn't mean that the reader will care.

Dream fiction, however, tells us a great deal about our obsessions, our fears and longings, and it does more than just tell us: it transports the reader into another, metaphorical, world.

But wait: now I am in Paris because a novel of mine, *The Feast of Love*, has been published in a French translation. I am being interviewed by a French critic, who, like many French critics, is intelligent, articulate, and sly. We are in a café—where else in Paris would we be? The critic, behind his tinted glasses, says my novel is like a dream of love and infatuation. "You Americans," he says, and I instantly stiffen with hostility because I don't like sentences that begin with "you" followed by a group population. "You Americans," he says, "fall into the dream of fiction more easily and faster than we do here in France. In France we have a rationalist, skeptical tradition descending from Descartes. We resist falling into the dream. That is why there is no great contemporary French fiction. Without the dream, there is no great fiction." Then he backtracks. "I'm certainly *not* saying your novel is great," he says, "just that great fiction has dream content in it."

For twenty years, I have thought about what that critic said to me that afternoon in a Parisian café. At first, for a few years, I thought he was dead wrong, and now I think he may have been correct.

But let's leave the French critic behind for a while and ask ourselves how considerations of implausibility arise—what grounds are used when such truth claims are made? Here at the outset I should say that I think there are logical problems with every argument about implausibility that I'll describe, but because they occur so frequently in workshops and elsewhere, I need to establish them first.

Implausibility claim #1: *That particular character would not do what she just did.* What we know about her is inconsistent with that behavior. This criticism falls under the category of incoherent portraiture. The portrait makes no sense. This is a genuine craft problem but is not strictly a problem of plausibility or belief, and for the most part, I will ignore it in what follows.

Implausibility claim #2: *People don't do such things. People don't act that way.* Or: *Such things never happen. Life isn't like that.* This story or novel is untrue; it does not represent accurately what I understand to be the possible spectrum of events given these particular characters and their environment, given what I know about human beings and how they typically act. This, too, is a problematic category because human beings, as we all know, are capable of astonishing or unbelievable actions, and we don't always know what someone in a community outside our own might do. All the same, we all know of TV shows that gin up the drama in the first ten minutes for the sake of getting attention. They don't feel real, or true; they feel like something that happens on TV. But remember that, after all, readers love to be astonished and taken to the very edge of what is believable, and most of us have been slightly corrupted narratively by movies and TV. I know I have been. Parenthetically, I need to add that our current cultural and political climate has plenty of examples of public actions that once would have been considered outlandish or incredible. I will return to this problem later.

Implausibility claim #3: *That coincidence is simply impossible; it makes no sense.* This argument is a tricky one, because in certain stories and circumstances we are usually willing to set aside our disbelief in coincidence—especially if a story embodies a set of longings or fears or anxieties or terrors. So here's the issue: Under what conditions does the reader willingly suspend her disbelief about a coincidence? By contrast, what conditions may lead her to drop out of the story and close the book and say, "This all just made up, and, I'm sorry, it's just fucking unbelievable"? Note the obscenity here: the feeling of implausibility is often accompanied by anger, as if the reader or viewer has been subjected to a con, a fake, a fraud—a story that has tried to put one over on you, or, to quote the charge against Socrates, "to make the worse appear the better cause." The problem of implausible coincidence and contrivance is the one I will address first, and my initial example will be Alfred Hitchcock's 1958 film Vertigo, based on a French novel by Pierre Boileau and Thomas Narcejac. I could have used almost any novel by Dickens, particularly Great Expectations, but I'm going to use this movie instead.

1. The Wish

In 2012, the British magazine Sight and Sound polled the film critics of the world to name "the best picture ever made," and the result, that year, was Hitchcock's Vertigo. David Thomson has described the film as a "piercing dream," but, possibly challenging common sense, I am not going to explicate the full plot of the film at length here, or make a claim for it, in case the reader has never seen it. I will simply say that in this movie, a detective is asked to follow a beautiful, glamorous woman who is thought to be suicidal. Notice that the plot really begins with a request moment based on friendship between the two men: the woman's husband has asked the detective to please follow his wife and protect her from harm. This detective soon falls in love with the beautiful suicidal wife. When the detective, played by James Stewart, is apparently unable to prevent the woman's suicide, he falls into terrible, disabling guilt—he goes crazy for a while—and when he recovers, he finds another woman, a retail clerk, on the street in

San Francisco, a woman who maybe resembles his lost love, where-upon he does his best to persuade this woman, Judy Barton (in a second request moment), to dress up and do her hair so that she will resemble the dead, lost woman he could not save. Two request moments shape the plot. Once Judy Barton does what the detective has asked her to do, she, miraculously, confoundingly, looks exactly like the woman who died—not similar to her, but *exactly* like her.

This synopsis includes only what happens on the surface; I am not explaining what *actually* is true in this story, what is truly the case in the movie, because our hero, the detective played by James Stewart, has been subjected to a confidence trick, a con, as has the viewer, and he, and we, wake up only twenty minutes before the end of the film. Like him, we have been deceived by appearances. But that's not the point, not exactly. The point is that this story embodies a wish, and a dream, a powerful, all-consuming longing: What if a person you felt love for, and a responsibility for, died, and out of grief and guilt, you could somehow bring him, or her, or a replica, back to life? What if you could do that?

You would be, in effect, inside a dream.

There's a giant coincidence at the center of this story that's absolutely implausible and, upon consideration, impossibly contrived. I once asked Robert Pippin, a Hegelian philosopher who teaches at the University of Chicago, about this coincidence. Pippin has been absorbed and obsessed by this film and has written a fine book about it. In answer to my question, Pippin said, well, Hitchcock loved surrealism and absurdity. He loved the films of Luis Buñuel. But for me that doesn't explain why many viewers accept the outrageous contrivance of *Vertigo*'s plot.

Those who accept this plot probably do so because they, too, share a consuming and almost unconscious wish that it might be possible to bring someone you once loved back to life. This wish, this longing, is so obsessional that it sweeps all considerations of plausibility away. You're hypnotized by it; you're in a dream world. You're spell-bound inside a semirealistic fairy tale. A story that's only a fantasy is not the truth—but a story that immerses you in a character's fantasy and then makes you wake up from it, *that* may be the truth.

The film is beautifully shot; the soundtrack music, by Bernard Herrmann, is derived from Wagner's *Tristan and Isolde* and is hypnosis music, with endlessly repeating sequence structures. Many viewers are simply overpowered by the entire show; skepticism dies under the force of that wish. As the novelist Joan Silber wrote to me in a letter about this, "The strength of a con isn't its plausibility but how much people want to believe it. This is why people buy face cream that will make them look young forever."

I first saw *Vertigo* in a theater in 1958 when I was eleven. I'd never seen anything like it. Later, in 1963 or so, it was broadcast on TV, and I saw it at home with my mother. My mother wasn't buying any of it. Every so often, sitting over there on our reupholstered sofa, she would make a noise, "Pffftttt," the sound of disbelief, of enraged skepticism. Maybe she had a stake in the matter: her first husband, my father, had died at the age of forty-five of a heart attack when I was eighteen months old, and he never came back to life, and nobody, and certainly not my stepfather, was ever like him, and that was the truth, and all those lived-through consequences had been my mother's life.

My mother, in her perpetual grief, didn't believe that movie. There on the sofa, she gave a Bronx cheer to the beautiful wish: the whole story was just narrative bullshit for her. She had awakened from that particular dream a long time ago.

Bringing the dead back to life? Finding a replica for the person you lost? *Pffftttt*. That was a wish and a longing for others, not for her. Such a longing is what Montaigne described as a *soul error*: desiring something that you know you can't have. In this world, you can't bring dead people back to life. A story that not only portrays a fantasy but also immerses the reader in it may be a con job, but fantasies, and the characters who are under their spell, are at the heart of much storytelling, especially among young people. Adolescents live in the iron grip of their fantasies. And some fantasies are nearly impossible to give up. Maybe we shouldn't have them, but storytelling gives us license to indulge them. Many adolescents are spellbound; I certainly was. In my adult lifetime, I've probably seen *Vertigo* at least twenty times. When I read, sometimes I still am spellbound.

But let's allow the film critic David Thomson to have the last word about *Vertigo*: "It's a test case: If you are moved by this film, you are a creature of cinema. But if you are alarmed by its implausibility, its hysteria, its cruelty—well, there are novels."

To which my answer is: *Sorry, but no.* Many classic novels do exactly what *Vertigo* does. *Vertigo* is, after all, adapted from a novel. We shouldn't kid ourselves. The question is: How do we cast a spell in a story so that the reader ignores all the implausibilities we've put there? And under what conditions could we honorably do that? When powerful desires or fears overpower our common sense and we deploy all the technical resources we have—that's when.

Worrying about the plausibility of dreams, I wrote a few months ago to my teacher in Buffalo in the 1970s, Irving Massey, a person of great wisdom, now in his old age. I asked him, "Irving, why do we always believe our dreams when we're dreaming?" He wrote back: "Maybe dreams aren't experienced as implausible because, as registers or transcriptions of what we feel, they aren't."

That's beautiful.

2. Some Practicalities

Realism, as I have been arguing throughout this book, only makes sense if everybody agrees about what reality is. When they don't, there can't be any such thing as realism, because nothing "real" is out there. The word *realism*, as it's commonly used when it's applied to fiction, usually refers to experiences that most people agree on: real-world settings; events that exist in a middle range of plausibility and experience uncontaminated by wishes, dreams, or terrors; characters who are more or less recognizable as human beings; and dialogue that resembles ordinary conversation (that is, not in blank verse, etc.). Obviously, some or any of these categories can be stylized when circumstances in the fiction are extreme, as in *Catch-22* or *Nightwood*, or *Miss Lonelyhearts* or *Invisible Man* or *Beloved*, but even those books might be labeled "realistic" by some people, though not by me. It's a very slippery category. One musician and writer in a letter to me more or less denied that the word had any meaning at all.

So let's suppose that you want to get the reader from this world of facts and realities, over there, to the world of dreams, fears, and wishes, where characters reside who *are* spellbound by love or desire or terror. You want to move, as the writer John Hawkes once called it, in *the necessary direction of true derangement*. How do you transport the reader there? And why does Hawkes say it's "necessary"?

Let's start with a purportedly realist novel, *The Great Gatsby*. Almost everybody assumes that this book is an American classic of plausible realism. Not me. In my opinion, Fitzgerald's novel is so contaminated by dreams and longings and glamour that, if you succumb to it, if you knuckle under, you're in a dream world yourself. The working out of the plot is a parade of implausibilities and coincidences, topped off by Myrtle Wilson being run over in a case of mistaken identity and a resulting act of bloody revenge on the titular character, Gatsby. Viewed objectively, this great American classic is completely preposterous. The novelist Sigrid Nunez has also said so, at length.

But most readers *want* to be in the glamorous haze of possibilities that the novel generates. Like *Vertigo*, *The Great Gatsby* has a catalyst of longing—the desire to repeat or to re-live the past. Entering a dream world of money and glamour, Nick Carraway, the book's narrator, comes to Long Island, to the house of Tom Buchanan, and no sooner has he done so than the register of the prose goes up a couple of octaves. We're still in chapter one when Nick first sees Daisy Buchanan. It's a famous passage, a set of transit sentences to get him and you from here, the world of factoids where nothing magical ever happens, to over there, where anything might happen, and does—the land of romance, enchantment, sex, and violence.

The techniques that Fitzgerald uses to transport the reader include elaborated and beautifully intricate syntax that you can get lost in, accompanied by imagery designed to hypnotize you, and a metaphor that stops being metaphoric and becomes literal or concrete. In such writing, imagery always takes precedence over statement; *the image makes the case, not the statement.* This is also the case in Murakami's novels; unrealism depends on imagery. The imagery is typically obsessive and insistent. You can argue with a statement, but you can't argue with a dramatic image. In this passage, there is also the animation of inanimate objects. So, these techniques—(1) intricately beautiful syntax; (2) hypnotic, insistent, obsessive imagery; (3) literalized metaphor; and (4) the animation or personification of the inanimate—are the hallmarks of transit sentences; they put readers under a spell. Here are Fitzgerald's:

> The windows were ajar and gleaming white against the fresh grass outside that seemed to grow a little way into the house. A breeze blew through the room, blew curtains in at one end and out the other like pale flags, twisting them up toward the frosted wedding-cake of the ceiling, and then rippled over the wine-colored rug, making a shadow on it as wind does on the sea.
>
> The only completely stationary object in the room was an enormous couch on which two young women were buoyed up as though upon an anchored balloon. They were both in white, and their dresses were rippling and fluttering as if they had just

been blown back in after a short flight around the house. I must have stood for a few moments listening to the whip and snap of the curtains and the groan of a picture on the wall. Then there was a boom as Tom Buchanan shut the rear windows and the caught wind died out about the room, and the curtains and the rugs and the two young women ballooned slowly to the floor.

Speaking of *Gatsby*, the memoirist Patricia Hampl once told me, "You can only get the reader into the dream if the sentences and the style permit it." You take the risk of writing lush prose. Flat factoid prose filled with statements and without lift will not transport you. Look at the techniques here: the grass is surreal; it's growing nearly into the house. In the following compound-complex sentence, we have no fewer than two similes and one metaphor, and by the time you've reached the end of the sentence you may well have forgotten how it started—and we're still talking about the curtains. There's a pile-up of associative figuration that pushes the real objects off to the side.

The next paragraph begins with a comparison—the "anchored balloon"—and the following sentence elaborates the comparison by almost literalizing it: it's as if the two women have been flying around the house. Hypnotized in the same way that we are, the narrator, Nick, is spellbound in the next sentence, listening to the "groan" of a picture on the wall. Hey, reader: pictures don't groan, remember? But pictures *do* start to groan if you're the enchanted Beauty, and you've entered the Beast's castle, where all the spellbound objects look at you and have something to say. And then, what? Tom Buchanan closes the window, and the women float down slowly to the floor, and we're back to the real world, sort of.

How do you react to this passage in *Gatsby*? Do you say, *Oh, my God, look at that, how beautiful!*—or *Pffffttt*? Nick Carraway, our narrator, has fallen deep into a spell, has dropped into the dream, and he doesn't awaken until around chapter seven or eight. The last thirty pages of this novel are one prolonged hangover. In stories of enchantment, the key moment is the one when a character finally wakes up and sees the world for what it is. Some of the greatest stories of awakenings—Henry James' *Portrait of a Lady*, Faulkner's *Absalom, Absalom!*, Toni Morrison's *Song of Solomon*, Louise Erdrich's *Shadow Tag* and much of her other work, Saul Bellow's *Herzog*, and John Cheever's story "The Swimmer"—are about trying to wake up after you have been, to quote Don DeLillo, "puddled in dream melt."

John Hawkes' post–World War II novels have the restless emotional logic of dreams, as does Djuna Barnes' *Nightwood* (1936), a novel that Hawkes admired. Advancing through Djuna Barnes' novel, a reader is confronted with long, hallucinatory speeches whose subject matter often disappears beneath the extended surface of feverish similes and metaphors. In this book, metaphors seem always ready and eager to overcome both characters and events in an effort to subsume them or to make them disappear. It is as if figurative language has taken over what remains of reality, throwing the whole category of "reality" into question, reality itself being intolerable, with the result that what is left of the physical world is almost impossible to see clearly:

> Waking, she [Nora] began to walk again, and looking out into the garden in the faint light of dawn, she saw a double shadow falling from the statue, as if it were multiplying, and thinking perhaps this was Robin, she called and was not answered. Standing motionless, straining her eyes, she saw emerge from the darkness the light of Robin's eyes, the fear in them developing their luminosity until, by the intensity of their double regard, Robin's eyes and hers met. So they gazed at each other. As if that light had power to bring what was dreaded into the zone of their catastrophe, Nora saw the body of another woman swim up into the statue's obscurity, with head hung down, that the

added eyes might not augment the illumination; her arms about Robin's neck, her body pressed to Robin's, her legs slackened in the hang of the embrace.

In this passage, Nora has spotted for the first time Robin Vote together with her new lover, Jenny Petherbridge, also known as "the squatter." But what the passage is really about are the shadows cast by a statue; and the way that an exchanged glance can summon into the scene a third person who doesn't belong there; and the way that statues and human beings can be exchanged somehow in this particular world, where even statues can replicate themselves. This scene creates a supercharged emotional landscape between night and day, peopled by statues and statue-like figures, but in some sense a critic cannot even say that the scene exists to create a dramatic situation and a landscape, both of which are secondary to the language in which they appear. The scene exists so that the sentences can unfurl in all their metaphoric and visual intensity, in the way that meaning in dreams all but vaporizes the events of the dream, leaving only the images still standing. The characters are merely pretexts for the metaphors. In much of Nightwood, one feels that the story has departed, leaving behind the words, singing frantically about everything that's missing.

Stanley Elkin once said, in a class I attended, that you shouldn't interrupt a realist story with a dream, partly because dreams are boring, but also because in a post-Freudian age, dreams don't lie, and therefore they give the reader a key that too easily unlocks a story's meaning. An interpolated dream is like a narrative shortcut and is always like someone at the blackboard with a pointer aimed at the story's core meaning.

But Stanley Elkin said nothing about entire stories that feel dreamlike or slightly hallucinated. He wrote them himself. They were his stock in trade.

3.

The issue of implausibility in what I would call "hallucinatory real-ism" becomes particularly acute when the world of fiction has been tilted so that everyone inside a particular novel or story is off-balance. Realism as we generally understand it and as I have defined it is often not up to the task of telling us what it feels like to live under oppres-sion, particularly when the authorities, the figures of power and en-forcement who loom over us, seem to be unpredictable, unreadable, or insane.

When we are at peace with ourselves and at peace with the structures of power that surround us and in which we may flour-ish, we are likely to tell stories of local, intricate behavior and mis-behavior. In such stories, subtle secrets and betrayals—think of Alice Munro's stories or William Trevor's or ZZ Packer's or Chekhov's, or the nineteenth-century English novel—take center stage, and the stories' particular focus is all on character, all the glories and frail-ties of human beings that constitute a story's normal heart.

But suppose, just suppose for the sake of argument, that the struc-tures of institutional power have no coherence and are no longer under the control of human reason. Suppose that an ordinary citizen looks around at the political and social world that she or he inhabits and is forced to say, as Captain Willard says in *Apocalypse Now*, in re-sponse to Kurtz's question about whether his methods are unsound, "I don't see any method at all, sir."

When the methods of our leaders and the authorities are un-sound, or unbelievable, or oppressive and insane, the world of the story may have tilt to represent the out-of-balance condition simply in order to be accurate and true to what it feels like to be alive in that period. Given its departure from strict realism, the story may start to seem implausible or wildly exaggerated or feverish to the common-sense crowd. In such writing, "plausibility" is no longer relevant. Suddenly we have entered the realm of Emily Brontë's *Wuthering*

Heights, or in our own time, the fiction of Mohsin Hamid, Kelly Link, Karen Russell, George Saunders, and Carmen Maria Machado. These writers insist that the world as given to us or to the characters is fundamentally out of order, is broken or criminal, and our leaders are murderous and mad. The prose in these works is not set at 98.6, but somewhere up near 104, the temperature at which you start to hallucinate.

But for a moment let's push the fiction writers aside and ask the poets to step up to the podium. Here is an excerpt from a poem (a composite from several versions) written by Robert Bly and first published in 1970:

> Now the Chief Executive enters, and the press
>   conference begins.
> First the President lies about the date the Appalachian
>   Mountains rose.
> Then he lies about the population of Chicago.
> Then the number of fish taken every year in the Arctic,
> Then about the weight of the adult eagle, then about the
>   acreage of the Everglades.
> He has learned the true birthplace of Attila the Hun,
> Then he lies about the composition of the amniotic fluid.
> He has private information about which city *is* the
>   capital of Wyoming.
>
> He insists that Luther was never a German,
> And insists that only the Protestants sold indulgences,
> That Pope Leo X *wanted* to reform the Church, but the
>   liberal elements prevented him.
> That the Peasants' War was fomented by Italians from
>   the North.
> And the Attorney General lies about the time the sun sets.

These lies mean we have a longing to die.
What is there now to hold us on earth?
It is the longing for someone to come and take us by the
    hand to where they are all sleeping:
Where the Egyptian pharaohs are asleep, and our own
    mothers,
And all those disappeared children, who went around
    with us on the rings at grade school.

Do not be angry at the President—
He is longing to take in his hands the locks of death-hair:
To meet his own children, dead, or never born . . .

He is drifting sideways toward the dusty places.

This is what it is like for a rich country to make war

    The poem goes on from there. It's hard to describe what category these lines fall into, but "surrealistic realism" is fairly accurate. The excerpt starts with presidential lies and then moves off into Jungian deep collective associative psychology. In the years since they were written, these lines have lost none of their relevance; they might have been written yesterday. Surrealism has turned into realism, given the passage of time. I myself heard Bly read these lines in the 1970s, and later, in Vermont, I heard Galway Kinnell read these lines in the period before the Iraq War in 2003. The line that I want to emphasize is "What is there now to hold us on earth?" This line does not appear in the original version of this poem, "The Teeth Mother Naked at Last" (a title that Bly came to regret) in the book *Sleepers Joining Hands*. The line appears only in the poem's revision in the *Selected and New Poems* published in 2013. It seems to me a brilliant recognition that those who do not care about the earth anymore are trying to float free of it, in some deluxe penthouse atmosphere where truth has ceased to matter, where science and facts are discredited—a realm, one might say, where money and glitz have replaced both truth and the sacred. Up there, the truth is held in contempt, and we are in a strange place, without realism, and are being fed, instead, "alternative facts," to quote a famous contemporary public figure.

Poetry has never really signed a pact with realism. It has always been slightly wary of empiricism; poetry almost never pretends, as fiction sometimes does, that it is a picture of life. Instead, poetry, just by being poetry, emphasizes its own metaphoric status—that is, poetry is always formally at one remove from life; it is *like* life, *about* life, a thickly filtered and mediated version of it, reality with a vision and a consciousness and a voice attached to it, life as seen through the lenses of lyric utterance. Poetry is life when you're singing about it, songs of praise and desolation. By contrast, fiction is spoken, usually, but poetry is sung; it is the singing that tells us that we are over there, and not quite here.

Which is why poetry usually doesn't worry over implausibility. It's like asking grand operas to calm down. Does the ancient mariner *actually* play dice with death? It's a meaningless question. The word *actually* has no place in poetry. It was Coleridge himself who coined the phrase "willing suspension of disbelief" in the *Biographia Literaria*. In Bly's poem, the president is not named as Nixon or Johnson or anyone else. Bly's poem does not clash with our understanding of any particular public figure; it's not implausible because we know from the start that its stance is that of metaphor, its technique is that of exaggeration and satire, and very quickly it moves from political satire to deep collective tragedy and sorrow. The enraged laugh that lives in the neighborhood of sorrow is closer to deep truth here than any literal truth could ever be.

4.

A final example of deep surrealist truths comes from Carmen Maria Machado's story "Real Women Have Bodies," from her book *Her Body and Other Parties* (2017). In this story, the narrator goes to work at a fashion store, Glam, at the mall. In the course of the story, she discovers in a matter-of-fact way that many women are mysteriously becoming transparent, and through some infernal process are fading and are also being stitched into dresses. I am oversimplifying the story, but that is the gist of it.

The story's central point—what amounts to its critique—is that women who give themselves over to high fashion become less visible *as themselves*. They fade, or disappear, into, and become, the clothes they wear. The metaphoric conversion of this idea goes somewhat as follows: a woman wearing a dress from Glam is *like* an invisible or disappearing woman. Therefore, in narrative storytelling, the simile "like" is liquidated, and you get a literalization of the simile: the woman is actually becoming invisible. And so you get paragraphs like this:

> We are not alone in the room. Petra's mother is hovering near a dress, a bracelet pincushion wrapped around her wrist. As my eyes adjust to the dark, the lights coalesce into silhouettes, and I realize the room is full of women. Women like the one in the viral video, see-through and glowing faintly, like afterthoughts. They drift and mill and occasionally look down at their bodies. One of them, with a hard and sorrowful face, is standing very close to Petra's mother. She moves toward the garment slung over the dress form—butter yellow, the skirt gathered in small places like a theater curtain. She presses herself into it, and there is no resistance, only a sense of an ice cube melting in the summer air. The needle—trailed by thread of guileless gold—winks as Petra's mother plunges it through the girl's skin. The fabric takes the needle, too.

Hypnotic, hypnotized prose. A dream. It should go almost without saying that the narrator's challenge is to liberate the disappearing women from their dresses; from their hypnosis; from their invisibility; from the metaphors in which they are trapped; and from their oppression. Jacques Lacan says that we must liberate ourselves from the circles of meaning in which we are imprisoned. Does Machado's narrator succeed? Yes, but only in a manner of speaking. It is unclear by the end of the story whether the disappearing, transparent women have re-established ownership over their own bodies. Such ownership may be one of those one-way gates like virginity and innocence that, once lost, cannot be restored.

Carmen Maria Machado writes about the female body the way John Cheever writes about the suburbs. I mean that as praise. For her, it is an endlessly renewable generator of meanings; in her stories, the female body is the primary site of semiotic constructions for oneself and for others, and it constitutes a landscape of endless exploitation, meanings, and desires. All meanings start at, and with, the body and then radiate outward. And who, after all, can deny the body's primacy in our lives? In her stories, women's bodies might be described as the location upon which men and other women inscribe their desire and themselves; in her fiction, the body (and therefore the person) have traces left upon it of those who have loved and desired it. No woman in these stories is unmarked. Men seem not to retain the marks of others' love for them on their bodies, but women—in her stories— certainly do; they are written upon, as if every woman carries with her an internal tattoo burned into her by those who have loved her.

The central question of whether a woman can retain total ownership over her own body therefore arises in the book's first story, "The Husband Stitch," at whose center is a ribbon around the narrator's neck; this ribbon is the narrator's sacred object, her most private possession and the nonverbal key to her inner self. Given the story's implacable logic, like that of a ghost story, her husband throughout their lives together wants to untie the ribbon, which stands in for the last part of herself that she has kept for herself and not given away to him. They love each other, but that is not the story's point. The point is that the ribbon is hers and not his. This ribbon is consequently the one thing that holds her together, something he should not possess, a literalized metaphor that, like a dream object, *and only in the proximate world of dreams*, provides her with her last form of integrity. When she finally gives him permission to untie this ribbon, what we have been expecting all along occurs: given that same literalized metaphor operating throughout the story, the narrator falls apart. And yet she goes on speaking, telling her story to us, as one does in dreams.

5.

Are writers and painters and composers partially in a dream world when they create their works? Tolstoy apparently thought they often were. In *Anna Karenina*, a painter, Mikhailov, forgets everything he went through while he was painting. "He had forgotten all the suffering and ecstasy he had experienced with this picture when for several months it alone had occupied him incessantly, day and night, forgotten, just as he always forgot the pictures he had completed." You forget the work you do creatively the way you forget your dreams.

We sit at our desks. We daydream. The real world falls away, and another world comes through a portal to take its place. This world doesn't have a name until we name it. Faulkner called his "Yoknapatawpha County," a half-garbled, concocted name that seems to have come out of a dream.

6.

The grade-school boy has a prominent overbite with what used to be called buckteeth, a malady that inspires a great deal of cruel teasing against him by his classmates. He is clumsy and is usually chosen last to be on any particular team. He lives out in the middle of nowhere on a sort of hobby farm with his stepfather and his mother, who is moody and alcoholic. He feels solitary. The world, in short, is a deeply unwelcoming place—to quote the German writer Christa Wolf, whose books he will read many years later, *there is no place on Earth* where he is welcome.

All this changes when the boy turns fifteen. He discovers a novel quite by accident, a paperback for sale for fifty cents in a drugstore in Excelsior, Minnesota. The book is called *The Night of the Hunter* by a West Virginia author named Davis Grubb. The boy, who is me, reads the novel, a highly lyrical nightmare about losing a father and gaining a stepfather, and nothing in his life has ever felt as true to his life as this book. When he finally sees the movie version, starring Robert Mitchum and directed by Charles Laughton, his feeling is reinforced: this story, this dream, he thinks, however frightening it may be, is my true home. I could have dreamed this story myself. You have to believe me when I say that reading this lyrically nightmarish novel was a great relief to me, a kind of recognition, and a portal to a new world.

Fifty-five years later, that person, me, is now writing about dreams and about a world that still—with its mass murders and its unreadable, unstable leaders—seems deeply untrustworthy and still unwelcoming. But there is that portal, an escape hatch, and it's always been there: the books that welcome you in are always there, eager to have you enter their world. Every artful story, every poem, constitutes—as the critic Lewis Hyde has claimed in his book *The Gift*—a gift of sorts, to take you into a place that is wiser and smarter and more emotional about the world than the world itself is. If you're lucky, you enter the story and the story gives you a home.

Bertolt Brecht says that capitalism wants to put everybody to sleep, and that it's the duty of theater and literature to wake us up.

Yes, I agree; we must wake up, but we have to do it by turning the techniques of dreaming to our own purposes; we have to inspire our dreams to lead us to hope and action, and to hope's companion, enlightenment.

So we must remember all the guides to writing, all the lectures and workshops. But my first and last piece of advice to my friends and fellow writers is this: "Go home, and when you are stuck, remember all our suggestions and advice, but more than that, become like a child again. Go home and dream."

Notes on the Dramatic Image:
An Essay in Six Parts

for Robert Boswell

1.

Imagine a residential city street, shaded during the summer by oaks and elms. The houses in this neighborhood were built in the early twentieth century, before air-conditioning insulated everyone from the heat, and the two structures across from our vantage point have large screened front porches. Porch swings, suspended by chains from the ceiling, sway almost imperceptibly. One of these houses has an upstairs sleeping porch where family members can go on particularly hot nights. These residences, while neither grand nor ostentatious, have a certain roominess, as if they were meant to shelter families with several children, and in fact you can hear kids calling out to each other from a nearby vacant lot. Because we are situated in the Upper Midwest, where the winters are severe, the windows of these houses are relatively small, and during the summer if you are inside and are not sitting near a window, you must turn on an electric light in order to read.

Across from us is a red house with a steep slanted roof. At ground level, the porch light of the red house, for some reason, is always on.

Three doors down from the red house is that vacant lot, where the children are playing. Next door to the vacant lot stands a large green-and-white house with a wraparound porch. The house was built on a kind of knoll—you could hardly call it a hill—with a stone wall facing the street, and the only peculiarity of this residence is that no one ever seems to go in or out of it. Even at night, the house stands dark. During the summer, the lawn stays mowed, and the grass is always green, as if ghosts are tending it.

The street is Girard Avenue South in Minneapolis, and every afternoon the little boy who lives across from the house with the wraparound porch climbs the stairs to his second-floor bedroom so that he can watch from an upstairs window for his father to come home from work. Every day the boy pulls himself up on a bed in front of the upstairs window, and there he waits, looking out at the street. When he sees his father, he leaves the bed and toddles back downstairs so that he can be in the doorway when his father enters. Every evening his father greets him and lifts him up into the air.

That summer the father dies very suddenly at a picnic, falling down stone dead of a heart attack at the age of forty-four. The fact of his death is explained to the little boy, but because the boy is not yet two years old, the information does not penetrate, cannot cohere in the boy's mind, cannot coalesce as meaning, or as anything.

Therefore, for several months afterward, the boy climbs the stairs as he always has and takes up his post at the window, waiting for his father to come home from work. Perhaps the thought enters the child's mind that he himself has done something terribly wrong, because when his father does not appear as he once did, the boy must be faithful to the ritual he has invented to celebrate his father's daily homecoming. No one can explain to him what the situation is. After all, death and its particulars are meaningless to a child of two. Patiently, therefore, every afternoon, the boy waits, until it is time for dinner.

The leaves fall from the oaks and maples, and in due course, the winter comes. The boy learns to talk. Once he does, he forgets about his afternoon vigils. The years pass.

2.

A few years ago I was asked by the Library of America to edit the short stories of Sherwood Anderson, including those that had never been published in book form. These stories were sent to me as photocopies of microfilm files taken from old issues of the *New Yorker* and other magazines. Some of these stories were almost illegible. Among them was "The Corn Planting," from 1934. I read it before putting it aside. Two or three days later I was still thinking about it, or, rather, I was still mulling over its concluding dramatic image. To use a locution much loved by Sherwood Anderson himself, *something* about the image had struck me. I want to tease out the power of certain kinds of lyrical dramatic images such as the one we find in "The Corn Planting," and to ask, in a somewhat circular way, what the source of that power might be.

"The Corn Planting" has almost no plot. As a writer, Anderson had little gift for horizontal sequential structures, and his fiction therefore has a somewhat haphazard quality. Because he tended to shun plot, his stories are open to the operations of chance, much like a man who stands out on a golf course during a thunderstorm with his putter raised in the air, hoping to be struck by lightning. And that's how Anderson's stories work: lightning hits them every now and then. Instead of linear sequence structures, Anderson substitutes echoing dramatic images of a certain type, and the linked images provoke the electrical charge, which is often static, like the leaping charge in a Tesla coil.

The events of "The Corn Planting" can be easily summarized. Hatch Hutchinson, a farmer in his middle age, marries a forty-year-old schoolteacher. They have one son, Will, their only child, whom they dote on. The boy grows up. Will has a friend, Hal Weyman, who also goes away to college in Chicago, as Will does. The story in which they appear has a first-person narrator, a nameless resident of the town, a Sherwood Anderson stand-in, who reports on these events for us. This narrator tells us what Hal Weyman (the friend of both the narrator and Will) has told him about the old couple, Hatch and his wife, and how they fill the hours after their son has left home for Chicago:

> Hal said it was touching how much the father and mother de-
> pended on their one son, how much they talked about him and
> dreamed of his future. . . . They were the sort who work all
> the time, from early morning until late in the evening; and on
> moonlight nights, Hal said, and after the little old wife had got
> the supper, they often went out into the fields and worked again.

That simple detail, that Hatch Hutchinson and his wife some-
times do field work at night, has been planted unobtrusively in the story, where most readers are not likely to pay much attention to it. But to continue: In Chicago, Will Hutchinson attends art school, and has some success as a commercial artist. He sends his drawings to his parents, and Hal sometimes explains these drawings when he visits the old couple.

Then the disaster: in the spring, Will Hutchinson is killed in an automobile accident during a night of drinking. That same night, a telegram with this news is sent to the town's telegraph operator, and the telegraph operator gives the telegram to Hal, asking him to take it out to the Hutchinson farm. Hal, in turn, asks his friend, the story's narrator, to accompany him out there, a request to which the narrator agrees. They walk out; they do not drive. After arriving at the house, Hal knocks on the door loudly. Hatch Hutchinson comes to the door, and Hal informs the old man of the death of his son, his only child. Hatch says nothing in response and slams the door.

At this point, the narrator and Hal stay there, "silently listening and watching," waiting for something. And what that "something" is reveals itself as they wait. The old farmer and his wife come outside in their pajamas to the field, which had been plowed that day. The narrator and Hal conceal themselves: "[we] got to where we could see what was going on without being seen."

The story then gives us these two lightning-struck paragraphs:

It was an incredible thing. The old man had got a hand corn-planter out of the barn and his wife had got a bag of seed corn, and there, in the moonlight, that night, after they got that news, they were planting corn.

It was a thing to curl your hair—it was so ghostly. They were both in their night clothes. They would do a row across the field, coming quite close to us as we stood in the shadow of the barn, and then, at the end of each row, they would kneel side by side by the fence and stay silent for a time. The whole thing went on in silence.

Anderson, in his customary way, then editorializes about what the narrator has seen, but the *story*, as opposed to the commentary, essentially ends with that phrase, "The whole thing went on in silence."

Our anonymous narrator, if we are to believe him, does not seem to understand the dramatic image that he himself has just given us. We therefore have a storyteller who claims not to know what his story means or is oblivious to the problem of narrative meaning altogether. Having given us the image accompanied by his perplexed commentary about it, he makes his own puzzlement as much a part of the story as the image itself. "I am far from sure now," he says, "that I can put down what I understood and felt that night." In the gasping and blandly inarticulate sentences that follow, the narrator simply intensifies and dramatizes his own bewilderment, trying out first this theory, then that one, each theory marked by the key word *something*, a diction choice that signifies his inability to find the correct noun. I think this failure to find meaning goes beyond the inarticulateness of many of Sherwood Anderson's protagonists and is characteristic of the professed ignorance planted at the center of much American writing. To paraphrase the German art critic Arnold Gehlen, speaking about Manet's painting *The Luncheon on the Grass*, what we have here is an image that produces intuitions for which there are no concepts. As a witty friend of mine once remarked, the intuition without a concept rouses all sorts of specters, drifting up like smoke from the Kantian treasure chest of undead ideas.

This absence of understanding exists despite our recognition that the old couple is acting *in character*, as theater people would say; they're doing what they have always done. We've already been told that they sometimes work on the fields at night, so what they're doing now is neither freakish nor weird. Their actions are taking on the burden of their feelings, but these actions are not objective correlatives or anything of the sort. The only weird misfit detail here is that the old couple are out there planting the fields while wearing their pajamas. The image here echoes a previous image, so the story has already set up a consistency of imagery, a kind of visual echo effect, a form of rhyming action.

Also, and very noticeably, the image presents a nonprogressive action. It's as if it has always been going on and has no true beginning and no true end. Planting corn is not like robbing a bank; it is not climactic and involves no rising tension and does not involve suspense. It simply is. This action isn't going anywhere. Although repetitive, the action has a ritual component and gently takes the viewer, almost by stealth, into the landscape of stillness. Nonprogressive actions are of a particular type (that is, they are repetitive) and can acquire an aura when viewed from the proper angle. We tend to think of repetitive actions as dulling, stress inducing, and mechanical, but repetition is often planted at the heart of ritual, even the rituals of daily life such as this one. These actions have very little urgency concerning their completion—they express fixedness rather than movement—which is why stories that contain them usually have to be short.

We should note also that the corn planting is a result of the old father having been struck dumb by the news of his son's death. Writers sometimes ask what their characters *would* do, *should* do, *might* do, if and when they are stunned into silence, and their actions have to substitute for the language that has gone missing. Out of the inability to speak or explain, some precipitous action occurs. Such moments were Sherwood Anderson's specialty, a kind of silent and nonviolent shouting. They turn up everywhere in his fiction and often carry with them a dreamlike quality.

Dramatic action often acquires a particularly unstable feeling when it's a result of the characters' inability to articulate what needs to be said, or when the moment of articulation has passed. Action, of whatever type, in such a situation becomes a kind of sign language.

To return to my argument: we need to observe that this is an image caught by chance. Hal and the narrator are, in effect, spies. Their spying seems like a prelude to writing—as if spying were a necessary component of the creative act. Hal and the narrator see this scene *together*, so it's not a solitary hallucination; there is a community of seers. And it seems important to me that in this scene, the old man and his wife do not know that they are being observed. People act differently when they know they are being looked at; an element of performance tends to corrupt behavior whenever we know other people are watching us. We begin to act *for* them.

In his essay "Words and Images," Irving Massey argues that images caught by chance have a whiff of the eternal about them. This formulation points to a quality of stop-time in the image. He put it this way:

The image, then, rescues us momentarily from time: it provides an exit through the walls of discourse, an escape into the realms of simultaneity: until the course of the sentence resumes (and syntax begins to dominate again) we are out of time.

Many efforts have been made to discredit the traditions of which this idea is a key element, but I find myself returning to it to explain how time and the image are linked. There seem to be few other resources in art apart from the image to effect such a suspension. Since Hal and the narrator had no idea that they were going to see what they are seeing, they do not stand up and identify themselves: they recognize that they're watching something that's essentially private—private and painful, that is, but not shameful. What they see is beautiful and eerie, a ritualized grieving, a dumb-show encompassed in a single dramatic image, dreamlike, lit by the light of the moon. When you catch the sight of some action and catch it by accident, you feel privileged. You've been admitted into a place of secrets and privacy.

Finally, the image of Hatch and his wife is what Irving Massey would have called a "widowed image"—that is, an image that has been detached of the meaning that once was married to it. What we have in Anderson's stories are quasi-epiphanies without any paraphrased content and without any foundational insight. The old couple is planting, but they are also doing something else. Taking it symbolically takes us in the wrong direction, and the image of the old couple planting corn, a planting interrupted by prayer, is not, I think, symbolic. I can hear my inner high school English teacher telling me that the corn planting is a ritual, *symbolizing how life goes on, how seed is planted in the ground despite everything*, yadda yadda yadda, and my reply is, "No, no, no." For me, the image resonates because mystery adheres to it, because its meaning escapes me, because it's not what I expected, and yet, because I know that Hatch and his wife are a farm couple, it seems absolutely right—inevitable and surprising and mind-haunting.

This feature of Sherwood Anderson's writing fascinated the poet Donald Justice. In his essay on the "prose sublime," Justice puts it this way: "In Anderson there is not the . . . push toward meaning; the rendering exhausts the interpretation. It has everything the Joycean epiphany has except for the crucial flash of understanding. . . . Such passage(s) seem hardly to bother with understanding at all [and instead give us] unspoken connections, unnamable affinities, a tissue of association without specified relations."

Justice claims that he cannot find this quality in Russian or European literature, but it is surely there in Tolstoy's story "A Snowstorm," with its flurry of unsorted memories, a drowning, the grandmother's "naive selfishness of love." But, of course, in Tolstoy, the juxtaposition of imagery is deliberate, whereas in Sherwood Anderson it just happens. Tolstoy plans his effects; Sherwood Anderson stumbles upon them.

3.

In 1987 I was teaching at Wayne State University. In those days I had a colleague, a dapper novelist named Samuel Astrachan, who'd studied under Lionel Trilling at Columbia. Sam's novels were about human history, specifically Jewish history, and more specifically the history of Jews in America and elsewhere after the Holocaust. Sam and I would talk occasionally about stories and novels, and one day I gave him a copy of Janet Kauffman's story "The Easter We Lived in Detroit," which subsequently appeared in her book *Obscene Gestures for Women* (1989). I liked the story and thought he might like it, too.

The next time I saw Sam, I asked him what he thought of the story. "I didn't care for it," he said, firmly. When I asked him why, he pointed at a paragraph, *this* paragraph:

In the kitchen, I took a blue-painted hard-boiled egg from the refrigerator, poured some milk, and let my eyes travel the walls in the indoor light. It was greenish, undersea light, very mild. I peeled the egg and sliced it with a steak knife onto a big plate, where the two halves slid together. They arranged themselves, it certainly seemed to me then, as downhearted, pitying eyes. I just whispered, Don't you worry, Not today.

"That's not fiction," Sam said irritably. "That's poetry."

Like Sherwood Anderson's story, which in some respects it resembles, "The Easter We Lived in Detroit" has very little plot: the narrator has one child, a daughter, who has run away with an evangelical preacher, who is also a book burner. The narrator is married to Loren, who has been disabled in some way—the narrator calls him "vacated"—and who has dead hands. To put it bluntly, the narrator is coping with her circumstances. The couple is living in an apartment in Detroit. That's the backstory, and within the story itself, which takes place on an Easter Sunday and is a day-in-the-life, almost nothing happens; the narrator listens to the radio; she and Loren make love; she eats a hard-boiled egg; Loren takes an afternoon nap; the narrator writes her daughter a letter, and they have steak for dinner.

Nevertheless, the story is about grief, about losing a daughter, but it compensates for this absence by heightening attention to each household object, so that each material possession acquires the "luminous halo" that Virginia Woolf once claimed was the necessary feature of great fiction. "The Easter We Lived in Detroit" is heavily invested in everyday objects. They are very plain indeed—humdrum household acquisitions: geraniums, floorboards, and a husband. What is extraordinary is the mode of seeing, the hard force of attention paid, and the intricately crafted, stop-and-start syntax and imagery and metaphor used to transform these objects into the haunts of reality. The minutiae of the story may seem small, but the concentrated force of attention paid to what's there makes them large. The point, narratively, is not to move the story forward—that was Sam Astrachan's objection to it, the story's obstinate resistance to history and time sequence—but to make all visible objects shimmer within a moment, which itself is passing:

> While he read and the radio man talked on, I washed dishes. From the kitchen, I didn't mind watching him. The past can cut itself off very smoothly. It's possible that Loren's life from birth had been surrounded with a silence nobody noticed, and I certainly never noticed, until he stopped working. But then the quiet accumulated; it polished him, waxy and definite. That Easter morning, at a distance of twenty feet, I could see the capsules, like layers of color, around him. I took some time, looking at him. I watched him the way you watch, unpitying, an insect going its way in the alley, working its legs over chunks of gravel.

We can see several of the features we noted in the Sherwood Anderson story reclaiming our attention here: the participants are *in character*; the actions of the story are repetitions of what has happened many times before; the action is nonprogressive; the characters seem to have been struck dumb, have been muted, and when they speak, they speak briefly and almost meaninglessly; there is a lost child at the center of the narrative; and the story eventually turns away from the light it has been celebrating and quietly states its allegiance to silence and night. Speaking of her husband, the narrator says that he was "a shadowy man who'd discovered silence and who made love much more carefully now." At the conclusion, the narrator tells us, "Loren and I sat on the windowsill while the dark took over the living room and took over the ground outside, too. The dark, which is like a shelter around each person, is a lovely thing to see, once you see it."

The attentive reader can sense in this story that joy and sorrow, seemingly incompatible, are being asked to inhabit the same fictional space, and they do so by means of the imagery, which can compound contradictory emotions without having to justify or explain their co-presence. Having these two emotions mixed together gives the story the joyfully proud desolation of an American precisionist painting by someone like George Ault or Charles Sheeler:

> It was a pale light that slowed people down and hushed them up. Kids on bicycles riding no-hands swerved smoothly and turned up the alley as if their bikes were on automatic. Nobody shouted to anybody.

Does the story give the impression of someone spying, or images caught by chance? In one sense it does, because at one point it gives us an image of such singular intimacy that most pornography would seem public and showy by comparison:

> Loren said, Hold my hand. I took his hand and held it up to my mouth. All his fingers pointed to the ground. The skin on his arm was soft, untanned, with fine brown hair, and I drew my tongue across the hairs.

Reading this passage, I feel as if I am peering through a window; I have been allowed to see what no outsider should see.

And, finally, I would argue that "The Easter We Lived in Detroit" escapes, or more properly evades, a symbolic reading. I know, I know: the story takes place on Easter Sunday, which points to a revival or a resurrection of sorts. But the God in this story is unofficial, belonging neither to the radio preachers or the book-burning evangelist. God belongs, in this narrative, to the sewing table, to the hard-boiled eggs, the typewriter, a book, a scrap of dust in a corner, the hairs on Loren's fingers, the floorboards, a whistling tea kettle, an old framed photograph of the narrator's grandmother. All these humble things aren't symbols, but the god-stuff, the thing itself, when looked at properly. And Detroit. Why *Detroit*? Of all places? What if the story were called "The Easter We Lived in Tuscany" or "The Easter We Lived on the French Riviera" or "The Easter We Lived in the Hamptons"? Those spots are already beautiful, they don't need anyone's help, and observers wouldn't have to bring anything of their own to them. Beauty like that is sufficient to itself. But Detroit, as a city, has already been humbled. As everyone knows, it is a post-industrial ruin. God is assumed not to be there. A transformation is required. You wouldn't expect to find the joyful and sorrowful mysteries in the Motor City, but in this story, there they are.

So far, I've been describing these images as a form of lyric expansion—that is, they seem to stop time for a moment in order to hold that moment and sear it into our memories, an exit, to quote Massey again, though the walls of discourse, the temporary and the eternal brought into conjunction. The point of the image is not just image itself but its effect on our sense of time. Such lyric images can rarely support an entire story, because their very frozenness prevents them from yielding logically to a subsequent scene, and narrative is what happens in time, through time. Chekhov loved images, as his notebooks show, but his stories do not depend only on them. It may be possible to imagine a novel that is made up solely of images—Timothy Findley's novel *The Wars* comes close, as do many graphic novels—but the Sam Astrachan position has almost the whole history of the novel on its side. Stories and novels require connecting tissue, dialogue, and dramatic action that has consequences in other actions, not merely other images.

All the same, when I think of the whole of Tolstoy's *War and Peace*, the part I always remember is that moment in which we encounter a displaced image in the midst of violent action. In volume 1, part 3, chapter sixteen, Prince Andrey is wounded in the Battle of Austerlitz. Lying on the ground, wanting to see the battle and to know who's winning, he sees, instead, the sky. "Above him was nothing, nothing but the sky—the lofty sky, not a clear sky, but still infinitely lofty, with gray clouds creeping gently across." Prince Andrey at this moment is astounded that he's never really seen the sky before or perceived its immensity. The image of the sky and clouds here is just about the last thing you'd expect to see in a description of a battle. But the eye of the observer has been displaced, the field of vision has been altered, and all at once we have a glimpse of the eternal serving as a background to the foreground of fighting, injury, and death.

The eternal is always there, Tolstoy seems to assert, but we often fail to see it until we're wounded, like Prince Andrey, and are lying flat on the ground.

Here is an image from Chekhov: "They undressed the corpse but had no time to take off the gloves; a corpse in gloves."

And here is Joy Williams' take on the image: "The Bible is constantly making use of image beyond words. A parable provides the imagery by means of words. The meaning, however, does not lie in the words but in the imagery. What is conjured, as it were, transcends words completely and speaks in another language. This is how Kafka wrote, why we are so fascinated by him, why he speaks so universally."

4. An Interlude

In 1964, I was a senior in high school, seventeen years old, and one fall afternoon I drove into Minneapolis to buy my first hardback literary novel. I had been reading about this book everywhere. The novel was called *Herzog*, and somebody named Saul Bellow had written it, and I wanted to read it. This purchase would be one of the first actions I ever took to lead me toward a life that, I had a feeling, would be devoted, however imperfectly, to literature.

Accordingly, I went to a downtown Minneapolis bookstore called the Book Case, owned by a man named Benton Case, and when I took my copy of *Herzog* up to the counter and fished out the princely sum of five dollars and seventy-five cents for the book (which I still have, by the way, a first edition), the clerk reached for my money and then took a long look at me. He seemed puzzled. And then he said to me, and this is a quote, "I don't know why anyone in the world would want to read that book."

Across the space of almost sixty years I still remember that remark.

I took *Herzog* home and started to read it. Some of it didn't make any sense to me: the main character, who was named Herzog, was writing letters to someone named Heidegger. He was writing other letters. Slowly it dawned on me that I was reading a book about a Jewish intellectual written by a Jewish novelist—an experience I had never had before—and that the Jewish content of the book accounted for the clerk's distaste for it. Nevertheless, despite my occasional incomprehension, I pressed on.

Herzog has been driven slightly mad by his wife's infidelity and is grief-stricken over the loss of his daughter to her custody. His wife's lover is a comic vulgarian named Valentine Gersbach, and in due course she has left Herzog to live with this Gersbach, taking their daughter, June, with her. Herzog, in a comic Dostoyevskian frenzy, halfway through the book decides to do great harm to Gersbach, and with a loaded gun he drives over to Harper Avenue in Chicago, where Gersbach lives. He intends to kill somebody. He approaches the house and moves a concrete block so that he can stand on it to peer in through the bathroom window. Holding his gun, Herzog sees his daughter in the bathtub:

It was Gersbach. He was going to bathe Herzog's daughter! Gersbach! Junie was giggling, twisting, splashing, dimpling, showing her tiny white teeth, wrinkling her nose, teasing. "Now hold still," said Gersbach. He got into her ears with the washrag as she screamed, cleansed off her face, wiped her mouth. He spoke with authority but affectionately and with grumbling smiles and occasionally with laughter he bathed her—soaped, rinsed, dipping water in her toy boats to rinse her back as she squealed and twisted. The man washed her tenderly.

Because of this scene, everything changes. A sudden reversal: Gersbach, whom Herzog has considered a monster, a fool, and a villain, is visibly capable of sweetness and tenderness. This is bad news for Herzog; the vision kills off his self-righteousness. It stops his madness cold.

What I didn't know then, but what I know now, was that Bellow was drawing on a long and honorable narrative tradition in which an observer sees something by chance (often through a window) or overhears a conversation, after which the story must change its direction. In *Paradise Lost*, Satan spies on Adam and Eve in the Garden of Eden; Frankenstein's creature looks through a knothole and sees a scene of domestic bliss in Mary Shelley's novel; Scrooge sees happiness in Bob Cratchit's Christmas family gathering; in Proust, everybody spies on everybody else, including Marcel spying through a transom glass at the Baron de Charlus and Jupien making love; and, more recently, post-Bellow, Fuckhead sees a Mennonite man washing the feet of his wife in Denis Johnson's *Jesus' Son*.

In Bellow's novel, there they are, all the elements: an image caught by chance. An episode of spying. An everyday action. Two people who think themselves unobserved. A nonprogressive undramatic inconsequential action. Not a symbol, not a myth, not an idea, but the thing itself! No English teachers were needed to interpret it! I loved it.

Across the space of many years I remember reading that passage, holding the image of Gersbach bathing Herzog's daughter.

5.

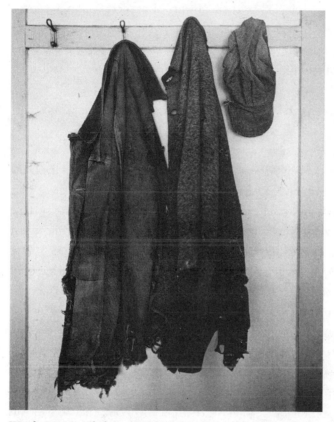

Wright Morris, *Clothes on Hooks, Home Place*, 1947

Saul Bellow's friend Wright Morris, in his book *Earthly Delights, Unearthly Adornments*, subtitled "American Writers as Image-Makers" (1978), writes of Sherwood Anderson that, when the stories are at their best, "The image is free of intrusion and self-indulgence." He should know. An American novelist who was also a great photographer (like Eudora Welty, come to think of it), Wright Morris wrote fiction that reads like a parade of images, accompanied by a set of meditations upon them. His work oscillates between the micro-detailed concrete image and the abstract thought, with characters who tend to be crippled by their powers of observation. No wonder one of his novels was titled *The Field of Vision*. Morris' own photographs are almost invariably of objects that have been well used and almost worn out, like these clothes hanging from hooks, objects that have acquired what the Japanese call *sabi*, the dignity and beauty of an object as it wears out—clothes so used, they are almost rags.

One of the shortest of Wright Morris' stories is the one with the longest title: "A Fight Between a White Boy and a Black Boy in the Dusk of a Fall Afternoon in Omaha, Nebraska." The story is a mere four pages long. It was published in the *New Yorker* in 1970. Its surface content is exactly what the story's title says it is: we are in the midst of the Great Depression, and two boys are fighting. The story at first seems to be about racial tension but does not analyze it. Other children are looking on, including a White boy who "observes the fight upside down as he hangs by his knees from the iron rail of the fence." But not everyone watches. A Black girl in a nearby annex goes on pasting cutouts of pumpkins onto a window. "Fights are not so unusual," the story informs us. "Halloween and pumpkins come but once a year."

Almost as soon as readers start in on the story, they're likely to notice that what's unusual about it is that the tone remains coolly objective and unruffled, although the angle of observation is unstable, moving from one point of view to another. The story seems to have almost no interest in the fight *as* a fight. Americans are expected to get aroused by violence, but this narrator will have none of that. Despite the heat of the action, the narration stays resolutely clinical.

Blood dripping to the pavement is of no particular interest. The tone is weirdly flat, judicious, distant, and hyperdetailed—completely at odds with the violence of the subject matter. Imagine: It is as if fighting is a rather dull subject. The action itself constitutes a tableau and hardly moves at all.

Instead, the story's interest locates itself entirely in the peripheries to the action: the stupidity of the White boy, the fact that he's been held back for three grades, that the bottom board of his desk has been removed to accommodate his knees, that each boy fears the Whiteness or the Blackness of the other, that the Black boy is barefoot. The details prevent the boys from becoming symbols or archetypes in an allegory. The fight is a nonprogressive action: the two boys, fighting, make their way down the alley, but neither wins or gets an advantage. This fight is going nowhere. At the end of the alley, we get a painterly effect: a gas streetlamp can be seen far at the end, described as if by an American precisionist painter: "the halo around it swimming with insects." But then the two boys disappear into darkness and all we hear is the shuffling feet of the White boy; "then that, too, dissolves into darkness."

At last we come to the last paragraph of this remarkable story. When the story appeared in the *New Yorker*, there was a space break between the last sentence of the previous section ("When the streetlights cast more light, he will go home") and the first sentence of the final paragraph. However, in Morris' *Collected Stories*, the space break is gone. Instead, readers, unaware that they have been placed in a catapult, are suddenly thrown out of the scene and are propelled through space-time. In this paragraph, the story breaks off from its field of vision, as if a camera had been jerked away from that alley in Omaha and had aimed itself at the horizon before it returned to a small domestic space. You have to make up a word for what this paragraph is doing. The inadequate word I have to resort to here for it is *horizoning*. Here is the story's final paragraph:

Somewhere, still running, there is a white boy who saw all of this and will swear to it; otherwise, nothing of what he saw remains. The Negro section, the bakery on the corner, the red-brick school with one second-floor window (the one that opens out on the fire escape) outlined by the chalk dust where they slapped the erasers—all that is gone, the earth leveled and displaced to accommodate the ramps of the new freeway. The cloverleaf approaches look great from the air. It saves the driving time of those headed east or west. Omaha is no longer the gateway to the West, but the plains remain, according to one traveler, a place where his wife still sleeps in the seat while he drives through the night.

If this paragraph doesn't give you chills, you're not paying attention. Where has the story gone? To its hidden subject, the passing away of all things in America, the old giving way to the new, with only the persistence of vision and memory tagging us to the places we remember. The boy who watched the fight has grown up; now, as an adult, he drives a car past Omaha, thinking of what he once saw there, still haunted by a single image. His wife sleeps on the passenger side. It is a solitary, unspoken memory, at least until now. A narrative has turned into an elegy. What is the narrator's emotion? Whatever it is, it's haunted.

Here is one last observation, nonfictional, from Wright Morris' book on American writers as image makers:

If I attempt to distinguish between fiction and memory, and press my nose to memory's glass to see more clearly, the remembered image grows more illusive, like the details in a Pointillist painting. I recognize it, more than I see it. The recognition is a fabric of emotion, as immaterial as music. In this defect of memory do we have the emergence of imagination? If we remember both vibrantly and accurately . . . the imaginative faculty would be blocked, lacking the stimulus necessary to fill in what is empty or create what is missing. . . . Precisely where memory is frail and emotion is strong, imagination takes fire.

The space of imagination, that is, constitutes a space vacated by memory. Emptiness is required for the imagination to function—to be called forth. The image and the imagination serve as the filled-in luminous packaging left by all that we have forgotten or somehow neglected to see the first time around, or something empty, totally empty, that we must dredge up and then fill in with more emptiness.

Anyone can write an image caught by chance, in silence, with nondirective action: such eloquent imagery is not hard to write. What's hard is not forcing a meaning down its throat. If you let out your inner high school English teacher and force a meaning on your imagery, making the meaning explicit, the reader will read it, get it, and rush onward. But if there's something widowed about the imagery, something that escapes meaning, the imagery will then stick to the reader, and begin to haunt.

Gertrude Stein once said that the reason people go on reading *Hamlet* is not because of what they understand about *Hamlet*. You reread something, she said, because of what you don't understand about it. An image that haunts you is one that escapes comprehension, that resists your appropriation of it. The truest ghosts are the ones that cannot speak. Instead, they seem to gesture, to beckon.

Gerard Manley Hopkins wrote in his notebooks about widowed images that they were images for which he had not "found the law." The feeling for what Hopkins called "inscape" somehow lies beyond the law, beyond total intelligibility. With such images, we are in unusual territory. Speaking of a Louise Glück poem in my presence years ago, the poet Larry Levis said, about a particular image in *The Wild Iris*, "I *want* to talk about it, but I can't."

6.

This particular Minnesota winter has set records for cold, and when the middle-aged man enters the house, he hears the steam radiators clacking. Inside the front door, whose security lock combination is three-one-four, is the waiting room. The same copies of the *New Yorker*, *Consumer Reports*, the *Atlantic*, and *Harper's* that were there last week are still there, in neat rows. The middle-aged man sits down near the radiator, unbuttons his overcoat, and begins to reread a *New Yorker*. No one else is waiting; he has the place to himself. He turns to a music column by Alex Ross and skims it, having first encountered it weeks ago. Nearby is a white-noise machine, meant to muffle the sound of any of the patients in any of the consulting rooms near where the man sits and waits, reading about Johannes Brahms.

A door opens upstairs, and a woman with a kindly, intelligent face calls down to him from the stairway to say that she is ready for his appointment. The man puts down the magazine, reaches for his overcoat, and makes his way up the stairs. Once he has crossed the threshold into her office, he hangs his coat on a coatrack and sits down in the appointed chair, the one where he always sits, across from where *she* always sits. She closes the door behind him.

"Well, how have you been?" she asks, smiling, as she always does whenever he is here. So the therapy session has started. She is from a large Irish American family, and she has acquired, or always has had, a talent for keeping her voice at a calm and peaceful level. She is the same age as the middle-aged man. This is important, this age equation.

The man opposite her tries, once again, to put into words what he has been feeling: that he is carrying around a sack of darkness, that the sack weighs on him no matter what he is doing, and that lately he has been trying to distinguish between sorrow and depression, because he believes that the two are distinct and he must learn to tell them apart.

"Sorrow," the therapist says. "No one uses that word anymore, do they?"

"No, they don't," the man replies. "It's an antique word. It's like that other word, *longing*. Nobody uses that word either. Longing is desire that's lost its way, lost its object. The Germans call it *Sehnsucht*. And maybe sorrow is grief that's lost its way, too, lost its object." Suddenly excited, he says, "It's a form of unhappiness that doesn't know how to define itself. And so there aren't any words for it. Only images."

The therapist thinks about this. She looks out the window, where a sparrow has alighted on a snow-covered branch. Behind her, the radiator continues to clank, as if someone were knocking, trying to get in. When she turns back to the middle-aged man, her face full of concern, she asks, almost out of the blue—it seems—"What's your first memory?"

And that's when I say that my first memory is of a street, Girard Avenue South. Across the street from where we live is a red house whose front porch light is always on, and next door to the red house is one that is white with green trim, a place that has a wraparound front porch. No one ever goes into or out of this house, I tell her, but the lawn is always green, and the grass is always trimmed, as if ghosts had mowed it and tended it.

"What about the sidewalk in front of the house where you were?" she asks. "Who's there?"

"Oh," I say. "That's easy. Nobody. No one is ever there."

"No one?" she asks. "Are you sure?"

"Yes, of course I'm sure," I tell her. "No one is *ever* there. No one ever will be. No one coming or going. The street is always empty."

"Empty," she repeats. She waits for a moment, apparently thinking about whether to say what's on the tip of her tongue. And then she says it. "That's sad, isn't it? Don't you think so?"

And that's when I say, "No, it's *not* sad." And I sit up in my chair, and I say, "It was the price of the ticket. It was the price I had to pay to get the ticket, and I paid it, and the ticket admitted me to my life, and it's been a lucky life, with all those books, and the people I've loved and the people who have loved me, and if it weren't for the emptiness of that street, I don't know where I'd be. Maybe I'd be selling insurance somewhere, just as my father did." I lean back and take a breath.

Red house, pointed roof, porch swing, porch light, white house, green trim, wraparound porch, and no one, ever, down on the sidewalk, no one there, no one coming or going as the street darkens toward evening, the lights clicking on in the houses.

No one is there. Call it a gift. All his life he will try to fill in that emptiness.

Acknowledgments

Earlier versions of some of these essays appeared in the following publications:

"Inventories and Undoings" (as "Undoings") appeared in the Spring 2012 issue of the *Colorado Review*.

"Lush Life" appeared in *A Kite in the Wind: Fiction Writers on their Craft*, edited by Andrea Barrett and Peter Turchi (San Antonio: Trinity University Press, 2011).

"Notes on the Dramatic Image" appeared in *Feed the Lake: Essays on the Craft of Fiction*, edited by Shelly Criswell and Grant Tracey (Cedar Falls: North American Review Press, 2016).

"What Happens in Hell" appeared in *Ploughshares* (Fall 2012), edited by Patricia Hampl; reprinted in *The Best American Essays 2013*, edited by Cheryl Strayed, and in *Pushcart Prize XXXVIII*, edited by Bill Henderson.

"All the Dark Nights" appeared as "Full of It" in *Letters to a Fiction Writer*, edited by Frederick Busch (New York: W. W. Norton & Co., 1999), and was reprinted in *The Writer's Reader*, edited by Robert Cohen and Jay Parini (New York: Bloomsbury, 2017).

The section on Haruki Murakami's *1Q84* in "Wonderlands" first appeared in a review of *1Q84* in the *New York Review of Books* (58:19) December 8, 2011, and the section on Don DeLillo's "Human Moments in World War III" in "Things About to Disappear: the Writer as Curator" first appeared in a review of DeLillo's *The Angel Esmeralda* in the *New York Review of Books* (59:2), February 9, 2012.

My thanks to the editors of these publications. Additional thanks to Fiona McCrae and Katie Dublinski of Graywolf Press and to copyeditor Lynn Marasco for their careful readings of these essays. Warm thanks to David Shields for his help in putting the essays in their right order, and great thanks also to the dedicatees of these essays, and to James Morrison, Joan Silber, Bill Lychack, Miles Harvey, Julie Schumacher, Dean Bakopoulos, Stacey D'Erasmo, Alan Shapiro, Ellen Bryant Voigt, Martha Southgate, and Lorrie Moore.

CHARLES BAXTER is the author of fourteen books, most recently the novel *The Sun Collective*. His stories have appeared in *The Best American Short Stories*, the Pushcart Prize anthology, and *The O. Henry Prize Stories*. He lives in Minneapolis.

The text of *Wonderlands* is set in Whitman.
Book design by Rachel Holscher.
Composition by Bookmobile Design & Digital
Publisher Services, Minneapolis, Minnesota.
Manufactured by McNaughton & Gunn on acid-free,
100 percent postconsumer wastepaper.